Learning Apache Drill
Query and Analyze Distributed Data Sources with SQL

Charles Givre and Paul Rogers

Beijing · Boston · Farnham · Sebastopol · Tokyo

Learning Apache Drill

by Charles Givre and Paul Rogers

Copyright © 2019 Charles Givre and Paul Rogers. All rights reserved.

Published by O'Reilly Media, Inc., 1005 Gravenstein Highway North, Sebastopol, CA 95472.

O'Reilly books may be purchased for educational, business, or sales promotional use. Online editions are also available for most titles (*http://oreilly.com/safari*). For more information, contact our corporate/institutional sales department: 800-998-9938 or *corporate@oreilly.com*.

Acquisitions Editor: Rachel Roumeliotis
Development Editor: Jeff Bleiel
Production Editor: Melanie Yarbrough
Copyeditor: Octal Publishing, LLC
Proofreader: Rachel Head

Indexer: Ellen Troutman-Zaig
Interior Designer: David Futato
Cover Designer: Karen Montgomery
Illustrator: Rebecca Demarest

October 2018:   First Edition

Revision History for the First Edition

2018-10-29:   First Release

See *http://oreilly.com/catalog/errata.csp?isbn=9781492032793* for release details.

978-1-492-03279-3

[LSI]

Table of Contents

Preface

The ability to analyze massive amounts of data is perhaps one of the most important developments of the 21st century. However, until recently, the tooling to analyze large datasets was exceedingly complex or expensive (or both). Apache Drill has the potential to change all that.

Apache Drill opens up incredible new possibilities for analyzing data because Drill enables you to query a variety of data sources using a standard language.

Who Should Read This Book

We envisioned this book for three groups of people: analysts or others who will be using Drill to query data, systems administrators who will be deploying and maintaining Drill in production environments, and developers who will be writing code to extend the functionality of Drill.

Why We Wrote This Book

Three years ago, Charles was introduced to Drill at the Strata Conference in San Jose, CA, and it sparked a realization that Drill could fundamentally change the way data is analyzed. After a few conversations with MapR chief scientist Ted Dunning, Charles realized that Drill had enormous unrealized potential for use with security-related datasets. However, at the time many of Drill's capabilities were undocumented, and the availability of information about how to develop for Drill ranged from limited to nonexistent. Charles wanted to extend the capabilities of Drill, but he had no idea where to begin. This book is everything that Charles would have wanted if he were starting his journey with Drill today.[1]

---

1 It feels very strange for Charles to write about himself in the third person.

Paul has worked at a number of business intelligence (BI) companies on a range of query and database tools. When he came across Drill, it seemed like the best of many different tools combined into one, while also being both open source and extensible. Paul joined the Drill team and has worked to get the word out about Drill's capabilities.

This book shows you how to use Drill to analyze data effectively. The book is not intended to replace Drill's documentation, but rather to serve as a guide to getting you on the right path with Drill. It represents the compilation of several years of lessons learned and should go a long way toward explaining what Drill is and how it solves user problems.

We also wrote this book for people who are interested in extending the capabilities of Drill. After you begin experimenting with Drill, you will likely develop ideas about missing functionality. When Charles started with Drill, the lack of documentation in this area was one of his biggest frustrations, and it is the goal of this book to remedy that situation. Chapters 8 through 12 cover in depth how to extend Drill's functionality in easy-to-understand language.

Navigating This Book

This book is intended for three rather distinct audiences, each with different skill sets. Here's how we address these audiences:

- Chapters 1 through 3 are a general introduction to Drill. They will give you a good idea of how to get up and running.
- Chapters 4 through 7 are intended for analysts, data scientists, and anyone who will be using Drill to analyze data. With the exception of Chapter 7, all of the chapters in this section require an understanding of SQL.
- Chapters 8, 10, 11, and 12 discuss how to extend the functionality of Drill. These chapters require an understanding of Java development to get the most out of them.
- Chapter 9 discusses the intricacies of installing and configuring Drill in a production environment. If you are a system administrator, you will want to read this chapter.
- Chapter 13 covers many different and diverse use cases for Drill. Regardless of your role, you will want to read this chapter to really understand the power of Drill.

Online Resources

All the code and data files referenced in the book are available at the following repository on GitHub (*https://github.com/cgivre/drillbook*). Please use the Issues tab in GitHub to report any errata in the code.

Drill has comprehensive documentation (*https://drill.apache.org*) as well.

Conventions Used in This Book

The following typographical conventions are used in this book:

Italic
> Indicates new terms, URLs, email addresses, filenames, and file extensions.

`Constant width`
> Used for program listings, as well as within paragraphs to refer to program elements such as variable or function names, databases, data types, environment variables, statements, and keywords.

`Constant width bold`
> Shows commands or other text that should be typed literally by the user.

`Constant width italic`
> Shows text that should be replaced with user-supplied values or by values determined by context.

 This element signifies a tip or suggestion.

 This element signifies a general note.

 This element indicates a warning or caution.

Using Code Examples

Supplemental material (code examples, exercises, etc.) is available for download at *https://github.com/cgivre/drillbook*.

This book is here to help you get your job done. In general, if example code is offered with this book, you may use it in your programs and documentation. You do not need to contact us for permission unless you're reproducing a significant portion of the code. For example, writing a program that uses several chunks of code from this book does not require permission. Selling or distributing a CD-ROM of examples from O'Reilly books does require permission. Answering a question by citing this book and quoting example code does not require permission. Incorporating a significant amount of example code from this book into your product's documentation does require permission.

We appreciate, but do not require, attribution. An attribution usually includes the title, author, publisher, and ISBN. For example: "*Learning Apache Drill* by Charles Givre and Paul Rogers (O'Reilly). Copyright 2019 Charles Givre and Paul Rogers, 978-1-492-03279-3."

If you feel your use of code examples falls outside fair use or the permission given above, feel free to contact us at *permissions@oreilly.com*.

O'Reilly Safari

 *Safari* (formerly Safari Books Online) is a membership-based training and reference platform for enterprise, government, educators, and individuals.

Members have access to thousands of books, training videos, Learning Paths, interactive tutorials, and curated playlists from over 250 publishers, including O'Reilly Media, Harvard Business Review, Prentice Hall Professional, Addison-Wesley Professional, Microsoft Press, Sams, Que, Peachpit Press, Adobe, Focal Press, Cisco Press, John Wiley & Sons, Syngress, Morgan Kaufmann, IBM Redbooks, Packt, Adobe Press, FT Press, Apress, Manning, New Riders, McGraw-Hill, Jones & Bartlett, and Course Technology, among others.

For more information, please visit *http://oreilly.com/safari*.

How to Contact Us

Please address comments and questions concerning this book to the publisher:

O'Reilly Media, Inc.
1005 Gravenstein Highway North
Sebastopol, CA 95472
800-998-9938 (in the United States or Canada)
707-829-0515 (international or local)
707-829-0104 (fax)

We have a web page for this book, where we list errata, examples, and any additional information. You can access this page at *http://bit.ly/learning-apache-drill*.

To comment or ask technical questions about this book, send email to *bookquestions@oreilly.com*.

For more information about our books, courses, conferences, and news, see our website at *http://www.oreilly.com*.

Find us on Facebook: *http://facebook.com/oreilly*

Follow us on Twitter: *http://twitter.com/oreillymedia*

Watch us on YouTube: *http://www.youtube.com/oreillymedia*

Acknowledgments

The authors would like to thank Arina Ielchiieva, John Omernik, Aman Sinha, and Parth Chandra for taking time from their busy schedules to provide us with thorough technical reviews. We would also like to thank Jeff Bleiel and the entire O'Reilly editorial team for working with us to see this book to completion. Finally, we would like to thank the dedicated contributors to the Drill project, without whom this book would not be possible.

Special Thanks from Charles

I would especially like to thank my wife, Alisheva, and children, Mel, Dovie, Rozie, and Goldie, for putting up with my absences and late nights while writing this book and for supporting me as I pursued my interest in Drill and geekery/nerdcraft in general. I definitely couldn't do it without you.

I would like thank all the members of the Drill development committee who worked with me and who have taught me so much about Java development, GitHub, and how to write production-quality code. I would also like to thank my coauthor, Paul, who has put up with countless questions and who has also taught me a lot about the internals of Drill.

Finally, thanks to Ted Dunning and Ellen Friedman for inviting me to contribute to this project, and the Drill Project Management Committee (PMC) for their lapses in judgment in making me a committer to the Drill project and most recently a PMC member.

Special Thanks from Paul

I wish to thank my wife, Anne, and children, Delaine, Forrest, and Pauline, for their patience as I disappeared on nights and weekends to peck away at this book.

I wish to also thank the Drill development team for their generous help during the two years I spent working on Drill and for the continued assistance in answering questions while writing the book. This book is a way to pass their knowledge along to others. Thanks to the original Drill developers, who built the product in record time, and to the later developers who continue to improve Drill. I am honored to serve on the Drill PMC with a wonderful group of contributors. Thanks also to Charles for driving the book to completion and for sharing his user perspective with all of us.

I would also like to thank MapR for funding the creation of Drill and for contributing it to the Apache Software Foundation (ASF) so that everyone can use it. Finally, thanks to the ASF for providing ongoing support for the Apache Drill project.

CHAPTER 1

Introduction to Apache Drill

If you do any kind of data analytics, you will most certainly agree that there is a major problem in the industry. As data volumes have increased exponentially in the past 10 years, so too have the types of systems and formats designed to analyze this data. All of this comes back to the basic fact that data is not optimally arranged for ad hoc analysis. Quite often, a data scientist or analyst will be confronted with data in a wide variety of formats, such as CSV, JSON, and XML, to say nothing of the various systems in which data can be stored, such as Hadoop, Hive, MongoDB, and relational databases. According to a 2016 article by Forbes (*http://bit.ly/2NBOrje*), data scientists spend nearly 80% of their time gathering and cleaning their data—88% of them say this is the least enjoyable part of their job.

In his book *Taming the Big Data Tidal Wave* (Wiley), Bill Franks, who was chief analytics officer at Teradata when he wrote it, introduces a metric called Time to Insight (TTI), which is the amount of time it takes from when an organization receives or generates data to when it is able to derive an actionable insight from that data. Driving down TTI is important because often the value of the insights decreases over time. Consider security information. If you are protecting a computer system, you want to detect intrusions as soon as possible to prevent the intruder from stealing data. If it takes you years to detect an intrusion, the value of that knowledge is pretty low because the intruder has likely already stolen all your valuable data, whereas if you can identify that intrusion within seconds, you can prevent the theft.

The cost of analytic insight also increases with the complexity of your tools. If your analysts need to write complex code to analyze your data, you will need higher-skilled, more costly analysts in order to extract insights from the data, and it will take them more time to do so, driving up the TTI.

Companies have approached this problem in different ways. Many have taken the route of simply storing all of their data into a massive Hadoop cluster, or *data lake*.

However, even though it does solve the problem of data being in multiple disparate systems, the data-lake approach does not (necessarily) solve the problem of data being in multiple formats.

Another approach is to use a central analytic platform that ingests an organization's data via an *extract, transform, and load* (ETL) process. This approach is also costly in that it requires you to send your data over a network, thereby increasing network usage; store copies of the same data in multiple systems; and transform the data from its original format into a standardized format, which might or might not be suitable for it. Additionally, it creates complexity when the original source systems want to change their schemas. More serious, however, is that this approach requires extensive involvement from an IT department to set up and configure.

Regardless of which approach you take, you can see that deriving value from these disparate datasets is time-consuming, costly, and difficult. This is where Drill can have a major impact.

Drill is an extremely versatile, powerful, extensible, and easy-to-use tool that can help you analyze your data more effectively, drive down your time to insight, and get more value from your data.

What Is Apache Drill?

At its core, Apache Drill is a SQL engine for big data. In practical terms, what this means is that Drill acts as an intermediary that allows you to query *self-describing data* using standard ANSI SQL. To use a comparison from the science fiction series *Star Trek*, Drill acts as a universal translator[1] for your data and enables you to use SQL to interact with your data as if it were a table in a database, whether it is or not. Bringing this down to earth, *Drill enables an analyst, armed only with a knowledge of SQL or a business intelligence (BI) tool such as Tableau, to analyze and query their data without having to transform the data or move it to a centralized data store.*

Drill Is Versatile

One of Drill's major strong points is its versatility. Out of the box, Drill can query a wide variety of file formats, including:

- CSV, TSV, PSV, or any delimited data
- JSON
- Parquet

---

[1] If you are not a *Star Trek* fan, the universal translator is a fictional device that instantly translates all alien languages into English (and presumably back to the alien language).

- Avro[2]
- Hadoop Sequence files
- Apache and Nginx web server logs
- Log files
- PCAP/PCAP-NG

Chapters 4 and 5 explain how to query these file formats.

In addition to being able to query a wide variety of file formats, Drill can query data in external systems including:

- HBase
- Hive
- Kafka for streaming data
- MapR-DB
- MongoDB
- Open Time Series Database
- Nearly any relational database with a JDBC driver

Finally, Drill supports files stored in a variety of distributed filesystems such as:

- Hadoop Distributed File System (HDFS)
- MapR-FS
- Amazon Simple Storage Service (S3)

Chapter 6 explains in detail how to connect Drill to these source systems and query them.

Additionally, Drill has extensive APIs that enable you to write your own custom functions, and readers for other data sources. You will learn how to write custom user-defined functions in Chapter 11 and storage and format plug-ins in Chapter 12.

Drill Is Easy to Use

One of the aspects of Drill that is striking to first-time users is how easy it actually is to use. Because Drill uses standard ANSI SQL with some additions, if you are comfortable with SQL, you already know 80 to 90% of what you need to execute queries using Drill. Drill has Open Database Connectivity (ODBC) and Java Database Con-

---

2 This feature is still experimental.

nectivity (JDBC) interfaces, so it can connect to most BI tools (such as Tableau, Qlix, and others) quite easily.

If you prefer a scripting language such as Python or R, modules exist that enable you to quickly and easily execute a query in Drill and import the results into those languages. Chapter 7 explains how to connect to Drill from a wide variety of other languages and platforms.

Drill does not require you to define a schema

One aspect of Drill that often intrigues new users is that you do not need to define a schema prior to querying your data. Relational databases require you to define a rigid schema prior to inserting the data into the schema. This schema enables databases to build indexes to enable rapid querying. Tools that follow this model are known as *schema-on-write*.

One of the limitations of a schema-on-write system is that schema modifications after the fact are quite difficult, if not impossible. As tools have progressed, a new technique of schema building has evolved, known as *schema-on-read*, whereby the data is inserted into the system without any schema definition; however, prior to querying the user must define the schema. This allows flexibility in the data model, but at a performance cost.

Drill does not follow either of these design paradigms. When using Drill, it is not necessary to define a schema at all prior to querying. Instead, Drill infers the schema from the structure of the data. This approach has its advantages, in that it is extremely flexible and does not have any time requirement from the users. It does have limitations, though, insomuch as Drill can struggle with malformed data. We discuss the technical details and limitations of this approach later in the book.

A Word About Drill's Performance

Drill makes extensive use of in-memory data buffers, CPU optimization, and transfers between clusters of nodes, the result of which is that Drill can process data much faster than MapReduce or Hive. Drill's performance (*http://bit.ly/2p0pzUo*) is comparable to if not better than Apache Spark's for various common operations such as joins and aggregation. What is interesting to note about Drill is that, unlike many big data tools, it also works very well with small datasets on a single-computer installation.

Drill's performance is best when querying data stored in Parquet format—a columnar format that is particularly well suited for use with Drill.

Drill Is Not a Database

Because Drill looks like a relational database to a user, users often expect database-like performance in all situations. Drill is very fast and does take advantage of many optimizations when querying data sources, but you should not expect nanosecond response times when using Drill to query data. We discuss performance tuning later in the book.

Where Drill offers a significant advantage over other big data tools is that it dramatically reduces the amount of human effort needed to query data sources. Because this is directly correlated with cost, Drill can quantifiably reduce the cost of accessing your big data systems.

A Very Brief History of Big Data

Since humans began processing digital data, there has been a perpetual struggle between not having enough processing power to deal with the data and not having the storage capacity to store the data. Before the turn of the century, most systems that stored great amounts of data were large databases developed by companies like Oracle, Teradata, and others. These systems were closed source, proprietary, and dependent on extremely expensive, high-end hardware to run.

In 2004, there was a watershed moment in computing that changed all that. That year, Google released a research paper titled "MapReduce: Simplified Data Processing on Large Clusters" (*https://ai.google/research/pubs/pub62*) by Jeffrey Dean and Sanjay Ghemawat that defined the MapReduce process—a relatively simple two-step process that enabled Google to process incredibly large amounts of data on commodity hardware. This paper and an earlier Google research paper titled "The Google File System" (*https://ai.google/research/pubs/pub51*) by Sanjay Ghemawat et al. inspired what became one of the most popular open source big data platforms: Apache Hadoop (*https://en.wikipedia.org/wiki/Apache_Hadoop*), which was first released in April 2006 and quickly set a new record by sorting 1.8 TB in 47.9 hours on 188 nodes of commodity hardware.

Hadoop

It became quickly apparent that Hadoop and MapReduce were going to change analytics. Around the same time, Amazon was releasing its Amazon Web Services (AWS) product, which enabled companies to quickly set up entire virtual systems to process ever-increasing amounts of data. The combination of Apache Hadoop and virtualization tools such as AWS made it much easier and less expensive for companies to store and process large datasets.

However, as more companies adopted Hadoop and MapReduce, they discovered a few problems with this system. Although it was now possible to process, store, and derive insights from extremely large datasets (now known as *big data*), it was extremely difficult and inefficient. Some problems, particularly those that involve grouping and counting things, are very easy to port to the MapReduce paradigm, but other problems, such as joining datasets together, were quite difficult. Additionally, MapReduce in Hadoop requires Java development skills and hence is out of the reach of most business analysts and many data scientists.

Facebook and Yahoo! both developed answers to this challenge in the form of higher-level platforms that abstracted the technical details of the MapReduce framework into a simpler language. Yahoo!'s solution, Apache Pig, was released in late 2008, and Facebook's became the Apache Hive project and was released in the same time frame. Hive and Pig both accomplish a similar goal of providing a high-level language with which a non–software developer can analyze large datasets; however, the two platforms took fundamentally different approaches to this problem. Hive uses a subset of SQL known as HiveQL to interact with the data, whereas Pig has its own language known as Pig Latin.

Pig, Hive, and a few other tools were major leaps forward in democratizing access to big data, but at the time they were basically wrappers for MapReduce, which by design relies on intense disk input/output (I/O) and as a result is slow. In 2012, there was another big shift in the big data landscape with the release of Apache Spark (*https://en.wikipedia.org/wiki/Apache_Spark*). Spark is an open source, distributed computing framework that works with Hadoop; but unlike the other systems, Spark makes extensive use of in-memory operations, which, when combined with other algorithmic improvements over MapReduce, results in performance improvements of several orders of magnitude. Spark also includes a robust machine learning library and interfaces for Python, SQL, Scala, Java, and R.

The 2010 Google Dremel paper (*https://ai.google/research/pubs/pub36632*) by Sergey Melnik et al. was another game changer in that it inspired a number of tools that enabled ad hoc analysis of very large datasets, including Drill, Impala, and Presto. Earlier tools such as MapReduce and Spark broke processing into stages, with the output of each stage materialized to disk and a shuffle that sent these results to the next stage. Dremel and the tools it inspired divide each stage into batches, then exchange batches from one node to another directly over the network, without the disk I/O of the prior generation of tools. This is often called "in-memory processing," though the term does not capture the exchange aspect of the Dremel model. See Chapter 3 for details.

Drill in the Big Data Ecosystem

Drill occupies a unique place in the big data ecosystem in that it facilitates ad hoc analysis of a wide variety of different data sources and formats using a common language: SQL. If you have a problem that can be expressed as a table—and many data analysis problems can—Drill might be a good addition to your toolkit.

With that said, Drill is not a good tool if you are doing operations that are highly iterative, such as machine learning, or cannot be expressed easily in SQL. Drill is a query engine, and it does not perform transactions and is not meant to write data (although Drill can create views and tables). You wouldn't want to use Drill to replace a database for tasks like a running a website.

Comparing Drill with Similar Tools

Throughout the years there have been various tools that attempt to provide a SQL layer on top of Hadoop. All of these tools, Drill included, were also inspired by the Google Dremel paper by Melnik et al. The tools that are most similar to Drill are Apache Impala and Presto. Both offer users the ability to query large datasets stored in Hadoop using SQL. Presto and Drill are both implemented in Java, whereas Impala is written in C++ and Java, which complicates development. Impala is linked with Hive's metastore: you cannot use it independently of the metastore.

Presto was developed by Facebook to be used on its large data stores. It offers a similar capability as Drill; however, unlike Drill, Presto requires users to define a schema prior to querying their data.

Additional Drill Resources

Comprehensive documentation for Drill is available on the Drill project website (*https://drill.apache.org/download/*). Drill's source code is published on GitHub (*https://github.com/apache/drill*). There is additional developer documentation available in the GitHub repository (*http://bit.ly/2qi8UMW*).

CHAPTER 2

Installing and Running Drill

Drill is a layered Java application. At the core is a set of Java JAR files that you can include in another Java application. Drill calls this the *embedded mode*. The sqlline tool we'll discuss is one example; the JDBC driver is another. The embedded mode is handy for learning Drill or to work with datasets stored on your local machine.

More typically, however, you run Drill as a server. Drill calls this the *server mode*. The Drill server, called a *Drillbit*, is just a wrapper around the core Drill library, so you get much of the same functionality either way. You can run a single Drillbit, or you can run multiple Drillbits on a cluster. Drill calls this *distributed mode*. The key advantage is that distributed mode provides much easier access to distributed filesystems, such as HDFS or S3.

You can run a single Drillbit on your laptop, which lets you try out the server features that you'll use in production, including working with distributed filesystems. It is important to note that you can do a lot with Drill without requiring a Hadoop cluster at your disposal. When it's installed on a cluster you work with Drill in exactly the same way as on your laptop, but now Drill will distribute its load across multiple machines. When you run Drill as a server, you will also need ZooKeeper running.

This chapter explains how to install Drill on your laptop, run it in both embedded and server modes, and configure your system to work with Drill. Chapter 9 explains how to run a distributed set of Drillbits on a production cluster.

After you install Drill, there are several ways of interacting with it. In addition to the command-line interface, you can interact with Drill via most BI tools through Drill's ODBC/JDBC interface. Drill also comes with a web interface, which we cover in Chapter 4.

If you just want to experiment with Drill, it is available preinstalled in a few publicly available virtual machines such as the Griffon Distribution for Data Science,[1] the MapR Sandbox, and others.

If you are interested in trying out Drill, it is sufficient to install Drill on your laptop and run it in embedded mode.

Preparing Your Machine for Drill

Before you install Drill on any machine, you need to have the Oracle Java SE Development Kit 8 (JDK 8) installed, which is available from Oracle's website.

If you already have the JDK installed, you can verify the version as shown here:

```
$ java -version
java version "1.8.0_65"
Java(TM) SE Runtime Environment (build 1.8.0_65-b17)
Java HotSpot(TM) 64-Bit Server VM (build 25.65-b01, mixed mode)
```

As long as your JDK is higher than version 1.8, you can run Drill. If you don't have the JDK on your machine, simply download the executable installer (*http://bit.ly/ 1X9h0Ea*) and run it.

Special Configuration Instructions for Windows Installations

On Windows machines, you will also need to have two environment variables set:

- A JAVA_HOME environment variable pointing to the JDK installation
- A PATH environment variable that includes the path to your JDK installation

To set these variables in Windows XP/Vista/7/8/10, perform the following steps:

1. Open the Control Panel, click System, and then click Advanced System Settings.
2. Switch to the Advanced tab and then click Environment Variables.
3. In the Environment Variables window, in the System Variables pane (see Figure 2-1), scroll down to PATH and then click Edit.
4. Add **C:\Program Files\Java\jdk1.*x.x_xx*\bin;**, replacing *x.x_xx* with the exact version number you downloaded in front of all existing entries. Do *not* delete any existing entries, because this can cause other applications to not run.
5. Repeat this process for the JAVA_HOME variable.

---

1 Griffon (*https://github.com/gtkcyber/griffon-vm*) is a version of Linux specially adapted for data science.

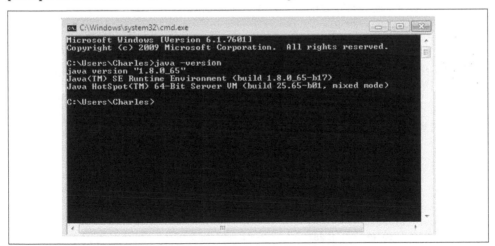

Figure 2-1. Configuring the environment variables

After you have installed Java and set the environment variables, you can confirm that your installation is working correctly by typing **java -version** at a command prompt. You should receive the result shown in Figure 2-2.

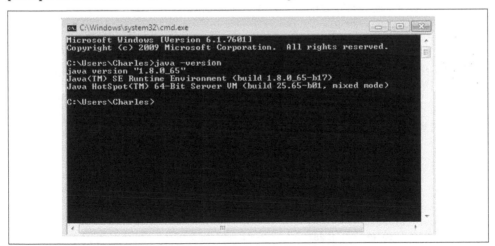

Figure 2-2. Confirmation that your installation is working correctly

Lastly, for Windows you will also need a program that can decompress TAR files, such as 7-Zip (*https://www.7-zip.org*).

Installing Drill on Windows

After you have Java correctly configured, installing Drill on a Windows machine is essentially the same process as for macOS or Linux:

1. Download the latest version of Drill (*https://drill.apache.org/download/*).
2. Move the file to the directory where you want to install Drill.
3. Using 7-Zip, or whichever extractor you have, unzip the file and the underlying TAR file into the directory of your choosing.

Starting Drill on a Windows Machine

Open a command prompt and navigate to the directory where you unzipped Drill. When you are there, navigate to the *bin* directory by typing **cd bin**. Next, at the command prompt, type the command **sqlline.bat -u "jdbc:drill:zk=local"**. If all went well, you should see the Drill prompt.

From here, you can enter SQL queries at the prompt. As part of the default installation, Drill includes a number of demonstration datasets, and among these is a file called *employee.json* that contains nominal data about an organization's employees. To verify that your installation is working properly, enter the following query at the Drill prompt:

```
SELECT education_level, COUNT( * ) AS person_count
FROM cp.`employee.json`
GROUP BY education_level
ORDER BY person_count DESC
```

If all is working properly, you should see an ASCII table of the data, as demonstrated here:

```
jdbc:drill:zk=local>
SELECT education_level, COUNT( * ) AS person_count
. . . . . . . . . . . >FROM cp.`employee.json`
. . . . . . . . . . . >GROUP BY education_level
. . . . . . . . . . . >ORDER BY person_count DESC;
+----------------------+----------------+
| education_level      | person_count   |
+----------------------+----------------+
| Partial College      | 288            |
| Bachelors Degree     | 287            |
| High School Degree   | 281            |
| Graduate Degree      | 170            |
| Partial High School  | 129            |
+----------------------+----------------+
5 rows selected (0.195 seconds)
```

Drill does not support server mode on Windows machines, so at this point your Drill installation is working and you can skip to the next chapter about connecting Drill to data sources.

To quit the Drill shell, type **!quit**.

Installing Drill in Embedded Mode on macOS or Linux

Installing Drill on a macOS or Linux machine is as simple as downloading and decompressing the TAR file. Depending on your system, either one of the following commands will download the Drill TAR file:

```
wget -O http://mirror.olnevhost.net/pub/apache/\
drill/drill-version/apache-drill-1.13.0.tar.gz

curl -o apache-drill-version.tar.gz \
http://mirror.olnevhost.net/pub/apache/drill/\
drill-version/apache-drill-1.13.0.tar.gz
```

After you have moved Drill to the desired location, simply decompress it:

```
tar -xvzf apache-drill-version.tar.gz
```

Adding Drill to the PATH

It is often convenient to define a variable to point to Drill's location. In your *.bashrc* or *.bash_profile* file, add the following line:

```
export DRILL_HOME=/path/to/drill
```

Then, all your commands can be of the form:

```
$DRILL_HOME/bin/drill-embedded
```

You might want to add the following line to your *.bash_profile* file as a convenience:

```
alias startDrill='$DRILL_HOME/bin/drill-embedded'
```

This will allow you to start Drill in embedded mode by typing **startDrill** at the command line. At this point, you are ready to run Drill.

Starting Drill on macOS or Linux in Embedded Mode

To start Drill after you've installed it, navigate to the path where you extracted the Drill files and execute the following command:

```
./bin/drill-embedded
```

You should see the following prompt:

```
Java HotSpot(TM) 64-Bit Server VM warning: ignoring option MaxPermSize=512M;
    support was removed in 8.0<&>
```

```
Jan 04, 2016 11:09:55 AM org.glassfish.jersey.server.ApplicationHandler
  initialize<>
INFO: Initiating Jersey application, version Jersey: 2.8 2014-04-29
  01:25:26.apache drill 1.14.0
"a drill is a terrible thing to waste"
0: jdbc:drill:zk=local>
```

From here, you can enter SQL queries at the prompt. As part of the default installation, Drill includes a number of demonstration datasets, and among these is a file called *employee.json* that contains nominal data about an organization's employees. To verify that your installation is working properly, enter the following query at the Drill prompt:

```
SELECT education_level, COUNT( * ) AS person_count
FROM cp.`employee.json`
GROUP BY education_level
ORDER BY person_count DESC;
```

If all is working properly, you should see an ASCII table of the data such as that shown here:

```
jdbc:drill:zk=local>
SELECT education_level, COUNT( * ) AS person_count
. . . . . . . . . . . >FROM cp.`employee.json`
. . . . . . . . . . . >GROUP BY education_level
. . . . . . . . . . . >ORDER BY person_count DESC;

+----------------------+---------------+
|   education_level    | person_count  |
+----------------------+---------------+
| Partial College      | 288           |
| Bachelors Degree     | 287           |
| High School Degree   | 281           |
| Graduate Degree      | 170           |
| Partial High School  | 129           |
+----------------------+---------------+
5 rows selected (0.195 seconds)
```

At this point, your Drill installation is working and you can skip to the next chapter about connecting Drill to data sources.

To quit the Drill shell, type **!quit**.

Installing Drill in Distributed Mode on macOS or Linux

Although Drill can significantly improve data exploration and analysis on one machine, its real power comes from running it in distributed mode, in which you can query multiple datasets *in situ*. This section assumes that you have a working cluster and covers how to set it up to work with Drill. We will not cover how to set up a Hadoop or MongoDB cluster. We discuss how to set up a production Drill cluster in Chapter 9.

Preparing Your Cluster for Drill

Before you install Drill on a cluster, your cluster must have the following installed:

- Oracle Java SE Development Kit 8 (JDK 8) (*https://bit.ly/1lO1FSV*) available
- ZooKeeper (*http://zookeeper.apache.org*)
- A distributed filesystem such as HDFS or S3

When running in embedded mode, or as a server on a single machine, Drill can read from either your local filesystem or a distributed filesystem. But when you run in distributed mode (with two or more Drill servers), you must use a distributed filesystem such as HDFS or Amazon S3.

Regardless of whether you run in embedded or server mode, Drill allows you to query any number of data sources in a single query in order to do joins, unions, and other SQL operations.

Drillbits form a Drill cluster using ZooKeeper, as described shortly. Even if you run a "single-node cluster" (a single Drillbit) on your laptop, you must also run ZooKeeper. For details on installing and configuring a ZooKeeper cluster, consult the "Getting Started Guide" (*https://zookeeper.apache.org/doc/current/zookeeperStarted.html*).

Depending on your system, either one of these commands will download the file:

```
wget http://drill.apache.org/download/apache-drill-version.tar.gz
curl -o apache-drill-version.tar.gz \
http://drill.apache.org/download/apache-drill-version.tar.gz
```

After you have moved Drill to the desired location, decompress it in the directory of your choice, such as */opt*:

```
tar -xvzf apache-drill-version.tar.gz
```

Finally, you may need to configure the node to communicate with ZooKeeper. The default file is fine for a single Drillbit with ZooKeeper running on the same host with default options. You must configure Drill for all other cases. To do this, you will need to modify the *drill-override.conf* file, which you can find at *path_to_drill/conf/drill-override.conf*. You will need to configure each node with the ZooKeeper host names and port numbers, as demonstrated in the following:

```
drill.exec:{
   cluster-id: "drillbits1",
   zk.connect: "zkhostname1:2181,
                zkhostname2:2181,
                zkhostname3:2181"
}
```

Configuration must be the same for all nodes in your Drill cluster. The default ZooKeeper port is 2181.

Starting Drill in Distributed Mode

To use Drill in distributed mode, each node in your cluster must have a Drillbit running on it. After you configure each node (as described in the previous section), you now have to start the Drillbit:

```
$DRILL_HOME/bin/drillbit.sh start
```

You can start, restart, stop, check the status of the daemon, or set it to autorestart with the same script, as follows:

```
$DRILL_HOME/bin/drillbit.sh [start|stop|restart|status|autorestart]
```

After you've started the Drill daemon on every node in your cluster, you are ready to connect to the cluster.

Connecting to the Cluster

The final step is starting the Drill shell. Execute the following command:

```
$DRILL_HOME/bin/sqlline -u jdbc:drill:zk=zkhost1,zkhost2,zkhost3:2181
```

If all goes well, the Drill shell will open. Execute the following query to verify the connection to the Drillbit:

```
SELECT * FROM sys.drillbits;
```

Drill also provides the *drill-localhost* script, which you can use to connect to Drill when ZooKeeper is installed on a local machine (typically when running a single Drillbit on your laptop).

Conclusion

If you've been following along on your computer, you should have a functioning installation of Apache Drill and are ready to query data on it. In the next few chapters, you will learn how to query various types of data using Drill.

CHAPTER 3

Overview of Apache Drill

Apache Drill is a distributed schema-on-read query engine loosely associated with the Hadoop ecosystem. This chapter unpacks this statement so you understand what Drill is and how it works before we dive into the details of using, deploying, and extending Drill.

The Apache Hadoop Ecosystem

Many excellent books exist to describe Apache Hadoop (*http://hadoop.apache.org/*) and its components. Here we expand on the introduction in Chapter 1 with the key concepts needed to understand Drill.

Hadoop consists of the Hadoop Distributed File System (HDFS), MapReduce, and the YARN job scheduler. Drill is best thought of as an alternative to YARN and Map-Reduce for processing data stored in HDFS.

The extended Hadoop ecosystem (sometimes called "Hadoop and Friends") includes a wide variety of tools. For our purposes these include the following:

- Alternative storage engines (e.g., MapR–FS, and Amazon S3)
- Database-like storage engines (e.g., HBase and MapR-DB)
- Compute engines (e.g., MapReduce and Apache Spark)
- Query engines (e.g., Apache Hive, Drill, Preso, Apache Impala, and Spark SQL)
- Coordination tools (e.g., Apache ZooKeeper and etcd)
- Cluster coordinators (e.g., manual, YARN, Mesos, and Docker/Kubernetes)

This list does not begin to touch on the many tools for coordinating workflows (e.g., Oozie and AirFlow), data ingest (e.g., Sqoop and Kafka), or many other purposes.

Drill Is a Low-Latency Query Engine

With so many options, you might wonder: where does Drill fit into this ecosystem? Drill is a low-latency query engine intended for interactive queries, especially those that power business intelligence tools such as Tableau.

Hadoop provides many query tool options.[1] The granddaddy is Apache Hive (*https://hive.apache.org*): a SQL-like engine that generates MapReduce jobs. Hive is like a freight train: it handles the massive scale needed for complex ETL tasks but moves too slowly for interactive queries. Apache Drill, Apache Impala (*https://impala.apache.org*), Hive LLAP (*https://cwiki.apache.org/confluence/display/Hive/LLAP*), and Presto (*https://prestodb.io*) are SQL query engines that target interactive uses. Although Impala is fast, it has historically been difficult to build and extend, works primarily with the Parquet file format and requires the Hive Metastore.

Drill's sweet spot is that it works with a wide variety of file formats and is extendable by savvy Java programmers. (Later chapters explain how to create extensions for user-defined functions and file format plug-ins.) Because Drill is developed in Java, it is far easier to build than the C++-based Impala.

Unlike other query engines, Drill can retrieve data not just from HDFS, but also from a wide variety of other storage systems (MapR-FS, Amazon S3, HBase, Kafka, and more). The Drill community continues to add integrations with other systems.

A key difference between Drill on the one hand and Hive or Impala on the other is that Drill does not require that you define metadata before querying files. Although Drill can use the Hive metastore, most users achieve great results by pointing Drill directly at their files without the complexity of metadata, metadata refreshes, and so on.

See Chapter 8 for more on the nuances of using Drill without metadata.

Distributed Processing with HDFS

HDFS stores data in (preferably) large files and provides a client API to access those files from any node in the Hadoop cluster. Historically, the best performance occurs when an application observes "data locality": moving processing to the nodes that contain the data of interest.

---

1 Distributed data storage is a complex and fascinating topic that we only touch upon here. For an in-depth discussion, see the excellent O'Reilly book *Designing Data-Intensive Applications* by Martin Kleppmann.

HDFS is a distributed filesystem. It divides each file into a set of blocks, typically 128 MB or 256 MB in size, and distributes the blocks across a set of data nodes. For resilience, it replicates each block, typically creating three copies. Data locality thus means moving computation to one of the three available nodes for each block and then combining the results. This is exactly what the classic MapReduce algorithm does: it "maps" work to data nodes and then "reduces" (collects) the results.

Conceptually Drill works the same way, though as we will see, the details differ to minimize query latency.

Elements of a Drill System

Figure 3-1 shows how Drill fits into a typical Hadoop system.

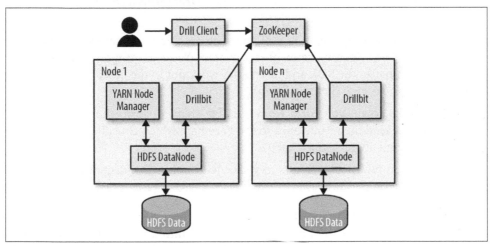

Figure 3-1. Overview of Drill in the Hadoop ecosystem

Drill runs on each data node, typically alongside YARN (which handles Spark and MapReduce jobs). Drill reads data from HDFS using the HDFS client API. Because Drill resides on the same nodes as the data, data reads are local, meaning that reads are often on a single node and almost always on the same rack.

When run in Amazon Elastic Compute Cloud (Amazon EC2), Drill resides on a set of EC2 instances and typically reads data from files stored in Amazon S3: a configuration called "separation of compute and storage." Such a configuration requires that all your data flows over the Amazon network.

Drill uses ZooKeeper to coordinate the Drill cluster. Each Drillbit registers itself in ZooKeeper so that it can be found by the other Drillbits and by Drill clients. Drill also uses ZooKeeper for its configuration (the storage and format configuration discussed in later chapters) and to implement its admission control mechanism (discussed in Chapter 9).

To connect to Drill, you use a Drill client—typically the JDBC or ODBC interfaces—and some client application such as SQLLine (discussed later) or Tableau. The client application connects to ZooKeeper to learn which Drillbits are running, and then (typically) connects to a random Drillbit, which acts as the "Foreman" to process your queries.

Drill Operation: The 30,000-Foot View

We now know enough to sketch out how Drill operates in the most general sense:

1. You store your data into a distributed filesystem (such as HDFS) in one of Drill's many supported formats (Parquet, JSON, CSV, and so on).

2. You start Drillbits on each of your data nodes. Drill forms a cluster through Zoo-Keeper.

3. You connect to Drill using a tool of your choice. The tool queries ZooKeeper to locate a Drillbit which becomes the Foreman. You submit queries to the Foreman, which parses the SQL and distributes work out to the other "worker" Drillbits (the equivalent of the "map" step).

4. The Drillbits obtain your data from the filesystem, perform the requested processing, and send the results back to the Foreman, which consolidates the results (the equivalent of the "reduce" step).

5. The Foreman returns the results to your client tool, which displays them, charts them, and so on.

Chapter 2 showed how to set up Drill in a simple single-node "cluster" for testing and development; Chapter 9 shows how to deploy Drill into a production Hadoop-like (HDFS, MapR-FS, or Amazon S3) cluster.

Drill Is a Query Engine, Not a Database

Chapter 1 mentioned that one common source of confusion for people coming from the relational database world is that Drill uses SQL. If databases such as MySQL, Postgres, and Oracle also use SQL, doesn't that mean that Drill is a database, too? Understanding this distinction is key to understanding Drill's place in the world.

A full relational database includes a storage layer and thus provides two kinds of operations:

- Data definition language (DDL) statements such as CREATE DATABASE, CREATE TABLE, CREATE INDEX, etc.)

- Data manipulation language (DML) (also called "CRUD" for Create, Read, Update, and Delete) statements such as INSERT, SELECT, UPDATE, DELETE

With Drill, HDFS (or a similar system) provides the storage layer. As a result, Drill needs no statements to create a database.

Drill treats files (actually, collections of files, which we discuss later) as tables. Drill's version of the CREATE TABLE statement is CREATE TABLE AS (CTAS), which writes files directly to HDFS. Further, because files are scanned sequentially (more on this momentarily), we do not have indexes, so there are no CREATE INDEX statements. (As discussed later, big data query engines use *partitioning* in place of indexes.)

Although you can add files to HDFS, each file is immutable after it is written. Thus, Drill supports no INSERT, UPDATE, or DELETE statements.

Files carry their own schema (the so-called "schema-free" or "schema-on-read" model). Thus, there are no DDL statements related to creating table, column, or index schemas.

If Drill does not handle storage or schema definition, what is left? In big data, the primary operation is the (distributed) execution of queries: the SELECT statement. Thus, to a first approximation, you can think of Drill as a SQL engine that performs SELECT statements across large distributed datasets.

Drill Operation Overview

We're now ready to look at the next level of detail of how Drill processes each query. Understanding these steps provides context for later chapters. Big data clusters are highly complex, and it can often be difficult to know where to look when problems occur. Understanding Drill's operation will help you determine whether the problem is in your query, your configuration, your files, and so on.

Drill Components

Drill is composed of four main parts:

- The Drill client, which connects to a Foreman, submits SQL statements, and receives results
- The Foreman, a Drill server selected to maintain your session state and process your queries. Drill clients distribute the Foreman roles for sessions by randomly selecting one of the Drillbits to act as Foreman for that session.
- The worker Drillbit servers, which do the actual work of running your query
- The ZooKeeper server, which coordinates the Drillbits within the Drill cluster

SQL Session State

Drill is a SQL engine. SQL is a stateful language: commands you issue in your session influence how later commands behave. As a trivial example, a session often begins with a USE DATABASE statement to select the database to use. Later SQL commands interpret names, such as SELECT * FROM `customers`, in the context of the selected database.

Although Drill is designed to be completely symmetrical, SQL requires that we break this symmetry at the connection level. In Drill you can connect to any random Drillbit, but after you're connected, all your subsequent queries must go to that same Drillbit so that they can reuse the session state stored in that Drillbit. In fact, the Foreman for a session is simply the Drillbit that maintains state for your specific connections. (Other Drillbits will act as the Foreman for other connections.)

The state that Drill maintains includes:

- The database (USE DATABASE) or workspace (USE WORKSPACE) that you've selected
- Session options selected with the UPDATE SESSION command
- The state for in-flight queries (the Drill client can run multiple queries in parallel)
- Temporary tables created by using the CREATE TEMPORARY TABLE AS (CTTAS) command

Session state lives only as long as the connection is active. If your connection drops, you will need to re-create session state when you reconnect. (This is why the Drill client cannot reconnect automatically. If it did, a query that worked fine one moment might fail the next because of the hidden loss of session state.)

Statement Preparation

Drill follows classic database practice to run a SQL statement:

- Prepare the statement (translate from SQL into a *physical execution plan*).
- Execute the physical plan to produce the desired results.

SQL is well known for providing a "relational calculus" format: you specify what you want, not how to get it. For example:

```
SELECT `name` FROM `customers.csv` WHERE `state` = 'CA'
```

to find the names of customers in California. Drill translates this to "relational algebra," such as "scan the *customers.csv* table, and then apply a filter that selects those where state equals CA"). Databases use the term "prepare" for this translation process.

The preparation phase itself consists of a number of phases:

1. Parse the SQL statement into an internal parse tree.
2. Perform semantic analysis on the parse tree by resolving names the selected database, against the schema (set of tables) in that database, the set of columns in those tables, and the set of functions defined within Drill.
3. Convert the SQL parse tree into a logical plan, which can be thought of as a block diagram of the major operations needed to perform the given query.
4. Convert the logical plan into a physical plan by performing a cost-based optimization step that looks for the most efficient way to execute the logical plan.
5. Convert the physical plan into an execution plan by determining how to distribute work across the available worker Drillbits.

Drill uses Apache Calcite (*https://calcite.apache.org/*) for much of the processing (up to the physical plan). Although the preceding steps apply to all SQL statements, as we saw earlier, Drill is a query engine so our primary focus in on SELECT statements.

Figure 3-2 illustrates the steps.

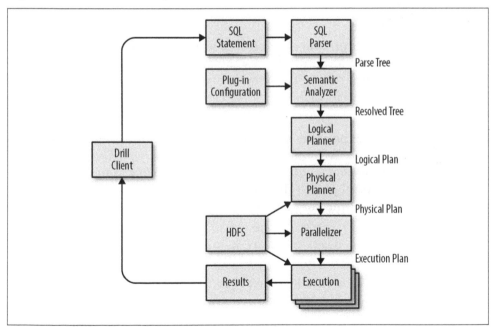

Figure 3-2. Life cycle of a Drill query

Parsing and semantic analysis

The parse phase is the one that checks your SQL syntax. If you make a SQL syntax error, Drill will display a long error message that attempts to explain the error. (Error reporting is a work in progress in Drill.)

The next step looks up names, and this can seem complex to those accustomed to databases with schemas. At prepare time, Drill knows the names of databases (called *storage plug-ins* in Drill) and tables. However, Drill *does not* know the names of columns. So, it postpones some decisions about columns to runtime. In particular, Drill does not know the data types of columns until it runs the query. This means that type-related errors that you might expect to be caught at prepare time are, in Drill, found only at runtime.

Furthermore, Drill will accept any column name, even the names of columns that don't actually exist in your table. Again, Drill does not know the set of available columns at prepare time. Because tables are just (collections of) files, it might even be that newer versions of the file have the requested column, but older files do not. Drill's schema-on-read system can handle such scenarios, whereas a system based on metadata cannot.

Logical and physical plans

Once the names are known, Drill uses Calcite to work out a logical plan for the query. For example, Drill might identify that you want to join tables A and B. The next step, the physical plan, works out the best way to implement the join. (Like most query engines, Drill implements multiple join *operators* and chooses the lowest-cost alternative for each query.)

The logical and physical plans are key to understanding how Drill operates and how to optimize queries. The Drill Web Console provides a *query profile* for each query. The query profile includes a visualization of the query plan in a form that is a hybrid of the logical and physical plans. (The diagram shows decisions made in the physical plan but omits many of the gory details, making the diagram closer to the logical plan.)

A query plan is a set of operators grouped into major fragments. An operator is a distinct operation such as "scan a file," "filter a result set," or "perform a join." Often, several operators can be combined into a pipeline. For example, the scan operation is typically combined with a filter operation.

Because Drill is distributed, data must sometimes be exchanged among Drillbits (called a "shuffle" in MapReduce and Spark). For example, to perform a GROUP BY operation, like rows are collected from all scan operators and sent to the Drillbit that will perform the aggregation for each group.

The set of operations that can be done without an exchange is grouped into a thread of execution called a *major fragment*. The Drill web console query profile view uses colors to show the set of operators that belong to the same major fragment. Every major fragment starts with either a scan or an exchange receiver. Each major fragment ends with either an exchange sender or (for the root fragment) a send back to the Drill client.

Operators make up a tree. The root is the *screen* operator (the one that talks to the Drill client). The leaves are scan operators that read data into Drill. Likewise, major fragments form a tree, but at a higher level of abstraction. The Drill web console displays the tree with the screen (root) operator at the top, and the scans (leaves) at the bottom.

Data flows from the leaves to the intermediate nodes and ultimately to the root (screen). From the perspective of an internal node, Drill uses the term *upstream* to indicate the source of data, which is toward the leaves. Similarly, the term *downstream* indicates the destination of the data, which is toward the root. (Confusingly, in the Drill web console, upstream is toward the bottom of the image; downstream is toward the top).

Distribution

The final step of query preparation is to distribute the physical plan across nodes. Because each major fragment is a single thread of execution, Drill performs distribution at the level of the major fragment. If, for instance, a major fragment scans a file, Drill will slice the fragment into pieces: one for each input file (if scanning a directory) and for each HDFS block in each file. The result is a set of slices (called *minor fragments*)—the smallest possible units of work in Drill.

Drill distributes the set of minor fragments to Drillbits for execution. The slicing process is a bit complex but well worth understanding because it helps you to understand the query profile and how best to tune query execution.

When parallelizing fragments, Drill considers where best to place each. For a scan, each fragment corresponds to one HDFS block for one file, so the best place to execute that fragment is on a node with the data. Because HDFS uses three-way replication, Drill has three "best" choices for the node to hold the fragment. Preferring to place a fragment on the same node as the data is called *data affinity*. Data affinity is only possible when Drill runs on the same node as the data. When compute and storage are separated (as when using Amazon S3), data affinity is ignored and Drill simply divides up work randomly.

Suppose that your file has 1,000 blocks, but your cluster has only 100 CPUs. Drill could create 1,000 different scan fragments, but doing so would simply create far more threads than CPUs, causing unnecessary CPU contention. Instead, Drill picks an ideal slice target per node. (By default, this number is 70% of the number of cores on the node.) Drill will create no more than this number of minor fragments. It then assigns files or file blocks to minor fragments, combining blocks if needed. In this example, with 100 cores, Drill will create 70 units of work, each of which will read approximately 14 blocks. Of course, if your query reads just a few blocks, Drill will create fewer minor fragments than the maximum.

Parallelizing of internal operators is similar, but without data affinity considerations. Instead, Drill might group data based on hash keys (for joins and grouping) or other considerations.

The slice target mentioned earlier applies to the slices of each major fragment. At present, Drill slices each major fragment independently. If your query is complex and has, say, 10 major fragments, Drill will parallelize each to 70% of the number of cores on your system. The result will be seven threads per core. Further, each query is parallelized independently of other queries (which might be planned on different Drillbits). As a result, in extreme cases Drill might create far more threads than the system has cores, leading to thrashing. If you find yourself pushing Drill to these extremes, consider enabling admission control (discussed in Chapter 9) to limit the number of queries.

Drill uses ZooKeeper to determine the set of Drillbits in the cluster. Thus, if you add a new Drillbit to the cluster, Drill will use it for new queries as soon as the Drillbit registers itself with ZooKeeper.

It is worth noting that the root fragment (the one with the screen operator) is special: it always has just one minor fragment, and that minor fragment always runs on the Foreman node for that session.

For those familiar with Apache Spark, Drill and Spark use similar structures but different names. Table 3-1 provides a quick reference.

Table 3-1. Comparison of distribution terminology

Drill	MapReduce	Spark
Query	Job	Job
Major fragment	Map or reduce	Stage
Minor fragment	Mapper, reducer	Stage
Operator	N/A	Task
Exchange	Shuffle	Shuffle

Statement Execution

After Drill has a finished query plan, the next step is to do something with the plan. Drill has two choices:

- Return the plan to the user (this is what happens if you use the EXPLAIN PLAN statement).

- Execute the plan on the cluster (the most common case).

The Foreman is responsible for orchestrating the query process. It will:

- Optionally wait for an opportunity to execute (if admission control is enabled).

- Send minor fragments to Drillbits for execution.

- Monitor progress of execution, watching for failures (due to problems in the query or the failure of a Drillbit).

- Track minor fragments as they complete.

- After the root fragment completes, shut down the query and write the query profile.

Drill uses a state machine for each query to track the progress of each minor fragment. The Drill web console collects this information to show the state of active queries. When a query completes, the final state of the query (along with a wealth of detailed data) is written to the query profile, which you can view in the Drill web console. In fact, the best way to develop a deeper understanding of the process described in this section is to spend time exploring the profile for a completed query.

Data representation

We have seen that Drill distributes work to Drillbits in the form of minor fragments, each of which contains a set of operators. Leaf fragments contain a set of one or more scan operators. The next question is: how does Drill represent the rows within the query?

Drill is a SQL engine, meaning that data is represented as rows and columns. JDBC and ODBC present query results one row at a time, with methods to access each column.

Drill, however, is a big data engine; processing data at the row level would not be very efficient. Thus, even though Drill processes data row by row, it does so by grouping rows into *record batches* that range in size from a few thousand up to 65,536 rows. Record batches are the unit of exchange at shuffles, and the units of data returned to the Drill client. The JDBC and ODBC drivers receive record batches and then iterate over them to return individual rows.

Suppose that your query reads a block of data that contains a million rows. Drill will read this data as a set of, say, 20 record batches with 50,000 records per batch. (The actual batch size varies depending on data format and size.) The minor fragment passes the record batches from one operator to the next, applying varying transforms.

When a batch reaches the top of the fragment, Drill sends the batch over the wire to the next minor fragment up the tree.

Query engines typically use one of two formats for data: *row oriented* or *columnar*. Drill is a columnar engine. This means that Drill stores data as columns, termed *value vectors*. Think of a value vector as an array of values. For example, if you have rows of data that contain an integer column N, all values for N are stored together in an array. Rows are simply a common index into a group of value vectors. The Drill record batch is thus simply a collection of value vectors.

Some of Drill's older materials talked about *vectorized processing*, the idea being that Drill might eventually use the Single Instruction, Multiple Data (SIMD) instructions of modern processors to speed up execution. At present, this is mostly still an aspiration, for two reasons. First, Drill uses SQL data types, which often include null values, which SIMD instructions do not support. Second, because Drill is SQL-based, it tends to work row by row rather than column by column, which makes it difficult to use a SIMD instruction to process a column. (The Drill project welcomes contributions to solve challenges such as this.)

You will encounter the columnar representation in two ways. First, the query profile displays the number of record batches processed by each operator and fragment. Second, if you create Drill extensions (as described in later chapters), you will work directly with Drill's value vectors and record batches.

Drill's value vectors were the starting point for the Apache Arrow (*https://arrow.apache.org/*) project, which provided a general-purpose columnar format for a variety of tools. Although Drill does not yet use Arrow, such use is possible in the future. (Drill has implemented substantial additional functionality not yet available in Arrow, so additional work is needed before the two can reconverge.)

Low-Latency Features

We mentioned earlier that Drill is a low-latency query engine. Drill uses a number of techniques to reduce latency.

Long-lived Drillbits

Even though MapReduce and thus Hive are known for extreme scalability, they are not particularly fast. Part of this is due to the way that MapReduce itself works: YARN must start a new process for each mapper or reducer.

Spark is faster because each application reuses the same set of Spark executors for each of its jobs. However, each application uses a separate set of executors, which incurs startup costs.

Drill takes the Spark idea one step further: it uses a single executor (the Drillbit) per node and for all minor fragments on that node. This architecture is similar to that used for Impala (the `impalad` process) and for Hive LLAP (Live Long and Process).

Because Drillbits are long-running, Drill can execute minor fragments immediately upon receipt without the overhead of starting a new process.

This speed-up comes at a cost, however: a loss of workload isolation. In some cases, excessive memory use by one query can cause another query to run out of memory. Excessive compution by one query can slow down all queries. This "noisy neighbor" problem occurs in many concurrent systems, and it typically becomes a problem in Drill only under heavy load. Because even separate processes will run into problems under heavy load, Drill's design is not an unreasonable trade-off. Drill's admission control mechanism can help reduce the noisy-neighbor problem if it does occur.

Code generation

Spark requires separate executors for each application because Spark users express their applications as code (in Scala, Java, or Python). Similarly, MapReduce must distribute application code to each mapper or reducer. Drill avoids the code distribution step for two reasons:

- Drill uses SQL as its input language, avoiding the need to execute application-specific code.
- Drill generates Java code on each Drillbit for each query, allowing a single Drillbit to handle any number of queries.

Earlier, we discussed that Drill translates a SQL statement into a physical plan sent to the Drillbits. To gain maximum performance, each operator translates its part of the physical plan to Java code, which the operator then executes against each of its incoming record batches.

Local code generation not only avoids the cost and complexity of code distribution but is an essential aspect of Drill's schema-on-read approach. Only when an operator sees the first batch of data will it know the type of each column. For example, a query might contain the clause `A + B`. Until we know the types of the columns, we don't know whether we need to perform integer, floating-point, or decimal arithmetic. Further, different scan operators might see different versions of the file schema, and so each fragment might, in some cases, see a slightly different schema and generate different code. Thus, Drill cannot generate code up front, nor can the same code be used by all fragments.

Drill processes this sample expression in a Project operator. As soon as that operator sees the first batch of data it can determine, say, that A is an `INT` and B is a `DOUBLE` (floating-point number). This allows the operator to generate Java code to convert A from INT to DOUBLE, and then add the two DOUBLEs.

This is a trivial example. Code generation is used heavily in filter, aggregation, join, and other operations. This not only allows Drill to use the same generic Drillbit for all queries, but also execute (Drill-generated) code specific to each query.

Network exchanges

The final key performance tool in Drill is its "in-memory" processing model. MapReduce writes shuffle data to disk after the map phase, to be read in the reduce phase. Drill avoids intermediate disk files by transferring data directly over the network from the Drillbit running an upstream (sending) fragment to the Drillbit running the downstream (receiving) fragment.

The Drill value vector format is designed to optimize exchanges: the same data buffers used for processing data within operators is used in Drill's Netty-based network layer. Drill uses a sophisticated handshake mechanism to implement backpressure: a signal to the producing fragments to stop sending if the downstream fragment can't keep up. You will see this delay reflected in the times reported in the query profile.

If a query runs slower than you expect, it might be due to a related issue: that some operators (such as the sort operator), cannot finish until they receive all of their inputs. If data is skewed (some fragments process much more than others), the sort must wait for the slowest sender, even if all other fragments are completed. The query profile timing numbers and timing charts help you to identify such cases.

Although Drill uses network exchanges to avoid shuffle files, there are times when Drill will still write to disk. *Buffering operators*, such as sort, hash aggregate, and hash join operators, must store all (or for a join, part) of their input in memory. If the query includes more data than will fit in memory, Drill operators will *spill* data to a temporary file on the local disk (or, if configured to do so, to the distributed filesystem). Operators that support spilling gather spill statistics that are available in the query profile. Although spilling ensures that queries complete, spilling is slower than in-memory processing. If a query begins to slow unexpectedly as data sizes increase, check the query profile to see whether operators have begun to spill.

Conclusion

People coming to big data from a traditional relational database sometimes expect Drill to "just work," assuming that, like a traditional database, Drill has full control over data layout, memory, CPU usage, plan optimization, and so on. The previous section should help you to understand the many complexities that Drill must manage in a big data system. Data is stored in HDFS. As we will soon see, the way that you store data (that is, partitioning) has a large impact on query performance. Because

Drill is query-on-read, the format of the file can affect query success if the file format is ambiguous or inconsistent.

The performance of a query is heavily influenced by disk I/O performance, by network performance, by the amount of memory available to Drill, and by the load placed on the system by other Drill queries and other compute tools.

Apache Drill is a very handy tool to have in your big data toolkit. But Drill is not magic: it is only as good as the design of your data and cluster. The preceding overview has introduced some of the concepts that you should be aware of as you tune your application; we expand on these ideas in later chapters.

This chapter provided only a high-level overview of Drill's operation. Much more detailed information is available online:

- Drill architecture (*https://drill.apache.org/docs/architecture-introduction/*)
- Query execution (*https://drill.apache.org/docs/drill-query-execution/*)
- Core modules (*https://drill.apache.org/docs/core-modules/*)
- Combination of the three (*http://bit.ly/2DbfugK*)

CHAPTER 4

Querying Delimited Data

In this chapter we get started with Apache Drill by querying simple data. We are defining "simple data" as data contained in a delimited file such as a spreadsheet or comma-separated values (CSV) file, from a single source. If you have worked with SQL databases, you will find that querying simple data with Drill is not much different than querying data from a relational database. However, there are some differences that are important to understand in order to unleash the full power of Drill. We assume that you are familiar with basic SQL syntax, but if you are not, we recommend *SQL Queries for Mere Mortals* (Addison-Wesley) by John Viescas as a good SQL primer.

To follow along, start Drill in embedded mode as explained in Chapter 2 and download the example files, which are available in the GitHub repository (*https://github.com/cgivre/drillbook*) for this book.

Ways of Querying Data with Drill

Drill is very flexible and provides you with several different ways of querying data. You've already seen that Drill has a command-line interface known as *SQLLine*. In addition to the command line, Drill has a web interface that you can access by opening a browser (after Drill is running) and navigating to *http://localhost:8047*, as shown in Figure 4-1.

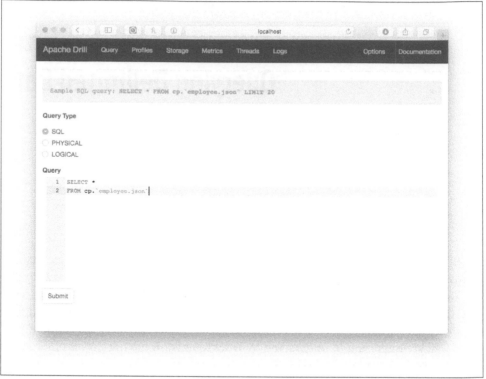

Figure 4-1. The Drill Web Console

Other Interfaces

You can also query data with Drill by using Drill's RESTful interface or by using a conventional tool such as Tableau and using Drill's ODBC or JDBC interfaces. We cover these interfaces later in the book and demonstrate how to query Drill using your favorite scripting languages, such as Python or R.

Lastly, if you install the MapR ODBC driver for Drill (*http://package.mapr.com/tools/ MapR-ODBC/MapR_Drill/*), bundled with that is a tool called *Drill Explorer*, which is another GUI for querying Drill.

For the beginning examples, we recommend that you start out by using the Web Console because there are certain features that are most easily accessed through it.

Drill SQL Query Format

Drill uses the ANSI SQL standard with some extensions around database table and schema naming. So, if you are comfortable with relational databases most of Drill's

SQL syntax will look very familiar to you. Let's begin with a basic query. Every SQL SELECT query essentially follows this format:

```
SELECT list_of_fields
FROM one_or_more_tables
WHERE some_logical_condition
GROUP BY some_field
```

As in standard SQL, the SELECT and FROM clauses are required, the WHERE and GROUP BY clauses are optional. Again, this should look relatively familiar to you, and this chapter will focus on Drill's unique features in SQL.

Choosing a Data Source

In most ways, Drill behaves like a traditional relational database, with the major difference being that Drill treats files (or directories) as tables. Drill can also connect to relational databases or other structured data stores, such as Hive or HBase, and join them with other data sources, but for now, let's look at querying a simple CSV file in Drill:

```
SELECT first_name, last_name, street_address, age
FROM dfs.user_data.`users.csv`
WHERE age > 21
```

This queries a sample data file called *users.csv* and returns the first name, last name, and street address of every user whose age is greater than 21. If you are familiar with relational databases, the only part that might look unusual is this line:

```
FROM dfs.user_data.`users.csv`
```

In a traditional database, the FROM clause contains the names of tables, or optionally the names of additional databases and associated tables. However, Drill treats files as tables, so in this example, you can see how to instruct Drill which file to query.

Drill accesses data sources using storage plug-ins, and the kind of system your data is stored in will dictate which storage plug-in you use. In Drill, the FROM clause has three components that do slightly different things depending on what kind of storage plug-in you are using. The components are the *storage plug-in* name, the *workspace* name, and the *table* name. In the previous example, dfs is one of the default storage plug-ins; "dfs" stands for *distributed filesystem* and is used to access data from sources such as HDFS, cloud storage, and files stored on the local system.[1] The next component is optional; it's the workspace, which is a shortcut to a file path on your system. If you didn't want to use a workspace, you could enter the following:

```
FROM dfs.`full_file_path/users.csv`
```

---

[1] The label "dfs" is actually arbitrary, and you can rename it whatever you want it to be. We will cover this later in this chapter.

Finally, there is the table, which this storage plug-in corresponds to a file or directory. In addition to the dfs plug-in, Drill ships with the cp or *classpath* plug-in enabled, which queries files stored in one of the directories in your Java classpath, typically used to access the example files included with Drill.

As illustrated in Figure 4-2, the Storage Configuration panel is where you can enable, disable, and configure the various storage plug-ins. You should resist the temptation to enable all the disabled plug-ins because you will get bad performance and strange error messages if you try to use Drill with an improperly configured storage plug-in enabled.

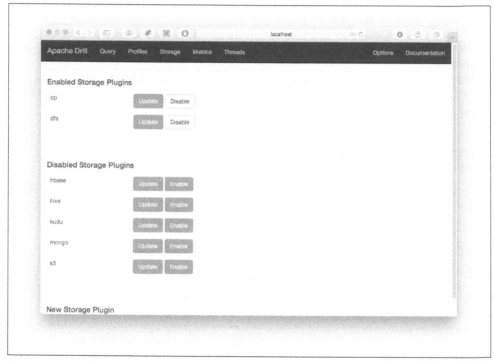

Figure 4-2. Drill storage plug-in configuration

Defining a Workspace

In Drill parlance, when you are using file-based systems, a workspace is a shortcut to a file path. To create a workspace, open the Drill web interface and then, at the top of the screen, click the Storage tab.

Next, click the Update button next to the dfs plug-in (see Figure 4-2) and you will see the configuration variables. You will see a section called workspaces, and there you will see the default workspaces, root and tmp, as shown here:

```
"workspaces": {
    "root": {
      "location": "/",
      "writable": false,
     "defaultInputFormat": null
    },
    "tmp": {
      "location": "/tmp",
      "writable": true,
     "defaultInputFormat": null
    }
  },
```

To create your own workspace, simply add another entry into the workspaces section with a path to a location on your local filesystem:

```
"drill_tutorial": {
  "location": "your_path",
  "writable": true,
  "defaultInputFormat": null
}
```

You must have read permission to be able to read data in your workspace, and it goes without saying that if you want to write to this path, you must have write permissions. You can configure workspaces as being writable or not, as well as setting a default file format. Often you will want to take the results of complex queries and create tables or views, and the workspace must be writable in order to store a view or new table. After you've created your workspace, at the bottom of the screen, click the Update button.

You can verify that your workspace was successfully created by executing a SHOW DATABASES statement; you should see your newly created workspace in the results.

View Your Configuration by Using the DESCRIBE Statement

In addition to the SHOW DATABASES statement, you can also view the plug-in configuration by using the DESCRIBE SCHEMA statement. For instance, you can view the configuration used in a notional workspace called test by using the statement DESCRIBE SCHEMA dfs.test.

Specifying a Default Data Source

The examples thus far use file paths in the FROM clause. In practice, these clauses can become long, and it is tedious to type them over and over in an interactive session. Drill has the idea of a *default data source*, which is used if you don't specify a data source (storage plug-in and workspace, also called a *namespace*) in your query. You use the USE statement to select the data source to use as the default, as shown here for dfs.data:

```
USE dfs.data;
SELECT *
FROM `users.csv`
WHERE age > 20
```

So, the preceding query is functionally equivalent to the query that follows.

```
SELECT *
FROM dfs.data.`users.csv`
WHERE age > 20
```

SQL Sessions

Drill is a SQL tool. SQL uses the idea of a session that is tied to a Drill connection. Session state, such as the USE statement, applies only to that one session.

JDBC, ODBC, and most BI tools create sessions; however, Drill's Web Console does not, and therefore the USE operator will not work in the Web Console. The Web Console uses Drill's RESTful interface. When you execute queries using the RESTful interface, each query is executed in its own session and the USE statement unhelpfully lasts only for the single REST request in which it was submitted.

Saving Your Settings

By default, in embedded mode Drill saves all settings in the */tmp* directory, which often does not persist if the machine is rebooted. To save your settings while running in embedded mode, you will need to modify the *drill-override.conf* file, which is located in the *DRILL_HOME/conf/* folder, by adding the following:

```
sys.store.provider.local.path="path to directory"
```

to the section drill.exec and supplying a nontemporary path, as shown here:

```
drill.exec: {
    cluster-id: "drillbits1",
    zk.connect: "localhost:2181",
    sys.store.provider.local.path="path_to_save_file"
}
```

It is a better practice to set up a single-node Drill cluster with Zoo-Keeper to save state correctly. When running Drill in server mode, Drill saves state in ZooKeeper so that it can be shared by multiple Drillbits and can be persisted across server restarts.

After you have specified a namespace with the USE operator, you can still access other namespaces, but you will need to explicitly list them, as shown here:

```
USE dfs.data
SELECT *
FROM `users.csv` AS u
INNER JOIN dfs.logs.`logfile.txt` AS l ON l.id=u.id
```

You can see in this example that the query joins data from *users.csv* with another file called *logfile.txt*, which is in a completely different namespace.

A Word About Case Sensitivity in Drill

In general, Drill is case insensitive. Books, including this one, generally show SQL keywords in uppercase. However, it is important to remember the few instances in which Drill is case sensitive. We would recommend treating database, table, and column names as if they were case sensitive, and then you won't have any Drill problems. Table 4-1 lists the instances for which Drill is case sensitive.

Table 4-1. Case sensitivity in Drill

Command/use	Case sensitive
Storage plug-in names	Yes[a]
Workspace names	Yes
File paths	Yes (on Linux and macOS, not Windows)
SQL commands	No
Column names	Generally no
JSON field names	No
Hive	No
HBase	Yes

[a] Starting with Drill 1.15, format and storage plug-in names will become case insensitive. To avoid future issues, we recommend naming all format and storage plug-ins using "camelCase".

Accessing Columns in a Query

Relational databases are considered *schema-on-write* in that the schema must be defined prior to writing the data on disk. More recently, tools such as Apache Spark use a technique called *schema-on-read*, which allows more flexibility because it allows users to modify the schema as the data is being ingested rather than being tied to a rigid, predefined schema.

Drill takes a different approach and relies on the data's natural structure for its queries. Suppose that we have a file called *customer_data.csv* that contains three columns of data: `first_name`, `last_name`, and `birthday`. Drill infers the schema directly from the structure of the data and, as such, you do not need to define any kind of schema prior to querying your data with Drill.

As an example, Drill will allow you to query this data directly by simply executing the following query:

```
SELECT *
FROM dfs.drill_tutorial.`customer_data.csv`
```

However, when you execute this query you will notice that Drill returns a single column for each row of data. This one column is called `columns` and is an array of VAR CHAR as shown in the following table:

columns
["Robert","Hernandez","5/3/67"]
["Steve","Smith","8/4/84"]
["Anne","Raps","9/13/91"]
["Alice","Muller","4/15/75"]

Drill infers a schema directly from your data. In this case, we have a CSV file without column headings. Since Drill doesn't know the name or number of fields, it instead returns the fields as an array. (We will see shortly how column headings change the results.) This represents a major difference between Drill and relational databases: Drill supports nested data structures such as arrays and maps, whereas conventional relational databases do not. In Drill, just as in many other programming languages, arrays are zero-indexed, meaning that the first item in an array is the *0th* item. Individual array items are accessed by using notation similar to most programming languages:

```
arrayName[n]
```

Where *n* is the numeric index of the item that you want to access. Although CSV uses a single array, other data sources (such as JSON) can contain a mix of nested columns and flat columns.

Getting back to our delimited data file, if you want to access the individual columns within this array, you will need to use the `columns` array in your query. Prior to Drill 1.15, the name `columns` must be in lowercase. The query that follows demonstrates how to access these columns within a query and filter data using one of these fields:

```
SELECT columns[0] AS first_name,
columns[1] AS last_name,
columns[2] AS birthday
FROM dfs.drill_tutorial.`customer_data.csv`
WHERE columns[1] = 'Smith'
```

This example first creates simple columns for some of the fields by using the AS clause. In SQL terminology, doing so *projects* the array elements to new columns. This query would return the data shown in the following table:

first_name	last_name	birthday
Robert	Hernandez	5/3/67
Steve	Smith	8/4/84
Anne	Raps	9/13/91
Alice	Muller	4/15/75

Delimited Data with Column Headers

If your delimited file contains headers with the column names in the first row, you can configure Drill to read those names, as well. To do this, you will need to open the web interface and go back to the screen where you configured the storage plug-in. In this case, click the button to edit the dfs plug-in and then scroll down until you see the section labeled formats. You should see some JSON that looks like this:

```
"formats": {
    "psv": {
        "type": "text",
        "extensions": [
            "tbl"
        ],
        "delimiter": "|"
    },
    "csv": {
        "type": "text",
        "extensions": [
            "csv"
        ],
        "delimiter": ","
    }, ...
    ,
    "csvh": {
        "type": "text",
        "extensions": [
            "csvh"
        ],
        "extractHeader": true,
        "delimiter": ","
    }
```

Drill includes a number of format plug-ins that parse data files and map data to Drill fields. The "text" format is the generic delimited data plug-in and provides you with a number of options to configure how Drill will read your files. Drill lets you give names to different collections of options, such as the "psv", "csv", and other formats in the previous example (see Table 4-2).

Table 4-2. Delimited data options

Options	Description
comment	Character used to start a comment line (optional)
escape	Character used to escape the quote character in a field
delimiter	Character used to delimit fields
quote	Character used to enclose fields
skipFirstLine	Skips the first line of a file if set to true (can be true or false)
extractHeader	Reads the header from the CSV file if set to true (can be true or false)

If you would like Drill to extract the headers from the file, simply add the line `"extractHeader": true,` to the section in the configuration that contains the file type that you are working on. Drill also ships configured with the *.csvh* file type configured to accept CSV files with headers. To use this, simply rename your CSV files *.csvh*. If you want to try this out for yourself, execute this query:

```
SELECT *
FROM dfs.drill_tutorial.`customer_data-headers.csvh`
```

This yields the results shown in the following table:

first_name	last_name	birthday
Robert	Hernandez	5/3/67
Steve	Smith	8/4/84
Anne	Raps	9/13/91
Alice	Muller	4/15/75

Table Functions

You should use the configuration options listed in Table 4-2 to set the configuration for a given storage plug-in or directory. However, you can also change these options in a query for a specific file, by using a Drill *table function* as seen here:

```
SELECT *
FROM table(dfs.drill_tutorial.`orders.csv`(
    type => 'text',
    extractHeader => true,
    fieldDelimiter => ',')
)
```

When you use a table function, the query does not inherit any default values defined in the storage plug-in configuration, and thus you need to specify values for all the mandatory options for the format. In the previous example, the `fieldDelimiter` field is required.

Querying Directories

In addition to querying single files, you also can use Drill to query directories. All of the files in the directory must have the same structure, and Drill effectively performs a union on the files. This strategy of placing data into nested folders is known as *partitioning* and is very commonly used in big data systems in lieu of indexes.

Querying a directory is fundamentally no different than querying a single file, but instead of pointing Drill to an individual file, you point it to a directory. Suppose that you have a directory called *logs* that contains subdirectories for each year, which finally contain the actual log files. You could query the entire collection by using the following query:

```
SELECT *
FROM dfs.`/var/logs`
```

If your directory contains subdirectories, you can access the subdirectory names by putting the dir*N* into the query. Thus, dir0 would be the first-level directory, dir1 the second, and so on. For instance, suppose that you have log files stored in directories nested in the following format:

```
logs
|__ year
    |__month
        |__day
```

You could access the directory structure by using the following query:

```
SELECT
    dir0 AS `year`,
    dir1 AS `month`,
    dir2 AS `day`
FROM dfs.`/var/logs/`
```

Additionally, you can use wildcards in the directory name. For instance, the following query uses wildcards to restrict Drill to opening only CSV files:

```
SELECT *
FROM dfs.`/user/data/*.csv`
```

Data Partitioning Depends on the Use Cases

The directory structure in this example is from an actual example from a client; however, this is not a good way to structure partitions to work with Drill because it makes querying date ranges very difficult as we discuss in Chapter 8. One better option might be to partition the data by date in ISO format. Ultimately, it depends on what you are trying to do with your data.

Directory functions

If you are using the `dir` variables with the `MAX()` or `MIN()` functions in the `WHERE` clause in a SQL query, it is best to use the directory functions rather than simple comparisons because it allows Drill to avoid having to make costly (and slow) full-directory scans. Drill has four directory functions:

- `MAXDIR()`
- `MINDIR()`
- `IMAXDIR()`
- `IMINDIR()`

These functions return the minimum or maximum values in a directory; `IMAXDIR()` and `IMINDIR()` return the minimum or maximum in case-insensitive order.

Directory Functions Have Limitations

The Drill directory functions perform a string comparison on the directory names. If you are trying to find the most recent directories, you cannot use these functions unless the most recent occurs first or last when compared as a string.

Using the previous example structure, the following query would find the most recent year's directory in the *logs* directory and return results from that directory:

```
SELECT *
FROM dfs.`/var/logs`
WHERE dir0 = MAXDIR('dfs/tmp', '/var/logs')
```

Understanding Drill Data Types

One of the challenges in using Drill is that although it in many ways acts like a relational database, there are key areas in which it does not, and understanding these is key to getting the most out of Drill. This section will cover the fundamentals of analyzing delimited data with Drill. The examples in this section use a sample data file, *baltimore_salaries_2015.csvh*, which is included in the GitHub repository (*https://github.com/cgivre/drillbook*).[2]

Although Drill can infer the structure of data from the files, when you are querying delimited data Drill cannot implicitly interpret the data type of each field, and because there are no predefined schemas, *you will need to explicitly cast data into a*

---

2 This data is also available on the US government's open data website (*http://bit.ly/2ESsAB7*).

particular data type in your queries to use it for other functions. For instance, the following query fails because Drill cannot infer that the `AnnualSalary` field is a numeric field:

```
SELECT AnnualSalary,
FROM dfs.drill_tutorial.`csv/baltimore_salaries_2015.csvh`
WHERE AnnualSalary > 35000
```

This query fails with a `NumberFormatException` because the `AnnualSalary` field is a string. You can check the column types by using the `typeof(<column>)` function as shown in the following query:

```
SELECT AnnualSalary, typeof(AnnualSalary) AS column_type
FROM dfs.drill_tutorial.`baltimore_salaries_2015.csvh`
LIMIT 1
```

This query produces the following result:

GrossPay	column_type
$53,626.04	VARCHAR

To fix this problem, you need to explicitly instruct Drill to convert the `AnnualSalary` field to a numeric data type. To use a comparison operator, both sides of the equation will need to be numeric, and to convert the field to a numeric data type, you will need to use the `CAST(field AS data_type)` function.

Table 4-3 lists the simple data types that Drill supports.

Table 4-3. Data types in Drill

Drill data types	Description
BIGINT	8-byte signed integer in the range −9,223,372,036,854,775,808 to 9,223,372,036,854,775,807
BINARY	Variable-length byte string
BOOLEAN	true or false
DATE	Date
DECIMAL(p,s)	38-digit precision number; precision is p and scale is s
DOUBLE	8-byte floating-point number
FLOAT	4-byte floating-point number
INTEGER or INT	4-byte signed integer in the range −2,147,483,648 to 2,147,483,647
TIME	Time
TIMESTAMP	JDBC timestamp in year, month, date hour, minute, second, and optional milliseconds
VARCHAR	UTF8-encoded variable-length string; the maximum character limit is 16,777,216

We discuss the date/time functions as well as complex data types later in the book, but it is important to understand these basic data types to do even the simplest calculations.

Suppose you would like to calculate some summary statistics about the various job roles present in this city. You might begin with a query like this:

```
SELECT JobTitle, AVG(AnnualSalary) AS avg_pay
FROM dfs.drillbook.`baltimore_salaries_2016.csvh`
GROUP BY JobTitle
ORDER BY avg_pay DESC
```

However, in Drill, this query will fail for the same reason as the earlier query: the GrossPay is not necessarily a number and thus must be converted into a numeric data type. The corrected query would be as follows:

```
SELECT JobTitle, AVG(CAST(AnnualSalary AS FLOAT))  AS avg_pay
FROM dfs.drillbook.`baltimore_salaries_2016.csvh`
GROUP BY JobTitle
ORDER BY avg_pay DESC
```

However, this query will unfortunately also fail because there are extraneous characters such as the $ in the AnnualSalary field. To successfully execute this query, you can either use the TO_NUMBER() function, as explained in the next section, or use one of Drill's string manipulation functions to remove the $. A working query would be:

```
SELECT JobTitle, AVG(CAST(LTRIM(AnnualSalary, '\$') AS FLOAT)) AS avg_pay
FROM dfs.drillbook.`baltimore_salaries_2016.csvh`
GROUP BY JobTitle
ORDER BY avg_pay DESC
```

A cleaner option might be to break this up using a subquery, as shown here:

```
SELECT JobTitle, AVG(annual_salary) AS avg_pay
FROM
( SELECT JobTitle,
    CAST(LTRIM(annual_salary, '\$') AS FLOAT) AS annual_salary
    FROM dfs.drillbook.`baltimore_salaries_2016.csvh`
)
GROUP BY JobTitle
ORDER BY avg_pay DESC
```

Cleaning and Preparing Data Using String Manipulation Functions

When querying data in Drill, often you will want to extract a data artifact from a source column. For instance, you might want to extract the country code from a phone number. Drill includes a series of string manipulation functions that you can use to prepare data for analysis. Table 4-4 contains a listing of all the string manipulation functions in Drill.

Table 4-4. Drill string manipulation functions

Function	Return type	Description
BYTE_SUBSTR(*string*, *start_index*)	BINARY or VARCHAR	Returns in binary format a substring of a string
CHAR_LENGTH(*string*)	INT	Returns the number of characters in a string
CONCAT(*list of strings*)	VARCHAR	Concatenates strings
ILIKE(*string*, *regex*)	BOOLEAN	Returns true if string matches the regular expression (case insensitive)
INITCAP(*string*)	VARCHAR	Returns a string with the first letter of each word capitalized
LENGTH(*string*)	INT	Returns the length of a string
LOWER(*string*)	VARCHAR	Converts a string to lowercase
LPAD(*string*, *length*, *fill text*)	VARCHAR	Pads a string to the specified length by prepending the fill or a space
LTRIM(*string 1*, *string 2*)	VARCHAR	Removes characters in string 2 from the beginning of string 1
POSITION(*needle* IN *haystack*)	INT	Returns the index of the needle string in the haystack string
REGEXP_REPLACE(*source*, *pattern*, *replacement*)	VARCHAR	Replaces text in the source that matches the pattern with the replacement text
RPAD(*string*, *length*[, *fill text*])	VARCHAR	Pads a string to the specified length by appending the fill or a space
RTRIM(*string 1*, *string 2*)	VARCHAR	Removes characters in string 2 from the end of string 1
SPLIT(*string*, *character*)	Array of VARCHAR	Splits a string on the character argument
STRPOS(*haystack*, *needle*)	INT	Returns the index of the needle string in the haystack string
SUBSTR(*string*, *x*, *y*)	VARCHAR	Extracts a portion of a string from a position 1–x an optional y
TRIM([*leading* | *trailing* | *both*] [*string1*] from *string2*)	VARCHAR	Removes characters in string 1 from string 2
UPPER(*string*)	VARCHAR	Converts a string to uppercase

A use case for some of these functions might be trying to determine which domains are most common among a series of email addresses. The available data just has the email addresses; to access the domain it will be necessary to split each one on the @ sign. Assuming that we have a field called email, the function SPLIT(email, '@') would split the column and return an array containing the accounts and domains. Therefore, if we wanted only the domains, we could add SPLIT(email, '@')[1] to the end, which would perform the split and return only the last half. Thus, the following query will return the domain and the number of users using that domain:

```
SELECT SPLIT(email, '@')[1] AS domain, COUNT(*) AS user_count
FROM dfs.book.`contacts.csvh`
GROUP BY SPLIT(email, '@')[1]
ORDER BY user_count DESC
```

Complex Data Conversion Functions

If you have data that is relatively clean, the CAST() function works well; however, let's look at a real-life situation in which it will fail and how to correct that problem with the TO_ methods.

Let's look again at the *baltimore_salaries_2015.csvh* file. This data contains two columns with salary data: AnnualSalary and GrossPay. However, if you wanted to do any kind of filtering or analysis using these columns, you'll notice that we have two problems that will prevent you from performing any kind of numeric operation on them:

- Each salary begins with a dollar sign ($).
- Each salary also has a comma separating the thousands field.

You already used string manipulation functions and CAST() to clean the data. This time, you will use the TO_NUMBER(*field, format*) function, which accomplishes both tasks in one step.

Table 4-5 lists the special characters that the format string accepts.

Table 4-5. Number formatting characters

Symbol	Location	Meaning
0	Number	Digit.
#	Number	Digit, zero shows as absent.
.	Number	Decimal separator or monetary decimal separator.
-	Number	Minus sign.
,	Number	Grouping separator.
E	Number	Separates mantissa and exponent in scientific notation. Does not need to be quoted in prefix or suffix.
;	Subpattern boundary	Separates positive and negative subpatterns.
%	Prefix or suffix	Multiplies by 100 and shows as percentage.
‰ (030)	Prefix or suffix	Multiplies by 1,000 and shows as per-mille value.
¤ (0A4)	Prefix or suffix	Currency sign, replaced by currency symbol. If doubled, replaced by international currency symbol. If present in a pattern, the monetary decimal separator is used instead of the decimal separator.
'	Prefix or suffix	Used to quote special characters in a prefix or suffix; for example, "'#'#'" formats 123 to ""#123"". To create a single quote itself, use two in a row: "# o''clock".

Therefore, to access the salary columns in the Baltimore Salaries data, you could use the following query:

```
SELECT TO_NUMBER(AnnualSalary, '¤000,000') AS ActualPay
FROM dfs.drill_tutorial.`baltimore_salaries_2015.csvh`
WHERE TO_NUMBER(AnnualSalary, '¤000,000')  >= 50000
```

Reformatting numbers

You can also use the TO_CHAR() function to round numbers or otherwise reformat them into a more human-readable VARCHAR format. If you are using TO_CHAR() for this purpose, you'll need to use the same formatting operators as with the TO_NUM BER() function.

Working with Dates and Times in Drill

Similar to numeric fields, if you have data that has dates or times that you would like to analyze, you first need to explicitly convert them into a format that Drill recognizes. For this section, we use a file called *dates.csvh*, which contains five columns of random dates in various formats (see Figure 4-3).

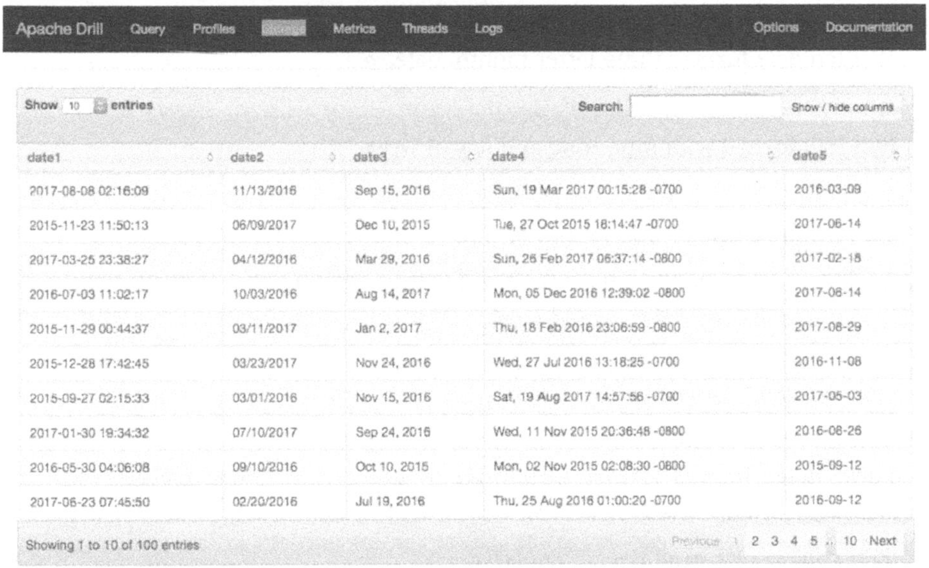

Figure 4-3. Results of a date/time query

There are several ways of converting dates into a usable format, but perhaps the most reliable way is to use the TO_DATE(*expression, format*) function. This function takes two arguments: an expression that usually will be a column, and a date format that specifies the formatting of the date that you are reading. Unlike many relational databases, Drill typically uses Joda—aka Java 8 Date Time or java.time format—formatting for the date strings for all date/time functions; however, there are several functions to convert dates that support ANSI format.[3] See Appendix A for a complete list of Drill functions, and see Table B-2 for a list of Joda date/time formatting characters.

Converting Strings to Dates

To demonstrate how to convert some dates, in the file *dates.csvh* you will see that there are five columns with random dates in the following formats:

date1
: ISO 8601 format

date2
: Standard "American" date with month/day/year

date3
: Written date format: three-letter month, date, year

date4
: Full ISO format with time zone and day of week

date5
: MySQL database format (*yyyy-mm-dd*)

The first one is easy. Drill's native CAST() function can interpret ISO 8601–formatted dates, so the following query would work:

```
SELECT CAST(date1 AS DATE)
FROM dfs.drill_tutorial.`dates.csvh`
```

The second column is a little trickier. Here, the month is first and the day is second. To ingest dates in this format, you need to use the TO_DATE(*expression, format_string*) function, as shown here:

```
SELECT date2, TO_DATE(date2, 'MM/dd/yyyy')
FROM dfs.drill_tutorial.`dates.csvh`
```

---

3 For more information, see Oracle's documentation on the DateTimeFormatter (*http://bit.ly/2oYt2D3*) class.

The third column contains dates that are formatted more in "plain text": Sep 18, 2016, for instance. For these dates you also need to use the TO_DATE() function, but with a slightly different format string:

```
SELECT date3, TO_DATE(date3, 'MMM dd, yyyy')
FROM dfs.drill_tutorial.`dates.csvh`
```

The fourth column introduces some additional complexity in that it has a time value as well as a time zone, as you can see here: Sun, 19 Mar 2017 00:15:28 –0700. It can be ingested using the TO_DATE() function; however, in doing so, you will lose the time portion of the timestamps. Drill has a function called TO_TIMESTAMP() that is similar to TO_DATE() but retains the time components of a date/time:

```
SELECT date4, TO_TIMESTAMP(date4, 'EEE, dd MMM yyyy HH:mm:ss Z')
FROM dfs.drill_tutorial.`dates.csvh`
```

The final column in this exercise, date5, has dates in the format of *yyyy-MM-dd*, which is very commonly found in databases. You can parse it easily using the TO_DATE() function, as shown in the following query:

```
SELECT date5, TO_DATE(date5, 'yyyy-MM-dd')
FROM dfs.drill_tutorial.`dates.csvh`
```

Reformatting Dates

If you have a date or a time that you would like to reformat for a report, you can use the TO_CHAR(*date/time_expression, format_string*) function to convert a Drill date/time into a formatted string. Like the TO_DATE() function, TO_CHAR() uses Joda date formatting. Table 4-6 presents the Drill date conversion functions.

Table 4-6. Drill date conversion functions

You have a...	You want a...	Use...
VARCHAR	DATE	TO_DATE() or CAST(*field* AS DATE)
VARCHAR	TIME	TO_TIMESTAMP()
DATE	VARCHAR	TO_CHAR(*field, format string*)

Date Arithmetic and Manipulation

Much like other databases, Drill has the ability to perform arithmetic operations on dates and times; however, Drill has a specific data type called an INTERVAL that is returned whenever you perform an operation on dates. When converted to a VAR CHAR, an INTERVAL is represented in the ISO 8601 duration syntax as depicted here:

```
P [quantity] Y [quantity] M [quantity] D T [quantity] H [quantity] M [quantity] S
P [quantity] D T [quantity] H [quantity] M [quantity] S
P [quantity] Y [quantity] M
```

It is important to understand this format because it is returned by every function that makes some calculation on dates. To try this out, using the *dates.csvh* file discussed earlier, the following query calculates the difference between two date columns:

```
SELECT date2,
       date5,
       (TO_DATE(date2, 'MM/dd/yyyy') - TO_DATE(date5, 'yyyy-MM-dd')) as date_diff
FROM dfs.drill_tutorial.`dates.csvh`
```

The resulting `date_diff` column contains values such as these:

- P249D
- P-5D
- P-312D

You can extract the various components of the `INTERVAL` by using the `EXTRACT()` function, the syntax for which is `EXTRACT(part FROM field)`.

Date and Time Functions in Drill

Drill has a series of date and time functions that are extremely useful in ad hoc data analysis and exploratory data analysis, which you can see listed in Table 4-7.

Table 4-7. Drill date/time functions

Function	Return type	Description
AGE(*timestamp*)	INTERVAL	Returns the age of the given time expression.
CURRENT_DATE	DATE	Returns the current date.
CURRENT_TIME	TIME	Returns the current time.
CURRENT_TIMESTAMP	TIMESTAMP	Returns the current timestamp.
DATE_ADD(*keyword, date, int or interval*)	DATE or TIME STAMP	Returns the sum of the date and the second argument. This function accepts various input formats.
DATE_PART(*keyword, date*)	DOUBLE	Returns a portion of a date expression, specified by the keyword.
DATE_SUB(*keyword, date, int or interval*)	DATE or TIME STAMP	Returns the difference between the date and the second argument. This function accepts various input formats.
EXTRACT(*field* FROM *expr*)	DOUBLE	Extracts and returns a part of the given date expression or interval.
LOCALTIME	TIME	Returns the local time.
LOCALTIMESTAMP	TIMESTAMP	Returns the current local time.
NOW()	TIMESTAMP	Returns the current local time.
TIMEOFDAY()	VARCHAR	Returns the current time with the time zone.

Function	Return type	Description
UNIX_TIME STAMP(*optional date string*)	BIGINT	Returns a Unix timestamp of the current time if a date string is not specified, or the Unix timestamp of the specified date.

Time Zone Limitation in Drill

At the time of writing, Drill does not support converting dates from one time zone to another. Drill uses the time zone from your operating system unless you override it, which can cause inconsistencies in your analysis if you are looking at data with timestamps from different time zones.

The best workaround at this point is to set up Drill to use UTC and to convert all your data to UTC, as well. To set Drill to use UTC you need to add the following line to the *drill-env.sh* file in the *DRILL_PATH/conf/* folder.

```
export DRILL_JAVA_OPTS=\
"$DRILL_JAVA_OPTS -Duser.timezone=UTC"
```

After you've done that, restart Drill and any Drillbits that might be running and then execute the following query to verify that Drill is running in UTC time:

```
SELECT TIMEOFDAY() FROM (VALUES(1))
```

Creating Views

Like many relational databases, Drill supports the creation of *views*. A view is a stored query that can include many data sources, functions, and other transformations of the data. You can use views to simplify queries, control access to your data, or even mask portions of it. As with relational databases, creating a view does not store the actual data, only the SELECT statement to retrieve the data.

Here's the basic syntax to create a view:

```
CREATE [ OR REPLACE] VIEW workspace.view_name AS query
```

You can also specify the columns after the view name. If you do not do this, the column names will be extrapolated from the query. After you have created a view, you can use the view name in the query as if it were a regular table.

For instance, let's say that you have a CSV file called *orders.csvh*, and you want to create a view of this data with data types already specified. You could use the following query to do so:

```
CREATE VIEW dfs.customers.order_data AS
SELECT columns[1] customer__first_name,
    columns[2] AS customer_last_name,
```

```
        CAST(columns[3] AS INT) AS product_id
        columns[4] AS product_name
        CAST(columns[5] AS FLOAT) AS price
    FROM dfs.data.`orders.csv`
```

Let's also say that you wanted to find each customer's average purchase amount. You could find that with the following query:

```
SELECT customer_last_name, customer_first_name, AVG(price)
FROM dfs.customers.order_data
GROUP BY customer_last_name, customer_first_name
```

In this example, by creating a view, you can eliminate all the data type conversions and assign readable field names to the data.[4]

Data Analysis Using Drill

Now that you know how to get Drill to recognize dates as well as numeric fields, you are ready to begin analyzing data. Much like any database, Drill has a variety of mathematical functions that you can use in the SELECT statements to perform calculations on your data. You can apply one of these functions to a column or nest functions, and the result will be a new column. Table 4-8 shows the operations that Drill currently supports.

Table 4-8. Drill mathematical functions

Function	Return type	Description
ABS(x)	Same as input	Returns the absolute value of the input argument x.
CBRT(x)	DOUBLE	Returns the cubic root of x.
CEIL(x)	Same as input	Returns the smallest integer not less than x.
CEILING(x)	Same as input	Same as CEIL().
DEGREES(x)	DOUBLE	Converts x radians to degrees.
E()	DOUBLE	Returns 2.718281828459045.
EXP(x)	DOUBLE	Returns e (Euler's number) to the power of x.
FLOOR(x)	Same as input	Returns the largest integer not greater than x.
LOG(x)	DOUBLE	Returns the natural log (base e) of x.
LOG(x, y)	DOUBLE	Returns log base x to the y power.
LOG10(x)	DOUBLE	Returns the common log of x.
LSHIFT(x, y)	Same as input	Shifts the binary x by y times to the left.
MOD(x, y)	DOUBLE	Returns the remainder of x divided by y.

---

4 Complete documentation for views in Drill is available on the Drill website (*https://drill.apache.org/docs/create-view/*).

Function	Return type	Description
NEGATIVE(x)	Same as input	Returns x as a negative number.
PI	DOUBLE	Returns pi.
POW(x, y)	DOUBLE	Returns the value of x to the y power.
RADIANS	DOUBLE	Converts x degrees to radians.
RAND	DOUBLE	Returns a random number from 0–1.
ROUND(x)	Same as input	Rounds to the nearest integer.
ROUND(x, y)	DECIMAL	Rounds x to y decimal places.
RSHIFT(x, y)	Same as input	Shifts the binary x by y times to the right.
SIGN(x)	INT	Returns the sign of x.
SQRT(x)	Same as input	Returns the square root of x.
TRUNC(x, y)	Same as input	Truncates x to y decimal places. Specifying y is optional; the default is 1.
TRUNC(x, y)	DECIMAL	Truncates x to y decimal places.

All of these functions require the inputs to be some numeric data type, so don't forget to convert your data into a numeric format before using one of these columns. The following example demonstrates how to calculate the square root of a column using Drill's SQRT() function:

```
SELECT x, SQRT(CAST(x AS FLOAT)) AS sqrt_x
FROM dfs.data.csv
```

Table 4-9 presents the results.

Table 4-9. SQRT() query results

x	sqrt_x
4	2
9	3
16	4

Summarizing Data with Aggregate Functions

In addition to the standard mathematical functions, Drill also includes the aggregate functions that follow, which perform a calculation on an entire column or grouping within a column. These functions are extremely useful when summarizing a dataset. A complete explanation of grouping in SQL is available in Chapters 13 and 14 of Viesca's *SQL Queries for Mere Mortals* (Addison-Wesley). However, the essential structure of a query that summarizes data is as follows:

```
SELECT unique field, aggregate function(field)
FROM data
WHERE logical condition (Optional)
```

```
GROUP BY unique field or fields
HAVING logical condition (Optional)
```

You can use aggregate functions to summarize a given column, and in these instances the aggregate function will return one row. Table 4-10 lists the aggregate functions included with Drill as of this writing.

Table 4-10. Drill aggregate functions

Function	Return type	Description
AVG(*column*)	Same as argument type	Returns the average of the expression
COUNT(*)	BIGINT	Returns the number of rows
COUNT(DISTINCT)	BIGINT	Returns the number of unique values and the number of times they occurred
MIN(*column*)	Same as argument type	Returns the smallest value in the expression
STDDEV(*column*)	DECIMAL	Returns the sample standard deviation of the column
STDDEV_POP(*column*)	DECIMAL	Returns the population standard deviation of the input column
STDDEV_SAMP(*column*)	DECIMAL	Returns the sample standard deviation of the input column
SUM(*column*)	Same as argument type	Returns the sum of the given column
VARIANCE(*column*)	DECIMAL	Returns the sample variance of the input values (sample standard deviation squared)
VAR_POP(*column*)	DECIMAL	Returns the population variance of the input values (the population standard deviation squared)
VAR_SAMP(*column*)	DECIMAL	Sample variance of input values (sample standard deviation squared)

As an example, this book's GitHub repository (*https://github.com/cgivre/drillbook*) contains a data file called *orders.csvh* which contains notional sales data for one month. If you wanted to calculate some monthly stats, you could use the following query to do so:

```
SELECT
    SUM(CAST(purchase_amount AS FLOAT)) AS monthly_total,
    MAX(CAST(purchase_amount AS FLOAT)) AS largest_order,
    MIN(CAST(purchase_amount AS FLOAT)) AS smallest_order,
    COUNT(order_id) AS order_count,
    AVG(CAST(purchase_amount  AS FLOAT)) AS average_order
FROM dfs.drill_tutorial.`orders.csvh`
```

Figure 4-4 shows the results.

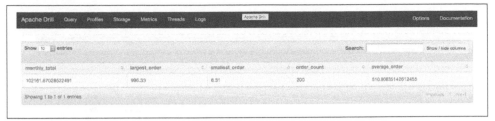

Figure 4-4. Stats query result

As you can see, the query calculates the total monthly sales, the largest order, the smallest order, the number of orders, and the average order amount for the month.

If you wanted to summarize this data by day, all you would need to do is add a GROUP BY statement at the end of the query, as shown in the following example:

```
SELECT
    EXTRACT(day FROM TO_DATE(order_date, 'yyyy-MM-dd')) AS day_of_month,
    SUM(CAST(purchase_amount AS FLOAT)) AS daily_total,
    MAX(CAST(purchase_amount AS FLOAT)) AS largest_order,
    MIN(CAST(purchase_amount AS FLOAT)) AS smallest_order,
    COUNT(order_id) AS order_count,
    AVG(CAST(purchase_amount AS FLOAT)) AS average_order
FROM dfs.drill_tutorial.`orders.csvh`
GROUP BY TO_DATE(order_date, 'yyyy-MM-dd')
ORDER BY EXTRACT(day FROM TO_DATE(order_date, 'yyyy-MM-dd'))
```

Figure 4-5 illustrates the results of this query.

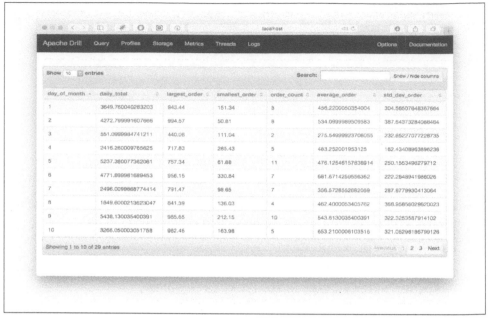

Figure 4-5. Data aggregated by day

If you wanted to present this data, you could format the numbers with a currency symbol and round them to the nearest decimal place by using the TO_NUMBER() function.

One major difference between Drill and relational databases is that Drill does not support column aliases in the GROUP BY clause. Thus, the following query would fail:

```
SELECT YEAR(date_field) AS year_field, COUNT(*)
FROM dfs.drill_tutorial.`data.csv`
GROUP BY year_field
```

To correct this you would simply need to replace GROUP BY year_field with GROUP BY YEAR(date_field).

Beware of Incorrect Column Names

If you include a field in the SELECT clause of a query that does not exist in your data, Drill will create an empty nullable INT column instead of throwing an error.

Other analytic functions: Window functions

In addition to the simple aggregate functions, Drill has a series of analytic functions known as *window functions*, which you can use to split the data and perform some operations on those sections. Although the window functions are similar to the aggregate functions used in a GROUP BY query, there is a difference in that window functions do not alter the number of rows returned. In addition to aggregating data, these functions are very useful for calculating metrics that relate to other rows, such as percentiles, rankings, and row numbers that do not necessarily need aggregation.

The basic structure of a query using a window function is as follows:

```
SELECT fields, FUNCTION(field)
OVER(
    PARTITION BY field
    ORDER BY field (Optional)
)
```

The PARTITION BY clause might look unfamiliar to you, but this is where you define the window or segment of the data upon which the aggregate function will operate.

In addition to AVG(), COUNT(), MAX(), MIN(), and SUM(), Drill includes several other window functions, as shown in Table 4-11.

Table 4-11. Drill window functions

Function	Return type	Description
CUME_DIST()	DOUBLE	Calculates the relative rank of the current row within the window: rows preceding/total rows.
DENSE_RANK()	BIGINT	Returns the rank of the row within the window. Does not create gaps in the event of duplicate values.
FIRST_VALUE()	Same as input	Returns the first value in the window.
LAG()	Same as input	Returns the value after the current value in the window, NULL if none exists.
LAST_VALUE()	Same as input	Returns the last value in the window.
LEAD()	Same as input	Returns the value prior to the current value in the window, or NULL if none exists.
NTILE()	INT	Divides the rows for each window into a number of ranked groups. Requires the ORDER BY clause in the OVER() clause.
PERCENT_RANK()	DOUBLE	Calculates the percent rank of the current row within the window: (rank − 1) / (rows − 1).
RANK()	BIGINT	Similar to DENSE_RANK() but includes rows with equal values in the calculation.
ROW_NUMBER()	BIGINT	Returns the number of the row within the window.

Comparison of aggregate and window analytic functions

The GitHub repository for this book (*https://github.com/cgivre/drillbook*) contains a file called *student_data.csvh*, which contains some notional test scores from 10 different students. If you wanted to find each student's average test score you could use either GROUP BY or window functions, but the GROUP BY option would be a simpler query. The following query accomplishes this task:

```
SELECT studentID,
    AVG(CAST(score AS FLOAT)) AS average_score,
```

```
        MIN(CAST(score AS FLOAT)) AS min_score,
        MAX(CAST(score AS FLOAT)) AS max_score
    FROM dfs.drill_tutorial.`student_data.csvh`
    GROUP BY studentID
```

Figure 4-6 demonstrates that this query produces the desired result.

Show 10 entries　　Search:　　Show / hide columns

studentID	average_score	min_score	max_score
student1	75.8	60.0	99.0
student2	84.8	76.0	101.0
student3	88.2	63.0	101.0
student4	76.4	60.0	97.0
student5	84.6	70.0	92.0
student6	75.8	61.0	94.0
student7	80.0	60.0	99.0
student8	83.0	70.0	99.0
student9	91.0	76.0	99.0
student10	79.8	63.0	98.0

Showing 1 to 10 of 10 entries　　Previous 1 Next

Figure 4-6. Aggregate query result

You could accomplish the same thing using window functions by using the following query:

```
    SELECT DISTINCT studentID,
        AVG(CAST(score AS FLOAT))
        OVER(
          PARTITION BY studentID
        ) AS avg_score,
        MIN(CAST(score AS FLOAT))
        OVER(
          PARTITION BY studentID) AS min_score,
        MAX(CAST(score AS FLOAT))
        OVER(
          PARTITION BY studentID
        ) AS max_score
    FROM dfs.drill_tutorial.`student_data.csvh`
```

Note that you must use the `DISTINCT` keyword; otherwise, you will get duplicate rows. If you are working with large datasets, it is useful to be aware of the different methods of summarizing datasets because one might perform better on your data than the other.

Another example would be ranking each student's score per test and calculating their quartile. In this example, it is not possible to do this using `GROUP BY`, so we must use the window functions `RANK()` and `NTILE()`. The following query demonstrates how to do this:

```
SELECT studentID,
    testnumber,
    score,
    RANK() OVER(
      PARTITION BY testnumber
      ORDER BY CAST(score  AS FLOAT) DESC
    ) AS ranking,
    NTILE(4) OVER(PARTITION BY testnumber) AS quartile
FROM dfs.drill_tutorial.`student_data.csvh`
```

Figure 4-7 presents the results of this query.

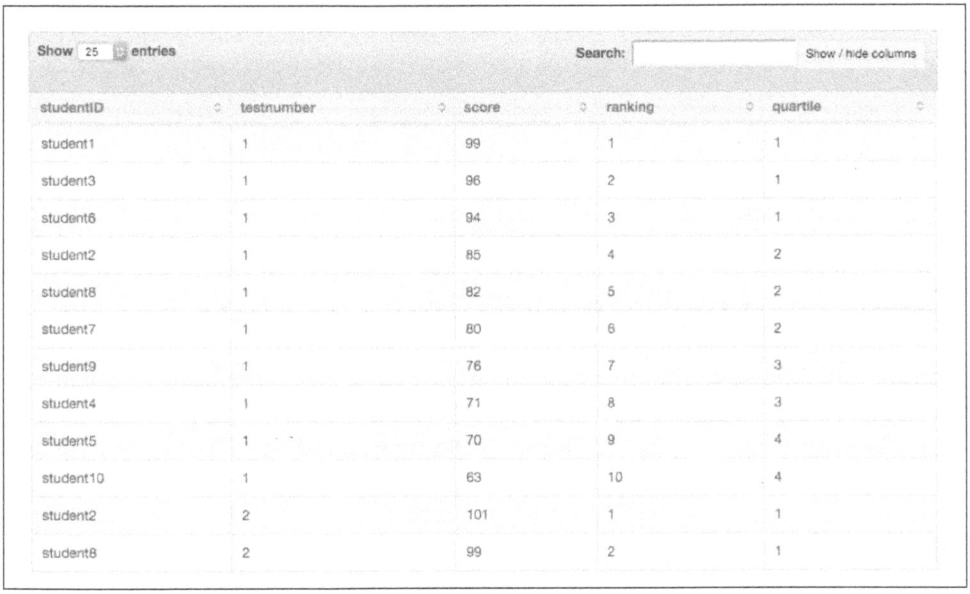
Show 25 entries Search: Show / hide columns

studentID	testnumber	score	ranking	quartile
student1	1	99	1	1
student3	1	96	2	1
student6	1	94	3	1
student2	1	85	4	2
student8	1	82	5	2
student7	1	80	6	2
student9	1	76	7	3
student4	1	71	8	3
student5	1	70	9	4
student10	1	63	10	4
student2	2	101	1	1
student8	2	99	2	1

Figure 4-7. Window query results

You cannot use the results from window functions directly in a `WHERE` clause; thus, if you want to filter results from a window function, you must place the original query in a subquery, as shown here:

```
SELECT *
FROM (
  SELECT
   studentID, testnumber, score,
   RANK() OVER(
    PARTITION BY testnumber
    ORDER BY CAST(score  AS FLOAT) DESC) AS ranking,
```

```
    NTILE(4) OVER(PARTITION BY testnumber) AS quartile
  FROM dfs.drill_tutorial.`student_data.csvh`) AS student_data
WHERE student_data.quartile <= 2
```

Figure 4-8 illustrates what this query returns.

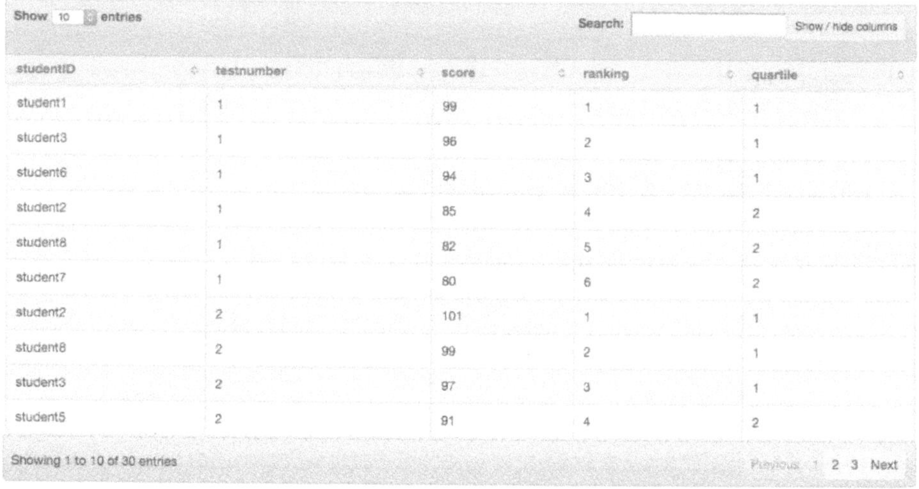

Show 10 entries Search: Show / hide columns

studentID	testnumber	score	ranking	quartile
student1	1	99	1	1
student3	1	96	2	1
student6	1	94	3	1
student2	1	85	4	2
student8	1	82	5	2
student7	1	80	6	2
student2	2	101	1	1
student8	2	99	2	1
student3	2	97	3	1
student5	2	91	4	2

Showing 1 to 10 of 30 entries Previous 1 2 3 Next

Figure 4-8. Window query results with filter

Common Problems in Querying Delimited Data

Because Drill allows you to query raw delimited data, it is quite likely that you will encounter certain problems along the way. We'll look at how Drill processes data in more detail in Chapter 8, but for now, a little understanding of Drill can help you quickly get around these problems.

Spaces in Column Names

If your data has spaces or other reserved characters in a column name, or the column name itself is a reserved word, this will present a problem for Drill when you try to use the column name in a query. The easiest solution for this problem is to enclose all the column names in backticks (`) throughout your query.

For instance, this query will throw an error:

```
SELECT customer name, dob
FROM dfs.`customers.csv`
```

This query will not:

```
SELECT `customer name`, `dob`
FROM dfs.`customers.csv`
```

Sometimes, columns can have spaces at the end of the field name. Enclosing the field name in backticks can solve this problem, as well—for example:

```
SELECT `field_1 `
FROM ...
```

Illegal Characters in Column Headers

We encountered this problem a while ago, and it took quite some time to diagnose. Essentially, we were querying a series of CSV files, and although we could query the files using SELECT * or most of the field names, the field we were interested in happened to be the last field in the row. When we tried to query that field specifically, we got an index out of bounds exception.

The reason for the error was that some of the CSV files were saved on a Windows machine, which encodes new lines with both a carriage return character (\r) and a newline character (\n), whereas Macs and Linux-based systems encode line endings with just the newline character (\n). In practice, what this meant was that the last field had an extra character in the field name; when we tried to query it without that character, Drill couldn't find the field and threw an exception.

The easiest solution is to make sure that all your files are encoded using the Mac/Linux standard; that way, you won't have any such problems.

Reserved Words in Column Names

A rather insidious problem that can bite you if you are not careful is when your data or column aliases are Drill reserved words.[5] Often, you will have a data file that has a column called year or date. Because both of these are reserved words, Drill will throw errors if you attempt to access these columns in a query.

The solution to this problem is twofold. First, be aware of the Drill reserved words list, and second, as with the other situations, if you enclose a field name in backticks it will allow you to use reserved words in the query. We recommend that if you have a data file with reserved words as column names, you should either rename them in the file or in the query with an AS clause. A good rule of thumb is to always use backticks around all column names.

---

5 You can find the complete list of Drill reserved words at the Apache Drill website (*https://drill.apache.org/docs/reserved-keywords/*).

Column Aliases

Drill treats column aliases a little differently than a relational database. In general, Drill is more restrictive than most relational databases as to where you can use a column alias, with the biggest difference being that you cannot use column aliases in a GROUP BY clause.

Conclusion

In this chapter, you learned how to query basic delimited data and to use Drill's vast array of analytic functions to clean, prepare, and summarize that data for further analysis. In Chapter 5, you'll take your analysis to the next level and learn how to apply these skills to nested datasets in formats such as JSON and Parquet, and other advanced formats.

Analyzing Complex and Nested Data

As Chapter 4 demonstrated, Apache Drill is a very powerful tool for analyzing data contained in delimited files. In this chapter, you will learn how to apply that power to complex and nested datasets and formats such as JavaScript Object Notation (JSON) and Parquet. Data contained in NoSQL stores such as MongoDB often contains nested data structures that make it difficult to query in the traditional SQL context. These data formats often require specialized tools to analyze, but with Drill you can query them just as you would any other dataset—albeit with some additional complexities. Before you dive into these datasets, however, you must understand how Drill deals with complex data objects.

A Word About Parquet Format

Parquet (*http://parquet.apache.org*) is a self-describing, compressed columnar format that supports nested data. Many big data systems such as Hadoop, Hive, Spark, and others support reading and writing Parquet files. Drill performs best reading Parquet files, so we recommend that if you are planning on querying large, complex data you convert the data into Parquet format.

Arrays and Maps

In Chapter 4 you learned about all the different data types that exist in Drill, such as INTEGER, DOUBLE, and VARCHAR. These data types are common in most databases and programming languages, but unlike most databases, Drill also features two complex data types, *array* and *map*, that you'll need to understand in order to analyze complex datasets.[1] Both of these data types differ from the standard data types in that they hold more than one value and can even hold other collections.

Arrays in Drill

In the previous chapter, you saw one of Drill's complex types: arrays. In Drill and many programming languages, an *array* is an ordered collection of data points that is indexed by number. Like many programming languages, Drill begins its indexing at 0, so the item at position 4 is actually the fifth item in the list, as demonstrated in Table 5-1.

Table 5-1. Array values

Index	Value
0	Steve
1	Stacy
2	Mary
3	Jose
4	Bob

In the array presented in Table 5-1, you can see that the value at index 2 is Mary, but that is actually the third item in the array.

Drill array syntax is similar to most programming languages, such as using brackets to reference individual items within an array. Table 5-1 would appear like this if you used SQLLine to display the column:

```
["Steve","Stacy","Mary","Jose","Bob"]
```

In practice, you will encounter arrays when querying CSV files or other delimited formats that do not include the field names in the header. In this book's GitHub repository (*https://github.com/cgivre/drillbook*), there is a file called *customer_data.csv* that contains the first names, last names, and birthdates of fictitious customers. If you were to execute a SELECT * query on this file, the result would look similar to that shown in Figure 5-1.

---

1 From a user's perspective, Drill supports arrays and maps that work as described in this chapter. As you will see when you develop user-defined functions or plug-ins for Drill, they are handled internally quite differently than in programming languages.

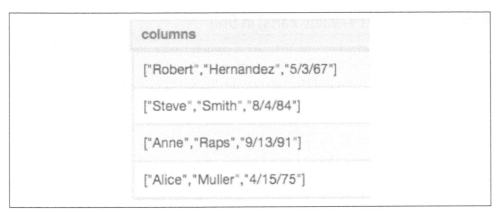

Figure 5-1. Arrays in Drill

You can see that each row contains an array with fields in it. If you wanted to access the birthday column, you could use the following query:

```
SELECT columns[2] AS birthday
FROM dfs.drill_tutorial.`customer_data.csv`
```

This would return the correct results. Likewise, if you wanted to break out all the elements of these arrays and make them more readable, you could execute the following query, which would return the results shown in Figure 5-2:

```
SELECT
    columns[0] AS first_name,
    columns[1] AS last_name,
    columns[2] AS birthday
FROM dfs.drill_tutorial.`customer_data.csv`
```

first_name	last_name	birthday
Robert	Hernandez	5/3/67
Steve	Smith	8/4/84
Anne	Raps	9/13/91
Alice	Muller	4/15/75
	Showing 1 to 4 of 4 entries	

Figure 5-2. Array query result

The most common use of arrays is to store the fields in a delimited file when that file has no header row with field names. Arrays are also used when reading JSON data.

Accessing Maps (Key–Value Pairs) in Drill

Maps are similar to arrays in that they are a complex data type that can hold more than one value; however, unlike arrays, maps are indexed by a key instead of a number.[2] JSON represents maps (called objects in JSON) using brackets, as follows:

```
{
  "key1":"value1",
  "key2":"value2"
}
```

You can access the individual fields within the map by referencing *table.map.field* in your query. For example, if the preceding map were called `data` and was found in a table called `customers`, you could access the individual fields by using the following query:

```
SELECT customers.data.key1, customers.data.key2
FROM...
```

As a more practical example, the book's GitHub repository (*https://github.com/cgivre/drillbook*) contains a file called *user_agents.csv*, which contains a bunch of user agent strings[3] from a web server log. If you were to query this file, the results would contain an array with the user agent string as the only array item. Here is a sample user agent string:

```
Mozilla/5.0 (Macintosh; Intel Mac OS X 10_10_1) AppleWebKit/537.36 \
    (KHTML, like Gecko) Chrome/39.0.2171.95 Safari/537.36
```

Although you can see there is a lot of information contained in that, it is difficult to map this information to fields. However, there is a Drill function called `parse_user_agent()` that returns a map of artifacts from the user agent string, as shown here:[4]

```
{
  "DeviceClass":"Desktop",
  "DeviceName":"Macintosh",
  "DeviceBrand":"Apple",
  "OperatingSystemClass":"Desktop",
  "OperatingSystemName":"Mac OS X",
```

---

2 Technically, maps in Drill are more analogous to structs in C, which are collections of nested tuples such that every record will have the same fields. Therefore, when reading `{a: {foo: 10}} {a: {bar: "fred"}}`, Drill will produce `{a: {foo: 10, bar: null} {a: {foo: null, bar: "fred"}`.

3 User agent strings are text sent to a web server as part of an HTTP request that contain information about the software and equipment that the user has. User agent strings can be very difficult to parse, but they contain a wealth of information and can be used for traffic analysis, or simply to send the appropriate version of a website to a client.

4 The `parse_user_agent()` function is not included with Drill because it needs to be regularly updated. You can download it from this GitHub repository (*https://github.com/cgivre/drill-useragent-function*).

```
    "OperatingSystemVersion":"10.10.1",
    "OperatingSystemNameVersion":"Mac OS X 10.10.1",
    "LayoutEngineClass":"Browser",
    "LayoutEngineName":"Blink",
    "LayoutEngineVersion":"39.0",
    "LayoutEngineVersionMajor":"39",
    "LayoutEngineNameVersion":"Blink 39.0",
    "LayoutEngineNameVersionMajor":"Blink 39",
    "AgentClass":"Browser",
    "AgentName":"Chrome",
    "AgentVersion":"39.0.2171.99",
    "AgentVersionMajor":"39",
    "AgentNameVersion":"Chrome 39.0.2171.99",
    "AgentNameVersionMajor":"Chrome 39",
    "DeviceCpu":"Intel"
}
```

If you want to access a few specific keys from this map, the best way to accomplish this is to write a query that retrieves the map itself. Then, using the *table.map.field* technique, you can access the individual fields as needed:

```
SELECT
    uadata.ua.AgentNameVersion AS Browser,
    COUNT(*) AS BrowserCount
FROM (
    SELECT parse_user_agent(columns[0]) AS ua
    FROM dfs.drill_tutorial.`user-agents.csv`
) AS uadata
GROUP BY uadata.ua.AgentNameVersion
ORDER BY BrowserCount DESC
```

This query extracts the AgentNameVersion field from the map and then aggregates that and counts unique values. The resulting dataset will indicate what browsers and versions were most popular on this website.

Querying Nested Data

Now that you have an understanding of how Drill handles complex data types, you are ready to start querying nested data formats such as JSON and Parquet. Drill can natively query data in these formats quickly and easily; however, data is often encoded in many ways using these formats. In this section you will learn how to use Drill's various functions to quickly and easily access nested data files.

Data types in JSON files

In Chapter 4, you learned that one of the big limitations of Drill is that it cannot infer data types from delimited data. When querying JSON or other nested formats, Drill is able to infer data types *if the data is formatted correctly.*[5] By default, Drill interprets any number with a decimal point as a `DOUBLE`, and numbers without a decimal point as `BIGINT`. Drill also interprets the unquoted words `true` and `false` as a `BOOLEAN` data type, and anything else will be treated as a `VARCHAR`.

Drill does not support mixed-type fields within a map, so if your data is inconsistent in this regard, you might encounter schema type errors when querying JSON files. To work around this issue, Drill has two configuration options that can fix this problem. Setting `store.json.read_numbers_as_double` to `true`, will alleviate number formatting errors. You can do this in the configuration files or with the following query:

```
ALTER SESSION SET `store.json.read_numbers_as_double` = true
```

If the JSON data you are reading did not correctly encode the various data types— such as putting quotation marks around numbers or capitalizing `True/False`, or something like that—you might encounter additional errors when reading JSON data files. If that is the case, the last resort is activating Drill's all-text mode, which causes Drill to interpret all fields as `VARCHAR`s. You can accomplish this by using the following query:

```
ALTER SESSION SET `store.json.all_text_mode` = true
```

---

5 A very common encoding error is when data has 0 instead of 0.0 in a column containing floating-point numbers.

JSON with Heterogeneous Data

If you have JSON data with mixed data types, you will not be able to directly query this in Drill. However, a new, experimental feature, the Union type, allows you to query JSON data with different types in the same field. Because this new feature is still considered experimental, you must explicitly enable it by setting the exec.enable_union_type option to true, as shown in this query:

```
ALTER SESSION SET `exec.enable_union_type` = true
```

You can use a field with a Union type inside of functions; however, you will need to consider how the function will react to different data types. If the data requires special handling for the different types, you can do this in a CASE statement using the new type functions:

```
SELECT 1 +
CASE
    WHEN is_list(a)
        THEN a[0]
        ELSE a
END
FROM table;
```

Formats of nested data

There are several different methods by which you can encode data in JSON format: column-oriented, record-oriented, and split. In this section, you'll learn how to convert all these formats into a basic table that you can further analyze.

This book's GitHub repository contains three JSON files containing the data from the file *customer_data.csv* but encoded in different formats: record-oriented, split, and column-oriented. You can try all the techniques with these sample datasets.

Querying record-oriented files.   The first example we will look at is *records.json*, which is encoded as shown in the code that follows. Note that in the JSON format, whitespace is ignored, but we have indented the fields to make the format easier for you to read:

```
[
    {
        "first_name":"Robert",
        "last_name":"Hernandez",
        "birthday":"5/3/67"
    },{
        "first_name":"Steve",
        "last_name":"Smith",
        "birthday":"8/4/84"},
    }
]
```

You can see that this data is encoded as an array of maps. This format is perhaps the easiest for Drill to query because it does not require the use of any specialized functions. Simply executing the query that follows results in Drill mapping the fields to the correct columns, as demonstrated in Figure 5-3:

```
SELECT *
FROM dfs.drill_tutorial.`records.json`
```

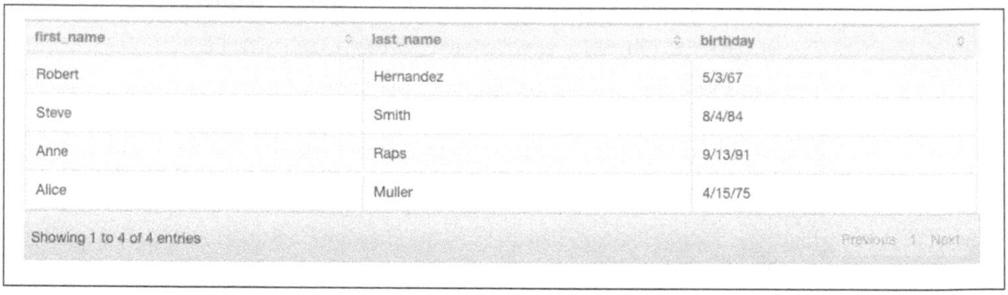

first_name	last_name	birthday
Robert	Hernandez	5/3/67
Steve	Smith	8/4/84
Anne	Raps	9/13/91
Alice	Muller	4/15/75

Showing 1 to 4 of 4 entries   Previous 1 Next

Figure 5-3. JSON query results

In practice, the array-of-objects formats is uncommon. More common (and efficient) is the non-standard list-of-objects format: {...}{...}.

Using the FLATTEN() function to query split JSON files.   Querying split JSON files introduces a bit of complexity into the equation. The following example demonstrates JSON data in the split format:

```
{
"columns":
  [
    "first_name",
    "last_name",
    "birthday"
  ],
"index":
  [0,1,2,3],
"data":
[
  [
    "Robert",
    "Hernandez",
    "5/3/67"
  ],[
    "Steve",
    "Smith",
    "8/4/84"
  ],[
    "Anne",
    "Raps",
    "9/13/91"
  ],[
```

```
      "Alice",
      "Muller",
      "4/15/75"
    ]
  ]
}
```

You can see in this format that the actual data is buried in an array called data. However, if you just execute the following query, it still will not produce the result we are looking for:

```
SELECT data
FROM dfs.drill_tutorial.`split.json`
```

Figure 5-4 shows the results.

Figure 5-4. Split JSON query results

In this case, you can see that we get one row with many arrays. To get the fields into a usable format, you must use the FLATTEN(x) function to break apart the array. This function breaks apart repeated elements in a column into rows. In this case, calling FLATTEN() on the data column will get you a dataset with each array as its own row (see Figure 5-5):

```
SELECT FLATTEN(data) AS row_data
FROM dfs.drill_tutorial.`split.json`
```

row_data
["Robert","Hernandez","5/3/67"]
["Steve","Smith","8/4/84"]
["Anne","Raps","9/13/91"]
["Alice","Muller","4/15/75"]
Showing 1 to 4 of 4 entries

Figure 5-5. Query results after flattening

Note that you now have each array in its own row. From this point you can access all of the fields by using this as a subquery, as demonstrated here, with the results shown in Figure 5-6:

```
SELECT
    row_data[0] AS first_name,
    row_data[1] AS last_name,
```

```
    row_data[2] AS birthday
FROM
(
  SELECT FLATTEN(data) AS row_data
  FROM dfs.drill_tutorial.`split.json`
) AS split_data
```

first_name	last_name	birthday
Robert	Hernandez	5/3/67
Steve	Smith	8/4/84
Anne	Raps	9/13/91
Alice	Muller	4/15/75

Showing 1 to 4 of 4 entries   Previous 1 Next

Figure 5-6. Query results after extracting fields

Because the FLATTEN(*nested_field*) function returns an array, you can also access individual items within that array; however, to create the table shown in Figure 5-6, you need to use a subquery.

Querying column-oriented JSON files with KVGEN().   The   following   example   shows another way in which you can encode data in JSON:

```
{
  "first_name":
  {
    "0":"Robert",
    "1":"Steve",
    "2":"Anne",
    "3":"Alice"
  },
  "last_name":
  {
    "0":"Hernandez",
    "1":"Smith",
    "2":"Raps",
    "3":"Muller"
  },
  "birthday":
  {
    "0":"5/3/67",
    "1":"8/4/84",
    "2":"9/13/91",
    "3":"4/15/75"
  }
}
```

In this example, the data is a map of key–value pairs. To access these columns, you need to use a new function: KVGEN(*nested_field*). As the name implies, the KVGEN(*nested_field*) function generates key–value pairs from a complex column. This next query generates key–value pairs for every entry in the first_name column:

```
SELECT KVGEN(first_name) AS kvgen_firstname
FROM dfs.drill_tutorial.`columns.json`
```

Figure 5-7 presents the results.

Figure 5-7. Unflattened query after KVGEN()

At this point, the formatting should look similar to the previous example in that we have an array of maps contained in a single row entry. And much like in the last example, to get the values, you should use the FLATTEN(*nested_field*) function on this column. You can see the results of this query in Figure 5-8:

```
SELECT FLATTEN(KVGEN(first_name)) AS kvgen_firstname
FROM dfs.book.`columns.json`
```

Figure 5-8. Query data after flattening

You still don't have the actual values; however, that is as simple as adding the key name after the function calls, as shown in the following query:

```
SELECT FLATTEN(KVGEN(first_name))['value'] AS firstname
FROM dfs.drill_tutorial.`columns.json`
```

Figure 5-9 displays the results.

firstname	
Robert	
Steve	
Anne	
Alice	
Showing 1 to 4 of 4 entries	Previous 1 Next

Figure 5-9. Query data with field extracted

Although this query successfully gets you one column, you'll find that if you try to do this with more than one column, the FLATTEN() method will cause a lot of undesired duplicate rows. Therefore, to produce a single table with all the columns, you need to extract each column and join them together in a series of subqueries.

However, you will run into another problem: there is no key with which to join the records. To join them together, you need to create a key using ROW_NUMBER() (one of the window functions that you learned about in Chapter 4). The following query extracts all of the fields as columns, which you can analyze (see Figure 5-10):

```
SELECT first_name, last_name, birthday
FROM
(
  SELECT row_number() over (ORDER BY '1')as rownum,
  FLATTEN( KVGEN(first_name))['value'] AS first_name
  FROM dfs.book.`columns.json`
) AS tbl1
JOIN
(
  SELECT row_number() over (ORDER BY '1')as rownum,
  FLATTEN( KVGEN(last_name))['value'] AS last_name
  FROM dfs.book.`columns.json`
) AS tbl2
ON tbl1.rownum=tbl2.rownum
JOIN
(
  SELECT row_number() over (ORDER BY '1')as rownum,
  FLATTEN( KVGEN(birthday))['value'] AS birthday
  FROM dfs.book.`columns.json`
) AS tbl3 ON tbl1.rownum=tbl3.rownum
```

first_name	last_name	birthday
Robert	Hernandez	5/3/67
Steve	Smith	8/4/84
Anne	Raps	9/13/91
Alice	Muller	4/15/75

Showing 1 to 4 of 4 entries   Previous 1 Next

Figure 5-10. Query data with all fields

There are other ways in which you can arrange data in JSON format, and although there might be occasional structures that Drill is not capable of reading, you will find that by using your knowledge of arrays and maps along with the FLATTEN() and KVGEN() functions you will be able to access most complex data sources.

Analyzing Log Files with Drill

One of Drill's most powerful features is that in addition to standard file formats, as of version 1.9, Drill can also read and query Apache web server logs. The ability to read and query other types of log files was added in version 1.14. You can aggregate and join these files with any other data source that Drill can read; however, getting the most out of this data requires an understanding of the nested data structures you have been learning about.

Configuring Drill to Read HTTPD Web Server Logs

To read web server logs, you must configure the storage plug-in that you are using to read the logs. Server administrators can customize the web server output to display whichever fields they are interested in recording. On your web server, these settings are typically located in */etc/apache2/apache2.conf*. In this file, there is a configuration option called LogFormat, which will look something like this:

```
LogFormat "%h %l %u %t \"%r\" %>s %O \"{Referer}i\" \"%{User-Agent}i\""
```

Once you've located the log format string, copy it to a location where you can readily access it because you will need this formatting string to configure Drill. The next step is to open the Storage tab in the Web Console and click the storage plug-in that you are configuring—probably dfs—and add the following code to the formats section:

```
"httpd": {
    "type": "httpd",
    "logFormat":"%h %l %u %t \"%r\" %>s %O \"{Referer}i\" \"%{User-Agent}i\"",
    "timestampFormat": null
}
```

Be sure to use the actual format string from your server. Table 5-2 shows some of the available fields.[6]

Table 5-2. Selected format string values

Format string	Description
%h	Remote hostname. Will log the IP address if HostnameLookups is set to Off, which is the default. If it logs the hostname for only a few hosts, you probably have access control directives mentioning them by name.
%{VARNAME}i	Contents of VARNAME: header line(s) in the request sent to the server. Changes made by other modules (e.g., mod_headers) affect this. If you're interested in what the request header was prior to when most modules would have modified it, use mod_setenvif to copy the header into an internal environment variable and log that value with %{VARNAME}e.
%l	Remote log name (from identd, if supplied). This returns a dash unless mod_ident is present and IdentityCheck is set to On.
%r	First line of request.
%s	Status. For requests that have been internally redirected, this is the status of the *original* request. Use %>s for the final status.
%t	Time the request was received, in the format [18/Sep/2011:19:18:28 -0400]. The last number indicates the time zone offset from GMT.
%u	Remote user if the request was authenticated. Might be bogus if return status (%s) is 401 (unauthorized).
%O	Bytes sent, including headers. Might be zero in rare cases such as when a request is aborted before a response is sent. You need to enable mod_logio to use this.

Querying Web Server Logs

After you have configured the plug-in, you are ready to begin querying web server logs. This book's GitHub repository contains a few sample web server logs for practice. Let's take a look at the file *hackers-access.httpd* (and note that the following code is broken for book formatting, but should be single lines in real data):

```
195.154.46.135 - - [25/Oct/2015:04:11:25 +0100] \
"GET /linux/doing-pxe-without-dhcp-control HTTP/1.1" 200 24323 \
"http://howto.basjes.nl/" "Mozilla/5.0 (Windows NT 5.1; rv:35.0) \
Gecko/20100101 Firefox/35.0"
23.95.237.180 - - [25/Oct/2015:04:11:26 +0100] \
"GET /join_form HTTP/1.0" 200 11114 "http://howto.basjes.nl/" \
"Mozilla/5.0 (Windows NT 5.1; rv:35.0) Gecko/20100101 Firefox/35.0"
```

By executing the following query, you will see all of the available fields:

```
SELECT *
FROM dfs.drill_tutorial.`log_files/hackers-access.httpd`
LIMIT 10
```

---

6 Complete documentation is available on the Apache website (*http://httpd.apache.org/docs/current/mod/mod_log_config.html*).

Note that this query returns many more fields than are in the format string. Drill's HTTPD parser breaks up many of the fields into their constituent parts. For example, the request_firstline field is broken into request_firstline_uri_userinfo and many more.

Analyzing user agent strings

There are a number of built-in functions that are very useful for analysis of web server logs and other network-related data. As we saw earlier, the web server logs contain user agent strings that hold a wealth of valuable data.

You can view the user agent strings by using the following query:

```
SELECT `request_user-agent`
FROM dfs.drill_tutorial.`log_files/hackers-access.httpd`
```

These sample results show that this request was made using Firefox 34 on a Windows machine:

```
Mozilla/5.0 (Windows NT 5.1; rv:34.0) Gecko/20100101 Firefox/34.0
```

However, parsing these details out of user agent strings is quite complicated; as a result, there is a function called parse_user_agent() that returns a map similar to the following:

```
{
    "DeviceClass":"Desktop",
    "DeviceName":"Macintosh",
    "DeviceBrand":"Apple",
    "OperatingSystemClass":"Desktop",
    "OperatingSystemName":"Mac OS X",
    "OperatingSystemVersion":"10.10.1",
    "OperatingSystemNameVersion":"Mac OS X 10.10.1",
    "LayoutEngineClass":"Browser",
    "LayoutEngineName":"Blink",
    "LayoutEngineVersion":"39.0",
    "LayoutEngineVersionMajor":"39",
    "LayoutEngineNameVersion":"Blink 39.0",
    "LayoutEngineNameVersionMajor":"Blink 39",
    "AgentClass":"Browser",
    "AgentName":"Chrome",
    "AgentVersion":"39.0.2171.99",
    "AgentVersionMajor":"39",
    "AgentNameVersion":"Chrome 39.0.2171.99",
    "AgentNameVersionMajor":"Chrome 39",
    "DeviceCpu":"Intel"
}
```

Installing the parse_user_agent() Function

Because user agents are constantly being updated, this function does not ship with Drill. You can view the complete installation instructions on GitHub (*https://github.com/cgivre/drill-useragent-function*).

Although not all user agents will contain all of these fields, you can access the individual fields by including them in a subquery, as shown here:

```
SELECT
    uadata.ua.AgentNameVersion AS Browser,
    COUNT( * ) AS BrowserCount
FROM (
    SELECT parse_user_agent( `request_user-agent` ) AS ua
    FROM dfs.drill_tutorial.`log_files/hackers-access.httpd`
    ) AS uadata
GROUP BY uadata.ua.AgentNameVersion
ORDER BY BrowserCount DESC
```

This query gets you a count of all the browsers and versions that accessed this server, as illustrated in Figure 5-11. You could of course aggregate any of the other fields in the same manner.

Browser	BrowserCount
Chrome 39.0.2171.95	614
Opera 26.0.1656.60	556
Chrome 36.0.1985.97	533
Firefox 34.0	527
Firefox 35.0	502
Firefox 32.0	326
Firefox 17.0	95
Internet Explorer 11.0	78
Chrome 39.0.2171.96	60
Chrome 39.0.2171.99	43
Showing 1 to 10 of 10 entries	Previous 1 Next

Figure 5-11. Browser count query result

Analyzing URLs and query strings

In web server logs, there are many URLs that will appear, and just like the user agent strings, there are many useful artifacts within these URLs that Drill can easily extract.

If you aren't familiar with URL structure, consider the following example URL:

```
http://somesite.com/login.php?username=bob&password=pass1234
```

Drill has a function called `parse_url()` that returns the following map when given the preceding URL:

```
{
    "protocol":"http",
    "authority":"somesite.com",
    "host":"somesite.com",
    "path":"/login.php?username=bob&password=pass1234"
}
```

In a web server log, the field `request_referer` contains URLs, and you can access these artifacts in the URLs by using the following query:

```
SELECT `request_referer`, parse_url(`request_referer`)
FROM dfs.drill_tutorial.`hackers-access.httpd`
WHERE `request_referer` IS NOT NULL
```

Figure 5-12 presents the results.

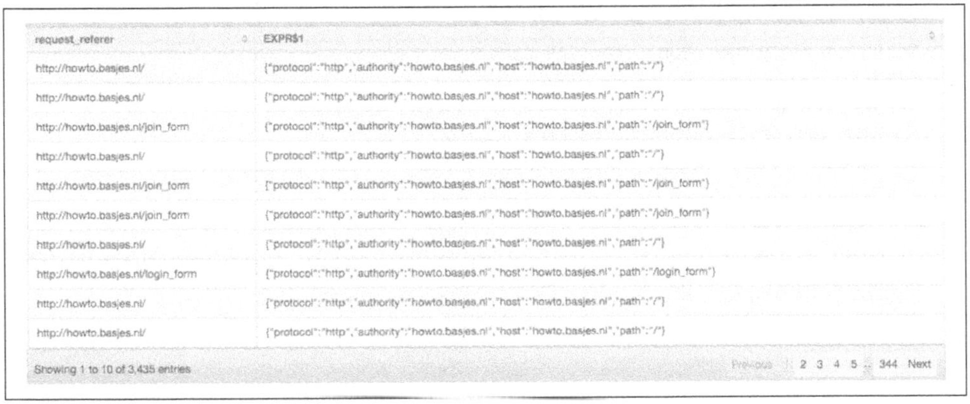

Figure 5-12. Query results with URL metadata

You can then access the newly extracted data artifacts just as you would any other map.

The query string can also be very useful for analysis. Recall from our fictitious URL that it contained `username=bob&amp;password=pass1234`, which is clearly a key–value pairing of variables. However, to analyze this data, you need to first break it up into a map. As you might imagine, Drill has the capability to do this by using the `parse_query()` function. This function takes a query string and returns a mapping of the key–value pairs from the query string. Note that this function will throw an error if you attempt to pass it a null string, so you need to check for empty query strings before you pass it anything. The following example demonstrates how to use the function in a query:

```
SELECT `request_referer_query`,
    parse_query(`request_referer_query`)
```

```
FROM dfs.drill_tutorial.`hackers-access.httpd`
WHERE LENGTH(`request_referer_query`) > 0
```

This query produces the result shown in Figure 5-13.

Figure 5-13. Query with key–value pairs extracted

This function can be very useful in identifying various attacks against a web server. Suppose that you wanted to extract all the values that were being passed to a specific key. You could execute the following query:

```
SELECT q.query_map.`came_from` AS came_from
FROM (
    SELECT parse_query(`request_referer_query`) AS query_map
    FROM dfs.drill_tutorial.`hackers-access.httpd`
    WHERE LENGTH(`request_referer_query`) > 0
) AS q
WHERE q.query_map.`came_from` IS NOT NULL
```

This could be very useful if you were looking at form submissions for malicious activity. Figure 5-14 displays the results of this particular query.

Figure 5-14. Query results showing URL referrer field

In this section, you've learned how to use Drill to analyze web server logs and how to use functions to extract valuable artifacts from this data. In the next section, we look at how to use Drill to analyze other types of log files. Much like web server log data, these log files will also contain nested data structures; thus, understanding nested data structures will be useful for getting the most out of your log files.

Other Log Analysis with Drill

In addition to web server logs, as of version 1.14, Drill can read any other kind of log files. Consider the following log file, which is a sample of a MySQL log:

```
070823 21:00:32      1 Connect     root@localhost on test1
070823 21:00:48      1 Query       show tables
070823 21:00:56      1 Query       select * from category
070917 16:29:01     21 Query       select * from location
070917 16:29:12     21 Query       select * from location where id = 1 LIMIT 1
```

Even though it might be possible to get Drill to parse this by splitting the fields by tabs, it would probably result in some needlessly complex queries.

Analyzing such log files using Drill is similar to how you just learned to get Drill to parse HTTPD server logs; however, instead of using the LogFormat string to define the file format, you must define a regular expression.[7] You will also need to use grouping parentheses to define the fields that you want to extract. Note that the log file extension uses Java-style regular expressions. You must escape backslashes within string constants, so you must double the backslashes. Thus, the regex \d{4} would become \\d{4}. For the previous log file, a regular expression to match the lines and extract the fields would be as follows:

```
(\\d{6})\\s(\\d{2}:\\d{2}:\\d{2})\\s+(\\d+)\\s(\\w+)\\s+(.+)
```

To configure Drill to read log files natively, you must add the following section to the storage plug-in configuration you will use to query your log files—probably hdfs or dfs. In the file formats section, add the following:

```
"log" : {
    "type" : "logRegex",
    "extension" : "log",
    "regex" : "(\\d{6})\\s(\\d{2}:\\d{2}:\\d{2})\\s+(\\d+)\\s(\\w+)\\s+(.+)",
    "maxErrors": 10,
    "schema": [
      {
        "fieldName": "eventDate",
        "fieldType": "DATE",
        "format": "yyMMdd"
      },
      {
        "fieldName": "eventTime",
        "fieldType": "TIME",
        "format": "HH:mm:ss"
      },
      {
        "fieldName": "PID",
        "fieldType": "INT"
      },
      {
        "fieldName": "action"
```

---

7 If you are unfamiliar with regular expressions, we recommend reading *Mastering Regular Expressions* by Jeffrey Friedl (O'Reilly).

```
        },
        {
          "fieldName": "query"
        }
      ]
    }
```

In addition to the regular expression, there are a few other fields that you must define in the storage plug-in configuration:

regex

> This is the regular expression that the logs should match. It must have grouping parentheses to extract the fields.

fields

> This is an array of the field names. If the number of field names is less than the number of groups from the regex, Drill will assign the name of field_*n* to any unnamed fields.

extension

> This is the file extension to be used with this configuration.

maxErrors

> This defines a limit for how many errors Drill will ignore before it halts execution of a query. Because logs can be inconsistent, you need to tune this parameter for best performance on your system.

schema

> This is where you define the schema of your log file. The schema is based on the number of capturing groups you defined in the regex variable. If you do not define the fields, they will be assigned a name of field_*n*, where *n* is the position index of the field, with the VARCHAR data type. The schema option is an array of objects that can contain the following fields:

fieldName

> This is the name of your field.

fieldType

> This allows you to define what data type Drill should apply to the column. This defaults to VARCHAR. At the time of writing, the log reader plug-in supports INT, FLOAT, VARCHAR, DATE, TIME, and TIMESTAMP.

format

> This field is mandatory if the field is a date or time data type. Uses Joda format strings.

Additional Implicit Columns

In addition to the columns extracted by the regex, the log format plug-in has two implicit columns: the _raw column, which displays the complete line from the log file; and the _unmatched_rows column, which displays rows that do not match the supplied regular expression.

Using the previous configuration, you can now analyze log files as you would any other data source in Drill. Figure 5-15 illustrates the query results from `SELECT * FROM dfs.book.`mysql.log``.

date	time	pid	action	query
070823	21:00:32	1	Connect	root@localhost on test1
070823	21:00:48	1	Query	show tables
070823	21:00:56	1	Query	select * from category
070917	16:29:01	21	Query	select * from location
070917	16:29:12	21	Query	select * from location where id = 1 LIMIT 1

Show 10 entries   Search: Show / hide columns

Showing 1 to 5 of 5 entries   Previous 1 Next

Figure 5-15. Results of log query

You can select individual fields, filter, aggregate, or perform any other type of analysis on this data.

Conclusion

In this chapter you learned how to query numerous complex data types, such as log files, JSON, and Parquet. You also learned about Drill's complex data types, maps and arrays, and how to combine all this to analyze nested datasets.

In Chapter 6, you will learn how to expand your ability to access data even further by learning how to connect Drill to other systems including relational databases, cloud storage, NoSQL data stores, and much more.

CHAPTER 6

Connecting Drill to Data Sources

In previous chapters you learned how to query individual files, but Apache Drill's real power is unleashed when you connect Drill to multiple data sources. You have already seen how Drill can natively query data in a file-based system, but it also can natively query the following data sources:

- Cloud storage (Amazon Simple Storage Service/Microsoft Azure/Google Cloud Platform)
- Hadoop
- HBase
- Hive
- Kafka
- Kudu
- MapR
- MongoDB
- Open Time Series Database (Open TSDB)

Additionally, Drill can query any system that provides a JDBC driver. In this chapter, you'll learn how to configure Drill to access and query all these different data sources. Drill accesses storage via a system of extensions known as *storage plug-ins* that require activation and configuration in order to query an external data source. This chapter assumes that you have a basic familiarity with the various data sources mentioned.

Querying Multiple Data Sources

Up to this point, you have seen only queries that use the dfs, or distributed filesystem, storage plug-in.[1] To query a different data source, you must configure a storage plug-in for that data source and then include it in the query. If you recall from Chapter 3, the FROM clause in a Drill query is structured as follows:

```
FROM storage_plugin.workspace.table
```

As an example, let's say you want to query a Hive cluster and you have created and configured the storage plug-in and given it the name hive. You could query that data by using the following (note that not all storage plug-ins have workspaces):

```
SELECT field
FROM hive.`table`
```

Additionally, you can join this data with other data sources simply by including it in a JOIN statement. As an example, if you had a Drill storage plug-in called hdfs connected to a Hadoop cluster, and a JDBC storage plug-in called mysql connected to a MySQL database, you could combine these data sources as demonstrated in the following query:

```
SELECT *
FROM hdfs.`data1` AS d1
INNER JOIN mysql.`database`.`table` AS m1
    ON m1.id = d1.id
```

As you can see, it is quite simple to query multiple data sources.

Configuring a New Storage Plug-in

To configure or add a new storage plug-in, in the Web Console, click the Storage tab at the top of the screen. From there, you will see the storage plug-ins that are available. By default, Drill ships with the cp and dfs storage plug-ins enabled and several others disabled. You can enable a storage plug-in simply by clicking the Enable button adjacent to the plug-in name, as shown in Figure 6-1. You can also update the storage plug-in's configuration by clicking the Update button (also shown in Figure 6-1). Finally, if you would like to add a new storage plug-in, you can do so in the New Storage Plugin section at the bottom of the page.

---

1 As indicated in Chapter 4, the plug-in name "dfs" is completely arbitrary.

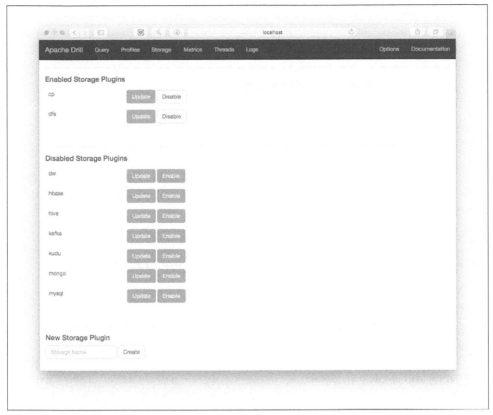

Figure 6-1. The storage configuration page

Connecting Drill to a Relational Database

Let's begin with the easiest data source to connect: a JDBC-compliant relational database management system (RDBMS). It might seem silly to connect Drill to a relational database; however, doing so allows you to join this data with other systems or files through standard SQL.

Before you set up the storage plug-in, you will need to download the database's JDBC driver and copy it to your Drill installation's */jar/3rdparty* directory. This is found in *$DRILL_HOME/jars/3rdparty*. If you are running Drill in distributed mode, you will need to copy the driver to the same path on every Drill node, then restart Drill.

In general, Drill will work with most conventional SQL databases that have a JDBC driver. The general format for the configuration is shown in the following snippet:

```
{
  "type": "jdbc",
  "driver": "JDBC Driver Artifact ID",
  "url": "jdbc connection string",
```

```
  "username": "username",
  "password": "password",
  "enabled": true
}
```

Be Cautious of Shared Credentials

At the time of writing, any credentials placed in storage plug-in configurations are visible to Drill administrators and should be considered shared passwords.

Drill has been tested with Microsoft SQL Server, MySQL/MariaDB, Oracle, PostgreSQL, and SQLite. The drivers for these databases are available at the following links:

- Microsoft SQL Server (*http://bit.ly/2JlZTLn*)

- MySQL (*https://dev.mysql.com/downloads/connector/j/5.1.html*)

- Oracle (*http://bit.ly/2qhw3PK*)

- PostgreSQL (*https://jdbc.postgresql.org*)

- SQLite (*https://bitbucket.org/xerial/sqlite-jdbc/downloads/*)

Configuring Drill to query an RDBMS

As indicated in the previous section, to connect Drill to a MySQL database, you first need to copy the JDBC driver to the *jars/3rdparty* folder, or for a production Drill, your site directory (see Chapter 9).

Next, start Drill and navigate to the Storage tab in the user interface. At the bottom of the page, go to the section labeled New Storage Plugin. Type a name for the storage plug-in, and then click the Create button. This name is how the storage plug-in will be accessed in queries. It should go without saying that *the RDBMS must be up and running to successfully query it from Drill.*

In the configuration panel, enter one of the configurations listed in the following subsections.

Microsoft SQL Server. To query a Microsoft SQL Server, use the following configuration settings:

```
{
  "type": "jdbc",
  "driver": "com.microsoft.sqlserver.jdbc.SQLServerDriver",
  "url": "jdbc:sqlserver://host:1433;databaseName=database_name",
  "username": "username",
  "password": "password",
```

```
    enabled: "true"

}
```

MySQL. To query a MySQL database through Drill, use the following:

```
{
  "type": "jdbc",
  "driver": "com.mysql.jdbc.Driver",
  "url": "jdbc:mysql://localhost:3306",
  "username": "username",
  "password": "password",
  "enabled": true
}
```

Oracle. To query an Oracle database through Drill, you need to specify the database name in the configuration, as shown here:

```
{
  "type": "jdbc",
  "driver": "oracle.jdbc.OracleDriver",
  "url": "jdbc:oracle:thin:username/password@host:1521/database"
  "enabled": true
}
```

PostgreSQL. Here's how to specify the database name to query a PostgreSQL database:

```
{
  "type": "jdbc",
  "driver": "org.postgresql.Driver",
  "url": "jdbc:postgresql://host/database",
  "username": "username",
  "password": "password",
  "enabled": true
}
```

SQLite. SQLite databases require you to enter the table name after the database alias when you query data:

```
{
  "type": "jdbc",
  "driver": "org.sqlite.JDBC",
  "url": "jdbc:sqlite:path_to_database_file",
  "enabled": true
}
```

Querying an RDBMS from Drill

After you have provided the configuration string, click Enable; if all went well, you should get a success message. You should now be able to use the database in a Drill query. You should structure the FROM clause as shown here:

```
FROM storage_plugin.database.table
```

Thus, a completed query would look like this:

```
SELECT *
FROM sqlite.`genres`;
```

This query returns all of the results from a table called `genres` in the chinook SQLite database.

Other uses of the drill JDBC storage plug-in

In addition to being able to query traditional databases that support JDBC, you can also access other data sources that have JDBC drivers. One example of this is data.world, an online platform that hosts open datasets for public use. As it turns out, a JDBC driver is available at the data.world GitHub repository (*https://github.com/datadotworld/dw-jdbc*).

After you have downloaded and installed the data.world JDBC driver, you can query data stored there as if it were hosted locally. To configure Drill to do this, open Drill's web interface and, at the top of the screen, click the Storage tab. In the New Storage Plugin section, click Create. In the blank window that opens, enter the following configuration:

```
{
  "type": "jdbc",
  "driver": "world.data.jdbc.Driver",
  "url": "jdbc:data:world:sql:username:dataset",
  "username": "username",
  "password": "API Key",
  "enabled": true
}
```

You will need to get an API key from data.world, which is available after you have an account. Save this plug-in as `dw`. After you've set up the storage plug-in, all you really need to do to query a data.world dataset is modify the `FROM` clause of your query.

The data.world driver is a little different than a regular Drill `FROM` clause in that it has four parts, whereas a traditional Drill data source has only three:

```
FROM dw.username.dataset.filename
```

We uploaded a spreadsheet to data.world that contained a listing of MAC addresses and the manufacturers of the associated devices. To query this data, you would enter a query like the following:

```
SELECT *
FROM dw.cgivre.`mac-address-manufacturers`.
`20170426mac_address.csv/20170426mac_address`
```

Querying Data in Hadoop from Drill

One of the primary use cases for Apache Drill is querying data in a Hadoop cluster. It is actually quite simple to configure Drill to query data stored in a distributed filesystem. You can query HDFS data from your laptop if the data is small. But, for large data sets, you typically run a Drillbit on each HDFS node as described in Chapter 9. Or, in specialized cases, you can run Drillbits on the same racks as your HDFS nodes, though this is an advanced configuration.

With that said, it is quite simple to connect Drill to query data stored in a Hadoop cluster. Simply copy the configuration settings from the dfs plug-in and change the connection as shown here:

```
"connection":"hdfs://name_node_host_name:port"
```

Authentication from Drill

When you connect to a distributed filesystem Drill uses user impersonation, as explained in "Security" on page 190. Therefore, the account that you are using to query Drill must have permission in HDFS to access the data you are trying to query.

Connecting to and Querying HBase from Drill

Apache HBase is a popular open source, nonrelational database modeled after Google's Bigtable. HBase has a few spinoff projects, such as OpenTSDB and Apache Accumulo.

Drill includes a default HBase storage plug-in configuration. It will be necessary to specify the IP addresses of your ZooKeeper quorum as a comma-separated list. After you've done that, enable the plug-in:

```
{
    "type": "hbase",
    "config": {
        "hbase.zookeeper.quorum": "hosts",
        "hbase.zookeeper.property.clientPort": "2181"
    },
    "size.calculator.enabled": false,
    "enabled": true
}
```

When you've done that, you are ready to query data in HBase.

Querying data from HBase

Querying data in HBase is *significantly more complicated than other data sources* because you will need to understand how data is stored in HBase. HBase stores data in bytes or byte arrays, and to be able to performantly query this data you need to understand the underlying data structure. From Drill, you can access individual columns can by using the following pattern:

```
table_name.column_family_name.column_name
```

HBase stores all columns as byte arrays stored in Drill as a VARBINARY column. To work with an HBase column, you first convert the VARBINARY column into another data type using either the CAST() function for numeric fields or CONVERT_FROM() for all other fields. The following example queries a fictitious table in HBase and converts the results into readable results:

```
SELECT
    CONVERT_FROM(tbl.sales.customerid, 'UTF8') AS customerID,
    CAST(tbl.sales.order_amount AS FLOAT) AS order_amount
FROM hbase.table
```

Little Endian Versus Big Endian

At the byte level, data is represented in two ways, *big endian* or *little endian*, which refers to the order in which the bytes of a number are stored in memory. As an example, the number 123 would be stored as "1-2-3" in big-endian format, and "3-2-1" in little-endian format. Normally, you don't really need to know this, but HBase stores information in both big- and little-endian formats and you can take advantage of performance enhancements if you are aware of the format of the data.

In production systems, HBase will use timestamps or dates as row keys that are encoded as big-endian. By default, however, Drill assumes that the data is unsorted little-endian. When you use the CONVERT_TO() and CONVERT_FROM() functions on big-endian data, Drill will optimize the scanning process. Drill also provides several data types for big-endian conversions that all end in _BE, which are intended to be used with HBase. You can find a complete list in the Drill documentation (*http://bit.ly/2NkK4ZX*).

The BYTE_SUBSTR() function is also very useful when querying HBase; it separates the components of a composite HBase row key. The following example shows a performant query in HBase:

```
SELECT
    CONVERT_FROM(BYTE_SUBSTR(row_key, 1, 8), 'BIGINT_BE') AS row_key
FROM hbase.table
```

When the data is encoded in sorted byte arrays Drill can take advantage of this to improve performance, but it requires you to convert your data into an _OB data type. The following example demonstrates how to improve the performance of an HBase query by limiting the data scanned to only those rows with keys between 0 and 100:

```
SELECT
    CONVERT_FROM(row_key, 'INT_OB') AS row_key
FROM hbase.table
WHERE CONVERT_FROM(row_key, 'INT_OB') >= CAST(0 AS INT)
    AND CONVERT_FROM(row_key ,'INT_OB') < 100
```

Querying Hive Data from Drill

Apache Hive is one of the first SQL-on-Hadoop software packages that was originally developed by Facebook and gives the user a SQL-like interface known as HiveQL to data stored in HDFS Amazon S3. Hive is a schema-on-read system, meaning that you must define a schema before you query data using Hive. The schema information is stored in a database known as a metastore and can be either on a remote system or embedded.

The Hive Metastore

One important thing to note about Hive is that it maintains a metastore—usually using Apache Derby or MySQL—which stores metadata about all the tables that users have queried. Unlike Drill, HiveQL queries generate MapReduce jobs, thus if you have data that is accessed using Hive, Drill can take advantage of Hive's metastore and query the data much faster than Hive can.

For more information about Hive, we recommend *Programming Hive* by Edward Capriolo, Dean Wampler, and Jason Rutherglen (O'Reilly).

Connecting Drill to Hive

To connect Drill to Hive, you must first determine whether the Hive cluster is using the embedded or a remote metastore. Normally, in a production environment, Hive uses a remote metastore; if it is not, you might want to talk with your systems administrator.

If you are using Hive with an embedded metastore, on the storage configuration page of the user interface, click the Update button adjacent to the Hive storage plug-in configuration. The default configuration for Hive is as follows:

```
{
  "type": "hive",
  "configProps": {
    "hive.metastore.uris": "",
    "javax.jdo.option.ConnectionURL":
        "jdbc:database://host:port/metastore database",
    "hive.metastore.warehouse.dir": "/tmp/drill_hive_wh",
    "fs.default.name": "file:///",
    "hive.metastore.sasl.enabled": "false"
  },
```

```
    "enabled": true,
}
```

Make Sure the Metastore Is Running

Before attempting to enable the Hive storage plug-in, make sure
your Hive metastore is up and running by executing the following
command:

```
hive --service metastore
```

For Drill to connect to Hive with an embedded metastore, you must first set the
`fs.default.name` to the default location of the files that you want to query. This can
be either the local filesystem (`file:///`), an HDFS root path on the default HDFS
namenode (`hdfs://`), or the path to a specific HDFS namenode (`hdfs://host:port`).

The configuration option `javax.jdo.option.ConnectionURL` requires a JDBC connection string to the metastore database. As with an RDBMS, you need to copy the
driver to the *DRILL_PATH/jars/3rdparty* folder for this to work.

After you have done all that, click Enable, and then you are ready to query Hive.

Connecting to Hive with a remote metastore.   If you are working with a production Hive
installation, you are more likely to have a remote metastore, and if you would like to
use Drill to query this data you will need to configure it to connect to the remote
metastore. As with the embedded metastore, you must first verify that the metastore
is running before you attempt to connect Drill. You can verify that the metastore is
running by using the following command:

```
hive --service metastore
```

Next, navigate to the Drill storage configuration and click the Hive storage plug-in:

```
{
    "type": "hive",
    "configProps": {
      "hive.metastore.uris": "thrift://host:port",
      "hive.metastore.sasl.enabled": "false",
      "fs.default.name": "hdfs://hdfs_host/",
    },
    "enabled": true
}
```

In the `configProps` section, set the `hive.metastore.uris` property to the thrift URI
and port for your metastore. Next, set the `fs.default.name` to the default location of
the files that you want to query. Note that if you include a hostname and port, the
URI must point to a main control node of a Hadoop cluster.

If your installation uses the `HBaseStorageHandler`, you will need to add the following two additional properties to the configuration to set the location of the ZooKeeper quorum hosts and ports:

```
"hbase.zookeeper.quorum": "zkhost1,zkhost2",
"hbase.zookeeper.property.clientPort":"2181"
```

At this point, you should be able to enable the Hive storage plug-in and query Hive directly from Drill.

Improving Performance of Parquet-Backed Tables

If you are querying Parquet files from Drill via Hive, you should set the `store.hive.optimize_scan_with_native_readers` option to true to enable Drill to use its native readers rather than those shipped with Hive. This option will be removed in Drill 1.15 and replaced with the following variable:

```
store.hive.parquet.optimize_scan_with_native_reader
```

Connecting to and Querying Streaming Data with Drill and Kafka

Apache Kafka is a popular, scalable real-time data and stream processor. According to Wikipedia (*https://en.wikipedia.org/wiki/Apache_Kafka?*), Kafka "aims to provide a unified, high-throughput, low-latency platform for handling real-time data feeds. Its storage layer is essentially a massively scalable pub/sub message queue architected as a distributed transaction log, making it highly valuable for enterprise infrastructures to process streaming data." If you are interested in learning more about Apache Kafka, we recommend *Kafka: The Definitive Guide* by Neha Narkhede, Gwen Shapira, and Todd Palino (O'Reilly).

To query Kafka from Drill, you must be running at least Kafka version 0.10 and Drill version 1.12 or greater. At the time of writing, the Kafka storage plug-in supports only JSON messages from Kafka.

JSON Configuration for the Kafka Plug-in

When querying data from Kafka, you might encounter some of the same issues as when querying JSON data in the filesystem. To set the JSON configurations for Kafka, you can use the following variables:

- `store.kafka.all_text_mode`
- `store.kafka.read_numbers_as_double`

As with the other storage plug-ins, to enable the Kafka storage plug-in, go to the Storage tab. There, you will see a disabled storage plug-in with the configuration shown here:

```
{
    "type": "kafka",
    "kafkaConsumerProps":
    {
        "key.deserializer":
            "org.apache.kafka.common.serialization.ByteArrayDeserializer",
        "auto.offset.reset": "earliest",
        "bootstrap.servers": "kafka_host:9092",
        "group.id": "drill-query-consumer-1",
        "enable.auto.commit": "true",
        "value.deserializer":
            "org.apache.kafka.common.serialization.ByteArrayDeserializer",
        "session.timeout.ms": "30000"
    },
    "enabled": true
}
```

How Drill Interprets Data from Kafka

When Drill queries Kafka, the storage plug-in maps Kafka *topics* to SQL *tables*. When you connect Drill to Kafka, it discovers all the available topics and maps them to tables with the same name. The rows of a topic are known in Kafka terminology as *messages*, and each message is mapped to a SQL row. Each message contains fields that are mapped to columns in Drill. Additionally, Drill generates the following metadata columns:

kafkaTopic
> The topic name from Kafka

kafkaPartitionid
> The partition ID from Kafka

kafkaMsgOffset
> The message offset from Kafka

kakfaMsgTimestamp
> The timestamp when Kafka received the message

kafkaMsgKey *(if not null)*
> The message key or ID if not null

Querying streaming data

After you have registered the Kafka storage plug-in, you can execute queries against data in Kafka as if it were any other data source. It is important to remember that Kafka contains *streaming data*, and when you query data from Drill, it will scan all the Kafka messages from the earliest (most recent) offset to the latest.

Because data is constantly flowing into Kafka, every time you query (or consume) data, Drill will reset the offset pointer. You can change this option in the configuration for the Kafka storage plug-in.

Avoid Endless Queries

When querying streaming data, it should go without saying that you should avoid SELECT * queries without limits. In the event of an endless query, Kafka will time out, but it is best to limit your queries as tightly as possible.

Improving the performance of Kafka queries

In Drill 1.14, there is an enhancement to the Kafka plug-in that significantly reduces query time. Prior to this version, Drill would scan all the data in a topic before filtering; however, as of version 1.14, Drill can filter on the Kafka metadata, which will greatly reduce the volume of data that Drill is scanning. At present, there are three fields that you can include in the WHERE clause of your queries that will enhance performance:

kafkaPartitionId
: Can be used with =, >, >=, <, <=.

kafkaMsgOffset
: Can be used with =, >, <=, <, <=.

kafkaMsgTimestamp
: Maps to the timestamp for each Kafka message. Drill can use this field only when you use the operators =, >, >=.

We recommend that you include these fields in predicates in the WHERE clause of your queries in your queries. For example:

```
WHERE kafkaMsgTimestamp > 'some date'
```

Connecting to and Querying Kudu

Apache Kudu is a low-latency storage system for tabular data. At the time of writing, Kudu is incubating with the Apache Software Foundation and the Drill integration is still experimental. Kudu is a true columnar store that supports key-indexed record lookup similar to HBase, but Kudu differs from HBase in that Kudu's data model more closely resembles a relational database.

To enable Drill to query Kudu, simply create a storage plug-in and enter the configuration that follows, replacing *master address* with the IP address or hostname of your Kudu master. After entering the IP address, enable the plug-in, and you should be able to query your data in Kudu!

```
{
  "type": "kudu",
  "masterAddresses": "master address",
  "enabled": true
}
```

Connecting to and Querying MongoDB from Drill

MongoDB is a popular NoSQL document-oriented database that can scale to enormous datasets. Installing and configuring MongoDB is beyond the scope of this book, but if you would like to read more about it, we recommend *MongoDB: The Definitive Guide* by Shannon Bradshaw and Kristina Chodorow (O'Reilly).

It is quite simple to connect Drill to MongoDB and to query the data in it. Make sure that MongoDB is running before you attempt to configure Drill. You'll notice on the Storage tab of the web console that Drill ships with a storage plug-in for MongoDB preconfigured. However, in the event that the configuration is missing, you can use the configuration shown here:

```
{
  "type": "mongo",
  "connection": "mongodb://mongodb_host:27017/"
  "enabled": true
}
```

After you have saved this configuration, you can verify the connection was successful by executing a SHOW DATABASES query in Drill. You should then see the tables from your MongoDB instance. You can now query your MongoDB instance using standard SQL from Drill!

Connecting Drill to Cloud Storage

In many instances, organizations store large amounts of data in various cloud storage services such as Amazon S3, Microsoft Azure, or Google Cloud Storage (GCS). As with other filesystems, you can use Drill to connect to these systems and directly query this data. The process for connecting to one of these services is essentially the same. First, you must download and install the appropriate driver for the cloud service you are using. Next, set your access credentials in the *core-site.xml* file, and then finally configure the storage plug-in (see "Working with Amazon S3" on page 185).

Querying data on Amazon S3

To query data on Amazon S3, you also need an access key and secret key.

Getting access credentials for S3.   To obtain access credentials, first log in to Amazon S3, and then, in the upper-right corner, click your name to open your personal settings menu, as shown in Figure 6-2. Click the My Security Credentials option.

Figure 6-2. AWS account menu

Next, click the "Access keys" link and generate the access and secret keys (see Figure 6-3).

 Be sure to save the keys in a safe place; you cannot retrieve them again after you have generated them.

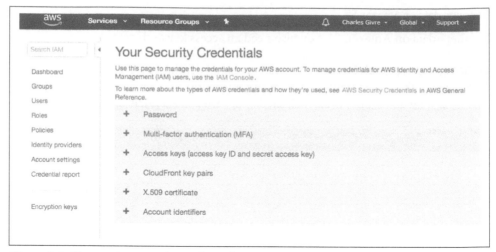

Figure 6-3. Generating security credentials

After you have obtained your access and secret keys, the next step is to configure Drill with your AWS credentials. To do this, add the following code to the file *$DRILL_HOME/conf/core-site.xml*, replacing the placeholder values with your credentials:

```
<configuration>
  <property>
    <name>fs.s3a.access.key</name>
    <value>YOUR_ACCESSKEY</value>
  </property>
  <property>
    <name>fs.s3a.secret.key</name>
    <value>YOUR_SECRETKEY</value>
  </property>
  <property>
    <name>fs.s3a.connection.maximum</name>
    <value>100</value>
  </property>
  <property>
    <name>fs.s3a.endpoint</name>
    <value>s3.REGION.amazonaws.com</value>
  </property>
</configuration>
```

When you have added these options to your configuration file, the next step is to install the driver and configure the storage plug-in.

Fundamentally, the configuration to query Amazon S3 is the same as querying the local filesystem (`dfs`), with the only difference being the configuration string having an `s3a` address instead of `file:///`:

```
    "connection":"s3a://your_S3_bucket"
```

Just as with the `dfs` storage plug-in, you can set up workspaces and file types; thus, a complete `s3a` configuration might look like this:

```
{
    "type": "file",
    "enabled": true,
    "connection": "s3a://your s3a bucket",
    "workspaces": {
        "root": {
            "location": "/",
            "writable": false,
            "defaultInputFormat": null
        },
        "formats": {
            "csv": {
                "type": "text",
                "extensions": [ "csv" ],
                "delimiter": ","
            }
        }
    }
}
```

Querying Minio datastores from drill

Minio (*https://www.minio.io*) is a high-performance distributed object storage server that you can easily set up to query with Drill. After you have Minio up and running from an accessible IP address, you need to modify the *core-site.xml* file as shown here:

```
<configuration>
    <property>
        <name>fs.s3a.access.key</name>
        <value>YOUR_ACCESS_KEY</value>
    </property>
    <property>
        <name>fs.s3a.secret.key</name>
        <value>YOUR_SECRET_KEY</value>
    </property>
    <property>
        <name>fs.s3a.endpoint</name>
        <value>http://minio_host:9000</value>
    </property>
    <property>
        <name>fs.s3a.connection.ssl.enabled</name>
        <value>false </value>
    </property>
    <property>
        <name>fs.s3a.path.style.access</name>
        <value>true</value>
    </property>
</configuration>
```

When this is complete, follow the instructions for connecting to an S3 bucket and you will be able to query your data stored using Minio!

Connecting to other cloud storage services

In addition to being able to directly query data in an Amazon S3 bucket, Drill can query data in GCS or Microsoft Azure. The basic procedure is similar: download and install the driver, set up the credentials in the *core-site.xml* file, and then create a storage plug-in similar to the `dfs` plug-in, with the connection string for the cloud storage provider.

The following steps download and unzip the Azure driver to the Drill *jars/3rdparty* folder (don't forget to restart your Drillbits after adding drivers):

```
$ cd $DRILL_HOME/jars/3rdparty/
$ sudo wget http://central.maven.org/maven2/org/apache/hadoop/hadoop-azure/\
2.7.1/hadoop-azure-2.7.1.jar
$ sudo wget http://central.maven.org/maven2/com/microsoft/azure/azure-storage/\
2.0.0/azure-storage-2.0.0.jar
```

Next, add the following property to the *core-site.xml* file:

```
<property>
    <name>fs.azure.account.key.your_data_files.blob.core.windows.net</name>
    <value><your_azure_account_key></value>
</property>
```

Finally, here's the connection string for Azure:

```
wasb://your_container@your_datafiles.blob.core.windows.net
```

To connect Drill to GCS, download the drivers from the GCS website (*http://bit.ly/2wNHLnP*) and copy them to the *$DRILL_HOME/jars/3rdparty* folder.

As with Azure, duplicate the settings for `dfs` and change the connection string to the one shown in the following snippet, replacing the placeholder with your bucket name:

```
"connection": "gs://your_bucket_name"
```

Querying Time Series Data from Drill and OpenTSDB

OpenTSDB is an open source, scalable time series database that is built on top of HBase. As of version 1.13, Drill can natively query time series data in OpenTSDB. It is quite simple to connect Drill to OpenTSDB, but querying time series data in Drill is a little more complicated than regular data.

As with the other storage plug-ins, we begin with the default configuration. To enable OpenTSDB, make sure it is running, navigate to the Drill storage configuration page, and then enable the storage plug-in, changing the `connection` property if necessary to point to your instance:

```
{
    "type": "openTSDB",
    "connection": "http://opentsdb_host:4242",
    "enabled": true
}
```

After you have enabled the storage plug-in, you are ready to query the time series data in OpenTSDB.

Special considerations for time series data

When you query time series data with Drill, you must specify certain configuration parameters in the FROM clause in your query. Table 6-1 lists the three mandatory parameters.

Table 6-1. OpenTSDB required query parameters

Parameter name	Description
metric	The name of the metric or field that you are querying.
start	The start time of your query. Can be specified as a relative or absolute timestamp.[a] For example, start=5y-ago.
aggregator	The aggregation function for your data. Some aggregation functions include count, sum, avg, std, and none.[b]

[a] A complete list of time formats for OpenTSDB is available in the OpenTSDB 2.3 documentation (*http://bit.ly/2D8T7bR*).
[b] A complete list of aggregation functions is available in the OpenTSDB documentation (*http://bit.ly/2JoeqGH*).

Additionally, there are two optional parameters, explained in Table 6-2.

Table 6-2. OpenTSDB optional query parameters

Parameter name	Description
downsample	Allows you to reduce the amount of data returned via a downsampling function.[a]
end	The desired end time for the query. If left blank, OpenTSDB assumes the current system time of the system as the end time.

[a] A complete list of available downsampling functions is available in the OpenTSDB documentation (*http://bit.ly/2qi4Xrl*).

The FROM clause of a Drill query must therefore look like the following example:

```
SELECT fields
FROM openTSDB.`(metric=metric_name,
    start=start_time,
    aggregator=aggregation_function)`
```

As a final example, the query that follows returns the aggregated and grouped values from the `clicks.speed.test` table, limited to the last year:

```
SELECT `timestamp`, SUM(`aggregated value`) AS avg_sum
FROM openTSDB.`(metric=clicks.speed.test,
        aggregator=avg,
        start=1y-ago)`
GROUP BY `timestamp`
```

Conclusion

One of Drill's most powerful use cases is the ability to query and join data from a wide variety of different data sources, including Hadoop, traditional relational databases, MongoDB, Kafka, and many others, all using standard SQL. In this chapter you have learned how to configure Drill to query all of these different data sources as well as the intricacies of querying particular data sources.

In the next section of the book, you will learn how to incorporate Drill into your data pipeline. You'll see how to connect to Drill, how to handle complex data formats with Drill, and how to deploy Drill in production.

CHAPTER 7

Connecting to Drill

In the past few chapters you have learned how to use Drill to query and explore data, and although this is extremely useful, you can get even more value out of Drill by using it as part of a larger data pipeline. Fortunately, Drill has many interfaces through which you can connect to it and query the results. In principle, the three methods are Open Database Connectivity (ODBC), Java Database Connectivity (JDBC), and Drill's RESTful interface. In this chapter, you will learn how to use these interfaces and connect to Drill using a wide variety of scripting languages and tools, including Python, R, Java, PHP, and Node.js, as well as some business intelligence (BI) tools such as Apache Superset, Zeppelin, and Tableau.

Understanding Drill's Interfaces

Before we get into the various language-specific libraries that enable you to easily connect to Drill, it is a good idea to understand the ways in which these libraries connect to Drill. Fundamentally, there are three ways to connect to it:[1]

- JDBC
- ODBC
- REST interface

In theory, you can use any program that implements one of these standards to programmatically connect to Drill. For instance, if you have some database explorer or

---

[1] There actually are two other ways of connecting to Drill: a native Drill client and a C clone of the Drill client. These are both beyond the scope of the book.

visualization tool that uses ODBC, you can use Drill's ODBC interface to connect the tool to Drill.

JDBC and Drill

Drill is implemented in Java, and as such it makes sense that Drill should implement the JDBC standard to enable other Java-based programs to connect to it. To use JDBC, you first need a copy of the Drill JDBC driver on your machine. The JDBC driver is included with Drill and is located at *$DRILL_HOME/jars/jdbc-driver/drill-jdbc-all-version.jar*. The driver class's name is *org.apache.drill.jdbc.Driver*.[2] Copy it to the machine that has the application you want to connect to Drill, then add it to that application's class path. Consult the documentation of your application for details.

Regardless of the application, to connect to Drill, you need to craft a JDBC connection URL. If you are using Drill in embedded mode on your local machine, that URL will be as follows:

```
jdbc:drill:drillbit=localhost:31010
```

You can of course, replace localhost with your hostname or IP address.

If you are connecting to Drill in distributed mode, you will need to know the name of your ZooKeeper cluster and you will use this form of URL: *jdbc:drill:zk=zkhost1:2818,zkhost2:2181,....* Additionally, there are various optional configuration variables that you can pass in your JDBC connection URL, including the following:

cluster ID
> The cluster name as set in *drill-override.conf*. The default is drillbits1. The default is typically fine unless you've customized this property in Drill's *drill-override.conf* file.

directory
> The ZooKeeper root znode for the Drill cluster. The default is root. Again, the default is typically fine unless you've customized this property in Drill's *drill-override.conf* file.

port
> The connection port. The port to connect directly to a Drillbit is 31010 (unless you changed this value in *drill-override.conf*.) The ZooKeeper default is 2181, and for a MapR cluster it is 5181.

---

2 There is an additional JDBC driver developed by MapR that has additional functionality beyond what is described here.

schema
> The default storage plug-in for the connection. This parameter is optional.

tries
> The number of connection attempts. The default is 5.

These values must be the same as those specified in the *drill-override.conf* file for the target Drill cluster.

In the following code snippet, you see the first of two examples of JDBC connection strings. This one demonstrates how to connect to Drill via a single ZooKeeper instance, as is used for development:

```
jdbc:drill:zk=zkhost:2181
```

The second example demonstrates how to connect to Drill via a multinode Zoo-Keeper cluster:

```
jdbc:drill:zk=10.20.100.20:2181,
            10.20.100.21:2181,
            10.20.100.22:2181;schema=mongodb
```

When there is more than one ZooKeeper node, Drill randomly connects to any of them and then randomly picks a Drillbit. If the ZooKeeper node happens to be down, Drill will try another. The complete documentation about connecting to Drill with JDBC is available in the documentation on the Drill website (*https://drill.apache.org/docs/using-the-jdbc-driver/*).

ODBC and Drill

In addition to connecting to Drill using JDBC, Drill supports using ODBC as a connection method. Configuring ODBC requires installing the ODBC driver on your system and configuring some files on your system.

Installing the ODBC driver

Installing the ODBC driver can be complicated. Complete instructions downloading it are available in the Drill documentation (*https://drill.apache.org/docs/installing-the-odbc-driver/*). After you've installed the ODBC driver, you need to configure it. Complete instructions to do so are also available in the Drill documentation (*https://drill.apache.org/docs/configuring-odbc/*).

Configuring ODBC on Linux or macOS. If you are installing the ODBC driver on a Mac or Unix machine, you must also install an ODBC driver manager, such as iODBC (*http://bit.ly/2JoRnLM*).

After downloading and installing the MapR ODBC driver (*http://bit.ly/2zct0wb*), there are three configuration files that you need to install and configure. These files will be copied to */opt/mapr/drill/Setup/* after you've installed the ODBC driver, and you'll need to copy them to your home directory and rename them as hidden files.

.odbc.ini
> Contains the definition of your ODBC data sources

.mapr.drillodbc.ini
> Contains driver configuration variables

.odbcinst.ini (optional)
> Defines the ODBC driver

Then you need to set the following environment variables to point to these files:

```
export ODBCINI=~/.odbc.ini
export MAPRDRILLINI=~/.mapr.drillodbc.ini
export LD_LIBRARY_PATH=/usr/local/lib
```

Configuring ODBC on Windows. After downloading and installing the MapR ODBC driver, navigate to the ODBC Data Source Administrator and click the Settings tab. On the System DSN tab, select MapR Drill, and then click Configure. To connect to Drill in embedded mode or as a single server on your local machine, define the following variables:

- HOST: localhost
- PORT: 31010
- Catalog: DRILL

If you are connecting to a cluster in distributed mode, you'll need to define the following variables:

ZKQuorum
> A comma-separated list of ZooKeeper nodes in the format *host or IP:port,host or IP:port*

ZKClusterID
> The name of the Drillbit cluster that can be found in the *drill-override.conf* file. Defaults to drillbits1.

Now that you've learned how to set up ODBC and JDBC to be used with Drill, in the next section, you'll learn how to write scripts to connect to Drill's various interfaces.

Drill's REST Interface

In addition to JDBC and ODBC, Drill also has a RESTful interface that you can use to execute queries as well as modify configuration settings. Drill's REST API uses the web console URL:

```
http://hostname:8047/function
```

The REST API has the following functions:

Cluster (cluster.json)
> Gets Drillbit information.

Options (options.json)
> Gets the name, default, and data type of the system and session options.

Query (query.json)
> Executes a query. You must use a POST request to execute a query.

Profiles (profiles.json)
> Gets the profiles of running queries.

Status (status.json)
> Gets the Drill status.

Storage (storage.json)
> Gets storage plug-in configuration and allows you to create, modify, or delete storage plug-in configurations. You must use a POST request to change the storage plug-in configuration.

Limitations of the RESTful Interface

Although the RESTful interface is the easiest to work with, it has two key limitations:

- The RESTful interface returns the entire result set in a single REST response, making it unsuitable for extremely large queries.

- The RESTful interface is stateless, so you cannot use the USE or ALTER SESSION commands.

The complete documentation for Drill's RESTful interface is available on the Apache Drill website (*https://drill.apache.org/docs/rest-api-introduction/*).

Connecting to Drill with Python

Python is certainly one of the most popular languages for data science and data analysis. Furthermore, Python has an ever-expanding ecosystem of data analysis, visualization, and machine learning libraries that makes it one of the best tools for data science.

At the core of this ecosystem is the Pandas library (*http://pandas.pydata.org*), which provides a collection of vectorized data structures. Most relevant to Drill is the `Data Frame`, which is a two-dimensional data structure. It is probably the most important component of the data science ecosystem in Python and is used as the basic container of data for visualization and machine learning. Therefore, in this section, we demonstrate how to quickly and easily get data directly from a Drill query into a Pandas `DataFrame`.

There are two Python modules, `drillpy` and `pydrill`, that you can use to connect to Drill. Both are wrappers for Drill's RESTful interface, so both have the limitations associated with that, but both work reasonably well, and as the Drill community improves the RESTful interface, so too will the drivers improve. `drillpy` is notably different in that it implements Python's DBAPI standard and thus you can use it with other modules that require a database connection.

Using drillpy to Query Drill

The basic steps for connecting to Drill with `drillpy` are as follows:

1. Create the connection object.
2. Create a cursor object.
3. Execute the query using the `execute()` method.
4. Retrieve the results by calling one of the `fetchone()`, `fetchmany(<n>)`, or `fetch all()` methods. `fetchall()` and `fetchmany()` both return Pandas `DataFrames`, and `fetchone()` returns a Pandas `Series` object.

If necessary, first install the module by running:

```
pip install drillpy
```

The snippet that follows demonstrates how to create a connection object in Python using `drillpy`. If you are using Drill in embedded mode, you can use `localhost` for the hostname. The default port is 8047 for the RESTful interface:

```
from drillpy import connect
con = connect(host="host",
```

```
db="database_name",
port=port_number)
```

After creating the connection object, call the `cursor()` function to create the cursor object, as shown in the following snippet:

```
cur = con.cursor()
```

Now you are ready to execute a query and get the results. The following snippet demonstrates how to execute a query and load the results directly into a `DataFrame`:

```
queryResult = cur.execute("query")
df = query.fetchall()
```

If you are executing multiple queries with variable parameters, you can use parameter substitution in a similar manner as with Python's SQLLite libraries, where the substitution is handled by a ? in the query string. For example:

```
query = cur.execute("SELECT * FROM mytable WHERE param1 = ? AND param2 = ?",
    (var1,var2))
```

Connecting to Drill Using pydrill

`pydrill` is another wrapper for Drill's RESTful interface, but it is a little more robust and includes access to many other aspects of Drill that are exposed in the RESTful interface besides just executing a query. `pydrill` is not DBAPI-compliant, and therefore if you want to use the database connection object in another module, it likely will not work. However `pydrill` can transfer query results directly into a Pandas `Data Frame`.

The process for connecting to Drill using `pydrill` is basically the same as with `drillpy`:

1. Create a connection object. `pydrill` has an `.isActive()` function to verify the connection was in fact successful.

2. Execute the query.

3. Iterate through the results or transfer them to a `DataFrame`.

Like `drillpy`, you can install `pydrill` by using `pip`, as shown here:

```
pip install pydrill
```

The following code snippet demonstrates how to query Drill using `pydrill`:

```
from pydrill.client import pydrill

#Connect to Drill
drill = pydrill(host='hostname', port=8047)

#Check to see if the connection succeeded
```

```
if not drill.is_active():
    raise ImproperlyConfigured('Please run Drill first')

#Execute the query
queryResult = drill.query('query')

#Export the results to a Pandas DataFrame
df = queryResult.to_dataframe()
```

Other functionality of pydrill

In addition to executing simple queries, pydrill has a lot of other functionality, including:

- Activating or deactivating a Drill storage plug-in as well as getting details about the available storage plug-ins
- Accessing usage statistics
- Accessing information about the query plans and much more

You can find the complete documentation for pydrill on the project's website (*http://pydrill.readthedocs.io/en/latest/*).

Other Ways of Connecting to Drill from Python

Because Drill is ODBC- and JDBC-compliant, it is possible to query Drill by using the pyODBC or JayDeBeApi modules. Although using these modules does get you access to additional functionality, they are also more difficult to configure and debug. JDBC has several key advantages over the RESTful interface; specifically, it can handle large result sets, security and authentication are easier to enforce using JDBC, and REST isn't usable in a large-scale cluster because there is no REST API to connect to ZooKeeper to determine whether a Drillbit is still alive and part of the cluster. You will find that it is easier to use the Python modules that are based on the RESTful interface such as PyDrill and DrillPy because you do not have to configure your system in order to use them.

The following code snippet demonstrates how to query Drill via JDBC using JayDeBeApi, Python's JDBC module. After importing the module, the most difficult step is creating the connection object using the jaydebeapi.connect() function. There are four arguments to this function, as shown here:

```
conn = jaydebeapi.connect("org.apache.drill.jdbc.Driver",
                          "jdbc connection string",
                          ["username", "password"],
                          "path_to_Drill_JDBC_driver",)
```

The following complete snippet demonstrates how to query Drill using `JayDeBeApi` and import the results into a Pandas `DataFrame`. The driver version will be different for each version of Drill, so make sure you are using the appropriate version:

```
import jaydebeapi
import pandas as pd

#Create the connection object
conn = jaydebeapi.connect("org.apache.drill.jdbc.Driver",
                    "jdbc:drill:drillbit=localhost:31010",
                     ["admin", "password"],
                     "drill_path/jars/jdbc-driver/drill-jdbc-all-version.jar")

#Create the cursor object
curs = conn.cursor()

#Execute the query
curs.execute("SELECT * FROM cp.`employee.json` LIMIT 20")

#Get the results
curs.fetchall()

#Read query results into a Pandas DataFrame
df = pd.read_sql("SELECT * FROM cp.`employee.json` LIMIT 20", conn)
```

The following snippet demonstrates how to query Drill in embedded mode in Python using Drill's ODBC interface with pyODBC. Using ODBC is a little more complex than JDBC because in order for this code to work properly, you must make sure the ODBC driver is correctly installed on your system. Also, crafting the DSN is more complex than the JDBC connection string:

```
import pyodbc
import re
import pandas as pd

#This section from https://github.com/cjmatta/drill_ipython_notebook
MY_DSN = """
Driver                    = /opt/mapr/drillodbc/lib/universal/libmaprdrillodbc.dylib
ConnectionType            = Direct
ZKQuorum                  =
ZKClusterID               =
Catalog                   = DRILL
AuthenticationType        = No Authentication
AdvancedProperties        = CastAnyToVarchar=true
HandshakeTimeout          = 5
QueryTimeout              = 180
TimestampTZDisplayTimezone = utc
ExcludedSchemas           = sys,INFORMATION_SCHEMA
NumberOfPrefetchBuffers    = 5
HOST                      = localhost
PORT                      = 31010
"""
```

```
#Build DSN
MY_DSN = ";".join(
    [re.sub(r'(\t+|\s+)=\s+', '=', i) for i in MY_DSN.split('\n') if i != '']
)

#Create the connection object and cursor
conn = pyodbc.connect(MY_DSN, UID='admin', PWD='password', autocommit=True)
cursor = conn.cursor()

#Set character encoding
conn.setdecoding(pyodbc.SQL_CHAR, encoding='utf-8')
conn.setdecoding(pyodbc.SQL_WCHAR, encoding='utf-8')
conn.setencoding(encoding='utf-8')

#Execute the query and get the results
sql = 'SELECT * FROM cp.`employee.json` LIMIT 20'
cursor.execute(sql)
sql_result = cursor.fetchall()

#Read the data into a DataFrame
df = pd.read_sql('SELECT * FROM cp.`employee.json` LIMIT 20', conn)
df.sample(5)
```

Connecting to Drill Using R

If you are an R user, fear not, as there is a module called sergeant[3] that enables you to query Drill directly from R and import the results into a DataFrame. sergeant allows you to connect to Drill in three ways: the DBI, RJDBC, and dplyr interfaces. sergeant also wraps all the functionality found in the Drill RESTful API, so you can activate, deactivate, or delete storage plug-ins. You can find the complete documentation at the sergeant website (*https://hrbrmstr.github.io/sergeant/*).

Querying Drill from R Using sergeant

To use sergeant, of course you must install it, which you can accomplish by using the following command:

```
devtools::install_github("hrbrmstr/sergeant")
```

After you've installed sergeant, the process for querying Drill is much like that for using one of the Python modules:

1. Create the connection.

2. Optionally check to see if the connection succeeded.

---

3 Get it?...Drill *sergeant*.

3. Execute the query.

The following code snippet demonstrates how to execute a query in Drill through R:

```
#Import sergeant
library(sergeant)

#Create the connection to Drill
conn <- drill_connection("hostname")

#Check to see if the connection was successful
drill_active(conn)

#Execute the query
drill_query(conn, "query")
```

As you can see, it really isn't too difficult to use R to query Drill.

Accessing other functionality in R

In addition to executing queries in Drill, sergeant can access other functionality in the Drill RESTful interface, much like pydrill. Here are some selected functions:

drill_active()
Tests whether the Drill HTTP REST API server is up

drill_metrics()
Gets the current memory metrics

drill_options()
Lists the name, default, and data type of the system and session options

drill_profile()
Gets the profile of the query that has the given query ID

drill_set()
Sets Drill SYSTEM or SESSION options

drill_show_files()
Shows files in a filesystem schema

drill_show_schemas()
Returns a list of available schemas

drill_stats()
Gets Drillbit information such as port numbers

drill_status()
Gets the status of Drill

```
drill_storage()
```
Gets the list of storage plug-in names and configurations

```
drill_uplift()
```
Turns columnar query results into a type-converted table

```
drill_use()
```
Changes to a particular schema

Connecting to Drill Using Java

Although there isn't a dedicated module for Drill, it is relatively straightforward to query Drill using JDBC. For this to work, you must install the JDBC JAR file in the classpath. The driver class name is `org.apache.drill.jdbc.Driver`.

To connect using JDBC and Java, the basic process is as follows:

1. Set the Drill driver.

2. Create a `Connection` object using a JDBC connection string and by calling the `DriverManager.getConnection()` function.

3. Create a `Statement` object by calling the `connection.createStatement()` function from your `Connection` object.

4. Execute the query by calling the `executeQuery()` function from your `Statement` object.

5. Iterate through the results by calling the appropriate `get()` function.

There are `get()` functions for every data type that exists in SQL databases, and a complete list of `get()` functions is available in the Java documentation (*http://bit.ly/2SsCHPS*).

This code snippet demonstrates how to query Drill in Java using JDBC:

```java
import java.sql.Connection;
import java.sql.DriverManager;
import java.sql.ResultSet;
import java.sql.Statement;

public class testDrillInterface {
  public static void main(String[] args) {
    try{
      //Choose the driver
      Class.forName("org.apache.drill.jdbc.Driver");

      //Create the Connection object
      Connection connection=DriverManager
                  .getConnection("jdbc:drill:drillbit=localhost:31010");
```

```
    //Create the Statement object
    Statement st = connection.createStatement();

    //Execute the query
    ResultSet rs = st.executeQuery("SELECT * from cp.`employees.json`");

    //Iterate through the results
    while(rs.next()){
      System.out.println(rs.getString(1));
    }
  } catch(Exception e){
    throw new RuntimeException(e);
  }
 }
}
```

Querying Drill with PHP

If PHP is your language or you are looking to write a web-based application using Drill as a backend, there is a PHP library to facilitate that. It is loosely modeled after PHP's MySQL interface, so if you are familiar with that, you already pretty much know how to use the Drill connector.

Installing the Connector

The connector is on Packagist (*http://bit.ly/2PuPbYz*) and can be installed by using composer, as follows:

```
composer require thedataist/drill-connector:dev-master
```

Using the Connector

The first step is to connect to Drill. The module uses Drill's RESTful interface, so it doesn't really make a "connection" in the same sense as with MySQL:

```
$drill = new DrillConnection('localhost', 8047);
```

As mentioned earlier, this creates the object, but doesn't actually send anything to Drill. You can use the is_active() method to verify that your connection is active:

```
if($drill->is_active()) {
   print("Connection Active");
 } else {
   print("Connection Inactive");
 }
```

Querying Drill from PHP

Now that you've connected to Drill, you can query it in a similar way as MySQL, by calling the query() method. After you've called the query() method, you can use one of the fetch() methods to retrieve the results. Currently the Drill connector has the following methods:

fetch_all()
: Returns all query results in an associative array

fetch_assoc()
: Returns a single query row as an associative array

fetch_object()
: Returns a single row as a PHP object

You might also find these functions useful:

data_seek($n)
: Returns the row at index $n and sets the current row to $n

num_rows()
: Returns the number of rows returned by the query

field_count()
: Returns the number of columns returned by the query

Thus, if you want to execute a query in Drill, you can do so as follows:

```
$query_result = $drill->query("SELECT * FROM cp.`employee.json` LIMIT 20");
while($row = $query_result->fetch_assoc()) {
  print("Field 1: {$row['field1']}\n");
  print("Field 2: {$row['field2']}\n");
}
```

Interacting with Drill from PHP

You can also use the connector to activate and deactivate Drill's storage as well as get information about Drill's plug-ins, with the following methods:

disable_plugin($plugin)
: Disables the given plug-in. Returns true if successful, false if not.

enable_plugin($plugin)
: Enables the given plug-in. Returns true if successful, false if not.

get_all_storage_plugins()
: Returns an array of all storage plug-ins.

```
get_disabled_storage_plugins()
```
Returns an array of all disabled plug-ins.

```
get_enabled_storage_plugins()
```
Returns an array of all enabled plug-ins.

```
get_storage_plugins()
```
Returns an associative array of plug-ins and associated configuration options for all plug-ins.

```
get_storage_plugin_info($plugin)
```
Returns an associative array of configuration options for a given plug-in.

Querying Drill Using Node.js

Lastly, in much the same manner as querying Drill in other languages, you can query Drill using Node.js with the `drill-client` module. You can install it with this command:

```
npm install drill-client
```

After you have installed the Drill client, the procedure is the same as in all other languages. Here are the basic steps:

1. Create the connection object by calling `Drill.Client()` with your connection parameters.

2. Call the `query()` function.

Because Node.js is asynchronous it is necessary to put the query processing logic in the callback function, as demonstrated here:

```
var client = new Drill.Client({hostname:'localhost', port:8047});

client.query('SELECT * FROM cp.`employee.json` LIMIT 10',
    function(error, data, columns){
        console.log({data: data['rows'],
        columns: data['columns'],
        error: error});
    }
);
```

Using Drill as a Data Source in BI Tools

In the previous sections, you saw how to connect to and query Drill in various programming languages. In this section, you will learn how to connect to Drill and use it as a data source in various popular BI and analytic tools to build interactive dashboards. This book cannot cover every possible tool, but you should be able to connect to most BI tools using either the JDBC or the ODBC interface.

Exploring Data with Apache Zeppelin and Drill

Apache Zeppelin is a notebooking tool that is becoming quite popular due to its tight integration with a variety of big data tools, such as Apache Spark. Zeppelin's simplicity and visualization capabilities, demonstrated in Figure 7-1, make it an ideal companion tool for working with Apache Drill.

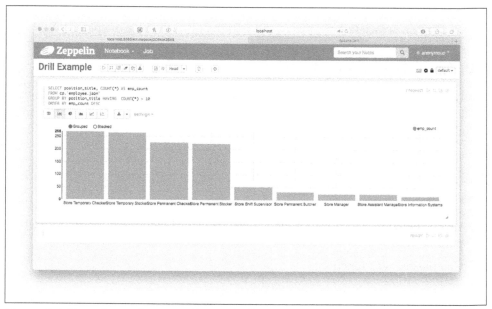

Figure 7-1. Zeppelin rendering Drill sample data

The easiest way to use Zeppelin with Apache Drill is to use the JDBC interpreter that ships with Zeppelin. If you didn't install the JDBC interpreter with Zeppelin, you'll need to install it using the following command:

```
$ZEPPELIN_HOME/bin/install-interpreter.sh --name jdbc
```

After you've installed the Zeppelin JDBC interpreter, you need to configure it within the Zeppelin interface.

Configuring Zeppelin to query Drill

The first step is to add Drill as a data source. To do that, in the upper-right corner of the screen, click the user settings menu, and then navigate to the Interpreter screen, as shown in Figure 7-2. Click +Create to create a new interpreter.

Figure 7-2. Zeppelin settings menu

On the Create screen, choose JDBC as the interface type, and then set the following configuration variables, as shown in Figure 7-3:

`default.driver`
> This should be set to `org.apache.drill.jdbc.Driver`.

`default.password`
> This is your account password.

`default.url`
> This is your JDBC connection string to Drill. To use Drill with Zeppelin in embedded mode or when a single Drillbit is running on your local machine, the connection string is `jdbc:drill:drillbit=localhost:31010`.

At the bottom of the screen, in the Dependencies section, add the path to the Drill JDBC driver as an artifact.

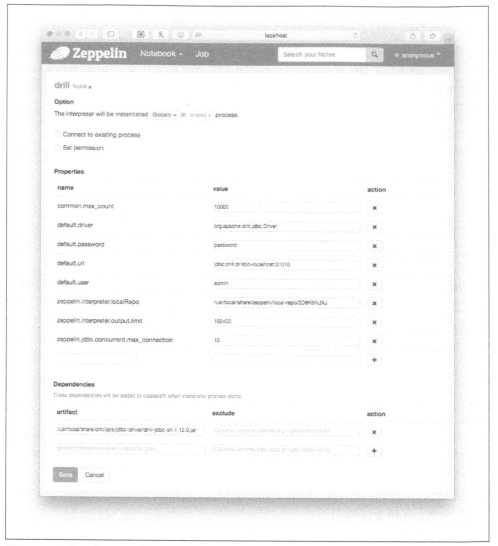

Figure 7-3. Configuring the Zeppelin interpreter

At this point, you should be able to query Drill in a Zeppelin notebook by simply setting the notebook's default interpreter to Drill.

Querying Drill from a Zeppelin notebook

If you've successfully set up Drill as an interpreter in Zeppelin, all you need to do to query Drill is simply type a SQL query into a box in a Zeppelin notebook, as illustrated here:

```
SELECT *
FROM cp.`employee.json`
```

This query is the default query for Drill. If you enter it in Zeppelin, you will see the query results depicted in Figure 7-4.

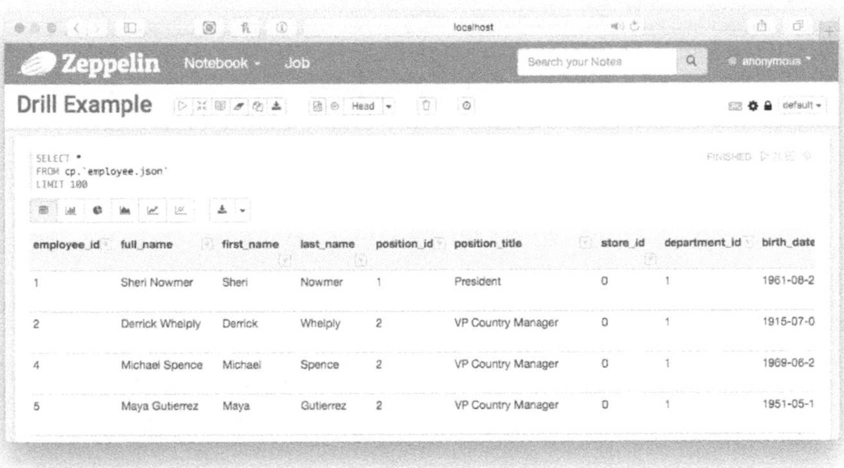

Figure 7-4. Query results in Zeppelin

By itself this doesn't really add much value beyond Drill's user interface; however, you can perform aggregations and other operations directly in the Zeppelin notebook. As an example, let's say that you wanted to find the average salary by education level in the sample data file included with Drill. You could write the following query:

```
SELECT education_level, AVG(CAST(salary AS FLOAT)) AS avg_salary
FROM cp.`employee.json`
GROUP BY education_level
```

However, in Zeppelin, you can accomplish the same task starting from the original query, which outputs all the results. In Figure 7-5, you can see how to take the original results, perform the aggregation, and visualize the results.

Figure 7-5. Query results in Zeppelin

Adding interactivity in Zeppelin

One of the features that makes Zeppelin powerful is the ability to create interactive reports directly from a SQL query. In the `WHERE` clause of a query, you can specify variables that you can change and cause Zeppelin to dynamically redraw the visualization.

The following query has a `WHERE` clause of `gender='${gender=M,M|F}'`, which creates a drop-down menu with two options for the gender:

```
SELECT *
FROM cp.`employee.json`
WHERE `gender`='${gender=M,M|F}'
```

Changing the drop-down menu selection causes the visualization to be redrawn, as shown in Figure 7-6.

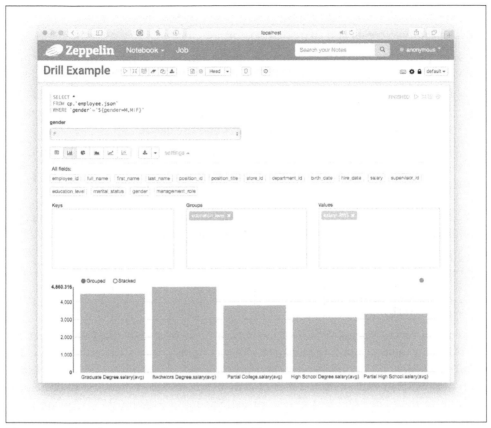

Figure 7-6. Visualization with dynamic variable

As you can see, Zeppelin is a good companion tool for Drill and requires little special configuration to quickly visualize and explore your query results.

Exploring Data with Apache Superset

Another open source BI tool that works well with Drill is a relatively new one, which as of this writing is in incubation with the Apache Software Foundation. This tool is called Superset, and it was developed by Airbnb and is implemented in Python using SQLAlchemy as a means of interacting with SQL-based data sources. Superset offers more sophisticated visualizations than Zeppelin, but at the time of writing, the project is still being developed and not all features work well with Drill.

According to the documentation (*https://superset.incubator.apache.org*), Superset's features include:

- A rich set of data visualizations

- An easy-to-use interface for exploring and visualizing data

- The ability to create and share dashboards

- Enterprise-ready authentication with integration with major authentication providers (database, OpenID, LDAP, OAuth, and REMOTE_USER through Flask AppBuilder)

- An extensible, high-granularity security/permission model allowing intricate rules on who can access individual features and the dataset

- A simple semantic layer, allowing users to control how data sources are displayed in the UI by defining which fields should show up in which drop-down and which aggregation and function metrics are made available to the user

Windows does not support Superset, but it works well on Linux and macOS machines. You can install Superset via the following commands:

```
pip install superset
fabmanager create-admin --app superset
superset db upgrade
superset load_examples
superset init
```

In addition to the standard SQLAlchemy, you need to install the Drill dialect for SQLAlchemy before running Superset. To accomplish this step, either clone the sqlalchemy-drill GitHub repository (*https://github.com/JohnOmernik/sqlalchemy-drill*) or download and unzip the files directly from GitHub. When you've done that, navigate to the folder you just cloned or extracted and execute the following command:

```
python setup.py install
```

At this point, you are ready to configure Superset to work with Drill.

Configuring Superset to work with Drill

After you install Superset and the additional drivers, you need to add Drill as a data source. Click the Sources menu and select the Databases option, as shown in Figure 7-7.

Figure 7-7. Adding Drill as a data source

When you are in the databases section, in the upper-right corner of the List Databases pane, click the + button to add a new data source, as shown in Figure 7-8.

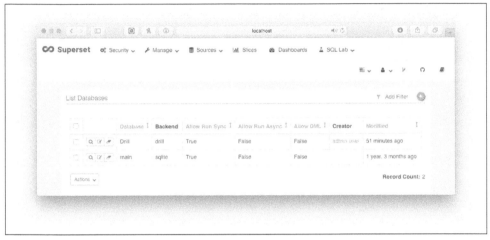

Figure 7-8. Adding Drill as a data source to Superset

On the Add Database screen, set up the configuration to allow Superset to communicate with Drill. You need to write a SQLAlchemy URI in the format shown here:

```
drill+sadrill://username:password@host:port/storage_plugin/workspace
?use_ssl=True
```

If you are connecting to Drill in embedded mode, you can use this connection string:

```
drill+sadrill://localhost:8047/dfs/drillclass?use_ssl=False
```

Enter your connection URI in the appropriate field, and you should be able to successfully test the connection, as demonstrated in Figure 7-9.

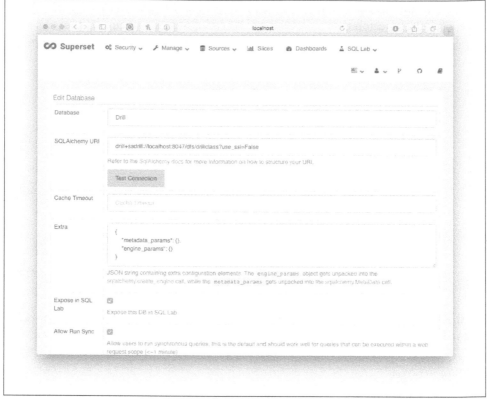

Figure 7-9. Drill configuration in Superset

You will want to select the "Expose in SQL Lab" and "Allow Run Sync" checkboxes. If you are querying large datasets or have queries that will take a long time to run, it would also be a good idea to set up Celery[4] to allow asynchronous connections.

Building a demonstration visualization using Drill and Superset

Now that you have Superset working with Drill, this section walks you through building a visualization. In the GitHub repository for this book, you will find a data file called *baltimore_salaries_2016.csvh*, which contains data about the salaries of all of the employees of the City of Baltimore.[5]

For this example, we will calculate the average salary per department and visualize the results. The following query will return those results:

---

4 Celery (*http://docs.celeryproject.org/en/latest/index.html*) is an open source distributed queue with a focus on real-time processing.

5 This dataset is available at the Baltimore City website (*http://bit.ly/2MZsvzc*).

```
SELECT Agency, TO_NUMBER(`AnnualSalary`, '¤') AS AnnualSalary
FROM dfs.demo.`baltimore_salaries_2016.csvh`
```

To visualize this data, the first step is to open SQL Lab and enter the query. Next, click the Run Query button; the results should look like those shown in Figure 7-10.

Figure 7-10. Query results in SQL Lab

When you have the query results, click the Visualize button, set the options as depicted in Figure 7-11, and then click Visualize.

Figure 7-11. Superset chart configuration

At this point, after some minor configuration changes, you should have a visualization similar to the one shown in Figure 7-12.

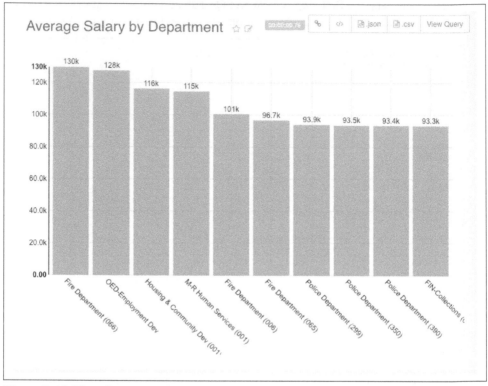

Figure 7-12. Visualization in Superset

When you save the visualization, you can add it to a pre-existing dashboard or create a new dashboard.

Using Drill with Other Visualization Tools

You can use Drill with many other visualization tools, including Tableau, Qlix, JReport, MicroStrategy Analytics, and others that have ODBC or JDBC support.

Conclusion

In this chapter, you learned how to programmatically connect to Drill using a variety of languages via Drill's interfaces. This capability enables you to use Drill to automate data flows as well as integrate Drill as a data source for various BI tools. Now that you know how to use Drill to query your data, the next step is to explore the details of Drill's schema-on-read approach.

CHAPTER 8

Data Engineering with Drill

Drill is a SQL engine that reads large data files stored in a distributed filesystem such as HDFS, MapR-FS, or Amazon S3. Drill works best with data stored in Parquet, but data seldom arrives in Parquet, and it is often handy to work with data in its original format. In this chapter, you will see that with Drill you can read data in many formats, and use specialized tricks to overcome schema-related issues. However, for production, Parquet is the preferred file format.

Although some of the material in this chapter has been covered in previous chapters, this chapter will go into much greater detail on how Drill actually processes data, which is vital to understand if you are developing extensions for Drill or if you encounter files with an ambiguous schema.

Schema-on-Read

Apache Drill is designed for the modern data lake, which consists of a very large number of files, organized into directories and stored in a wide variety of file formats. Although Drill is optimized for Parquet files, it can read data from many different file formats using extensible storage plug-ins.

Unlike Hive, which requires a schema to define a file, Drill uses the structure within the file itself. This strategy, known as *schema-on-read*, works very well for file formats such as Parquet, which carry a clear, unambiguous schema within the file itself. But as you will see in this chapter, you must provide Drill a bit of help to read other file formats, such as CSV or JSON, for which the schema can be ambiguous in subtle ways.

The SQL Relational Model

Drill takes on a daunting challenge: to infer schemas from a variety of file formats and map those schemas into the SQL relational model. We use the term *schema infer-*

ence for this process. (Drill itself does not use this term; it is borrowed from Apache Spark.) Making Drill work for you entails understanding the strengths (and limitations) of Drill's schema inference mechanism. The relational model describes a set of relations (tables) comprising a fixed set of domains (columns). Each column is described by a name and a type. (Columns often also have a defined position, as we will see shortly for CSV files.)

Drill uses JSON as its reference model. Although JSON can represent relational data, it also can represent additional data structures such as arrays and maps. Drill extends the SQL relational model to include these types. Because SQL itself does not support these extended types, Drill provides a number of techniques to bridge the gap between JSON and SQL.

Relational databases use a *schema-on-write* approach to store data in a predefined format. The big data world uses schema-on-read, but in two distinct ways.

Hive and Impala define a schema separately from the data, with the schema stored in the Hive metastore. When data is ambiguous, the Hive schema instructs each tool how to interpret the data. The cost, however, is that the user must maintain this schema, which becomes a complex task for large deployments and is awkward during data exploration. Drill can work with Hive data and the Hive metastore when available, but it can also work without them.

To work without a predefined schema, Drill takes a pragmatic approach: the schema is defined as a negotiation between the query and the file. For example, the same JSON file can be thought of as having typed fields or text fields. The same CSV file can be thought of as containing a single column (an array of VARCHAR) or as a set of columns. Yesterday's version of a JSON file might have had four fields per record; today's has six after an enhancement to the source of the data.

Data Life Cycle: Data Exploration to Production

When you start a new data project, you are presented with a collection of files, perhaps in a variety of formats. Drill's schema inference rules allow you to do *data exploration* quickly and easily, directly on the source data. Because that data might have an ambiguous structure, part of the exploration is to identify the issues and workarounds.

As you work, you can capture what you learn in SQL *views*. With views, you can rename columns, clean up formats, convert data types, and more.

Then, as a project moves into production, Drill encourages you to extract, transform, and load (ETL) your data into partitioned Parquet files. Parquet carries a clear schema, avoiding schema ambiguities. Parquet is also fast to read, especially if a query reads just a subset of columns. Partitioning data reduces the number of files that must be read to produce a result, further speeding up the query. (Think of partitioning as big data's answer to a table index.)

Sample Data

When learning Drill, it is often handy to have some sample data available. Drill provides the FoodMart (*https://github.com/julian hyde/foodmart-data-hsqldb*) sample dataset using the `cp` schema. (The FoodMart dataset is originally from Microsoft, and was made available to Drill by Julian Hyde of the Calcite project.) The data is available without the "test." prefix shown in the ER diagram in the link just provided. In fact, it is the FoodMart data that you query with the sample query in the Drill Web Console:

```
SELECT * FROM cp.`employee.json` LIMIT 20
```

The FoodMart dataset is very rich and allows you to try out many advanced features on known good data before trying them on your own data. The data is available in JSON format.

Drill also includes some TPC-H sample data in Parquet format in the *tpch* directory:

```
SELECT * FROM cp.`tpch/partsupp.parquet` LIMIT 20
```

The schema is described in the TPC-H specification available from the TPC website (*http://bit.ly/2CLhLy8*).

See also the "Sample Datasets" and "Analyzing the Yelp Academic Dataset" sections in the online Drill documentation (*http://drill.apache.org/docs/*) for more datasets.

Schema Inference

Whether during data exploration or in a production system, Drill uses the same schema inference steps. Inference starts with the type of storage system, then proceeds to the type of file and to how to split up a file for reading. As the file is read, Drill must infer the type of each column, then determine how to combine schemas from different files and blocks within a file. Much of this is automatic, especially with Parquet files.

When doing data exploration with other kinds of files, proper inference often requires that you either set things up correctly within Drill, or write your query to resolve ambiguities. The next few sections walk through the overall process so that you know how the pieces work and how to resolve issues when things don't go as expected.

Further, because Drill is distributed, each fragment of a query (parallel execution path) makes its own independent decision about the schema. That is, fragments do not communicate to negotiate a shared view of the schema. Instead, each fragment infers the schema from the first record that it reads (or from metadata stored in the particular file that it reads for CSV or Parquet files).

The key issue to keep in mind when using Drill is this: Drill cannot predict the future. That is, Drill cannot choose types based on what might appear in the file in the future. Further, when running a distributed query, one scan operator cannot predict what another scan will infer about the schema.

Data Source Inference

Drill supports a wide range of file formats. Its first step in scanning any file is to infer the type of the file from the filename. Drill does this using a file type inference process that uses a storage configuration and an associated format configuration.

Storage Plug-ins

Drill is extensible. It accesses your data via a storage plug-in. By now you are familiar with storage plug-ins for distributed filesystems HBase, Hive, and so on. Here, we focus on the dfs plug-in that provides access to files on your local system, in HDFS, in MapR–FS, in Amazon S3, and so on.

Elsewhere in this book, for convenience, we refer to data sources such as HDFS, the local filesystem, Amazon S3, and MapR as different storage plug-ins. Truth be told, they are all just different configurations of the same dfs plug-in. Internally, dfs uses the HDFS client to work with the other storage formats. This means that Drill can work with any format for which an HDFS client implementation is available, including Isilon, Alluxio, Microsoft ADSL, and many more. Apache Drill does not test these add-on formats, but if they adhere to the HDFS standard, they have a good chance of working in Drill.

Storage Configurations

A storage plug-in is a piece of Java code, built into Drill or delivered as a JAR. To use a storage plug-in, you must define a *storage configuration* for the plug-in.

Confusingly, the Drill UI uses the terms "storage" and "storage plug-in" for the storage configuration. Some people use the term "storage plug-in configuration" for the same idea. Just remember that if you edit it in the Drill Web Console, it is a "configuration." If you write code in Java, it is a "plug-in."

Each storage plug-in can have multiple configurations. For example, you might have different storage configurations for the dfs plug-in depending on your needs. You create the storage configuration in the Drill web console. When run as a daemon, Drill stores the configurations in ZooKeeper so that they are visible to all Drillbits in your cluster. When run embedded in SQLLine (or in unit tests), the configurations are saved to local disk and are generally discarded at the end of the run.

Each storage configuration is given a name when you create the configuration. This is the name you use in queries. Each configuration also has a `type`, which connects the configuration to the plug-in implementation in code. For example, the `dfs` storage configuration that Drill ships with maps to the `file` storage plug-in, as shown here:

```
{
  "type": "file",
```

You can use the Web Console to create a second storage configuration for the `file` plug-in using the Storage tab. Drill provides no default; it is handy to copy and paste an existing JSON definition.

The default `dfs` configuration points to your local filesystem and is handy for learning Drill. Change this to point to HDFS or Amazon S3 for a production system.

There is nothing magic about the `dfs` name, by the way. Feel free to instead create a `local` configuration for your local filesystem, and an `hdfs` or `s3` configuration for your distributed storage.

Here is how to create the example `local` storage configuration we'll use in this section:

1. Start Drill, as explained earlier.
2. Start the Drill web console, as explained earlier.
3. Click the Storage tab.
4. Find the default `dfs` plug-in, and then click Update.
5. Select all the JSON text and copy it to the clipboard.
6. Click Back.
7. In the New Storage Plugin area, enter the name `local`, and then click Create.
8. Paste the JSON into the editor.
9. Replace the contents of the `workspaces` object with the following:

```
"workspaces": {},
```

10. Click Update.

Workspaces

File storage configurations provide several properties to customize behavior. The storage configuration by itself refers to the root of the target filesystem. The `local` configuration you just defined points to the root of your local filesystem: that's what the file:// in the configuration means.

The GitHub repositiory for this book contains a data directory that contains the files used in this section. Suppose your download these files to your home directory in /Users/arina/drillbook. You can query the files using the following:

```
SELECT * FROM `local`.`/Users/arina/drillbook/data/drill/cust.csv`
```

The backticks are sometimes optional, but they are required if a name contains a character that is not a valid symbol character in SQL or if the name is the same as a SQL keyword. The simplest rule is to always enclose schema, table, and column names with backticks.

Using an absolute path is often unwieldy, however. You might have test and production filesets. If you share local queries with others, they will need to edit the file paths to work for their machines before running the queries. And data might move around in HDFS, for various reasons.

To avoid this issue, Drill defines the idea of a *workspace*, which is just a named subdirectory. So, you might define a data workspace for the book's data directory:

1. In the Drill Web Console, click the Storage tab.

2. Find the local configuration that you created earlier, and click Update.

3. Edit the JSON to revise the workspaces element as shown here:

```
"workspaces": {
  "data": {
      "location": "/Users/arina/drillbook",
      "writable": true,
      "defaultInputFormat": null,
      "allowAccessOutsideWorkspace": false
  }
}
```

   Replace the path in the preceding example with the location where you stored the book files.

4. Click Update.

Then, you can reference the workspace in a query:

```
SELECT * FROM `local`.`data`.`cust.csv`
```

In SQL terms, the configuration (with optional workspace) is like a database (MySQL) or schema (Oracle). The end result is that, either way, Drill now knows the location of the file that you want to query.

Querying Directories

If you have multiple files in a directory, you can use the directory name as a table name in a query. Drill will query all files within that directory. Suppose that you have a directory *cust* containing multiple customer CSV files. Here's how to query all of the files within that directory:

```
SELECT * FROM `local`.`data`.`cust`
```

For this to work, the files must be of the same type (all CSV, for example). However, you cannot query the workspace directly. That is, both of the following are invalid:

```
SELECT * FROM `local`.`data`  -- Not legal
SELECT * FROM `local`.`data`.`/` -- Not legal
```

Thus, you need to define the workspace to point one level above your data directory.

Workspaces are particularly useful when working with partitioned data, as explained in "Partitioning Data Directories" on page 169.

Special Files in Directory Scans

When scanning a directory, Drill ignores files whose names begin with either a period or an underscore. Indeed, Drill creates such files for its cached Parquet metadata. If, for some odd reason, you are presented with such a file, you can query it by spelling out the filename. For example: `SELECT * FROM `_oddFile.csv``.

Default Schema

Drill supports the SQL USE command to declare a default schema. To try this, start a local Drill:

```
cd $DRILL_HOME
bin/sqlline -u jdbc:drill:drillbit=localhost
```

Now you can use `local` as your default schema:

```
USE `local`;
SELECT * FROM `/Users/arina/drillbook/data/cust.csv`;
```

Both storage configurations and workspaces can become the default schema:

```
USE `local`.`data`;
SELECT * FROM `cust.csv`;
```

The default workspace is a session property: it remains in effect as long as you are connected to Drill and must be defined on each new connection. If you have authentication enabled, the Web Console is also stateful and USE (along with ALTER SESSION) will work. Without authentication, the Web Console is stateless and the USE statement is in effect only for the single request.

File Type Inference

The storage configuration and optional workspace instruct Drill where to look for files. Next, Drill must figure out the type of each file that it will scan. Drill uses the format plug-in mechanism to support an extensible set of formats.

Format Plug-ins and Format Configuration

Storage plug-ins have two parts: the plug-in (code) and configuration (JSON). Format plug-ins follow this same pattern. In Drill, file formats are extensible; we describe how to write your own format plug-in in Chapter 12.

Storage configurations appear in the Storage section of the UI. However, format plug-ins appear as part of some dfs-based storage plug-in: be it local, hdfs, s3, or similar. (Format plug-ins are supported only for the dfs storage plug-in, other plug-ins do not support format plug-ins.)

Format configurations allows us to fine-tune file formats for different types of data files, as we discuss in a few moments. You will see the default set of format configurations when you use the Drill Web Console to update a storage configuration as we did previously. If you delete a format configuration from a storage configuration, that file type won't be available within that configuration. Similarly, if you write or obtain a new format plug-in, you must add a format configuration to your storage configuration in order to use the new format.

Drill ships with a default set of format configurations in the default dfs storage configuration. Here is one example:

```
"csv": {
    "type": "text",
    "extensions": [
        "csv"
    ],
    "delimiter": ","
},
```

The name csv is purely for documentation; Drill does not use it. The important bits are what follows. The type names the underlying format plug-in—text, in this case. The text format plug-in is actually quite flexible and is used to define the psv and tsv formats as well. What makes this a CSV format are the property values. The extensions field identifies the file suffix (extension) used for this format. The delim iter field specifies that this is a comma-separated file.

You can customize these as needed, often by creating a custom storage configuration to hold your custom format configurations. Just be sure to give each a unique name and to map each to a distinct file suffix (more on this shortly).

Drill uses the file suffix to associate the file with a format configuration. It then uses the format configuration to locate the underlying format plug-in.

Format Inference

We can now assemble the all of this information to describe how Drill picks a format configuration for each file. Suppose that you have this query:

```
SELECT * FROM `local`.`data`.`cust.csv`
```

Drill proceeds according to the following steps:

1. Look up the schema local to find the storage configuration.
2. Use the type field in the storage configuration to find the storage plug-in implementation.
3. Use the next name, data, to find a workspace within the configuration.
4. Use the workspace to find the working directory for the query.
5. Use the working directory to find the target file(s).
6. Use the file suffix (in the query or by scanning a directory of files) to find the associated format configuration.
7. Use the type of the format configuration to find the format plug-in implementation. The format plug-in provides the reader to use to deserialize the data, as discussed in a few moments.

Drill now has all the information it needs to perform the file scan: the filesystem, the directory that contains the file, the name of the file to scan, and the format of the file.

Knowing this format inference process can be handy when things go wrong. (Drill's error messages are, to put it kindly, cryptic, so you must often figure out the problem yourself.)

File Format Variations

Files come in many varied formats. CSV files are notorious for having many standards (with or without headers, quoted or nonquoted strings, allowing multiline field values or not, etc.). As we saw, CSV files themselves are one variation of a more general "text" format with other variations such as pipe-separated values (PSV), tab-separated values (TSV), and so on.

The format configurations allow you to fine-tune the scan to your exact file format. This works well as long as each format variation has its own distinct file suffix: *.csv* for CSV files with a header, *.psv* for pipe-separated values, *.tsv* for tab-separated values, and so on.

However, because CSV has so much variation, you might find a situation in which some of your CSV files have headers whereas others do not, yet both variations end with *.csv*. To handle this, store the different file formats in different directories and define a storage configuration (not just workspace) for each. So, you might pull your store sales files into a *stores* directory and define a `stores` storage configuration for that directory. Then, in the `stores` configuration, you can configure the *.csv* extension to refer to a CSV format configuration that includes headers.

The general rule is that if files have distinct formats that require distinct format configurations, you must give them distinct suffixes. If you cannot do that, you must store them in separate directories, referenced by distinct storage configurations.

Schema Inference Overview

Internally, Drill uses a unique late-binding schema model. Unlike traditional schema-driven engines, the Drill query planner makes very few assumptions about the columns in your tables. This is why Drill (or at least its query planner) is sometimes called "schema-less."

As discussed in Chapter 9, the planner converts your SQL query into a directed acyclic graph (DAG), which consists of operators grouped into fragments. The leaf operators are file scans. You might at first think that Drill discovers the schema when it reads the data in the scan operators. However, this is only partly true. The implementation is actually much more subtle—and it is this subtlety that we discuss in this chapter so that you can get the most out of Drill.

The scan operator itself discovers the schema of each file (or file block) as the scan operator proceeds. But because Drill runs many scan operators in parallel, it is possible for some scan operators to read one schema (perhaps the current version of the schema), whereas others read a *different* schema (perhaps an older version of the schema).

Allowing a single query to read two distinct schemas is not actually a bug, as it might first seem; instead, it is an important feature because it allows Drill to work with a collection of files even as the schemas of those files evolve (often called *schema evolution*).

Recall that Drill divides a query into *major fragments*. Perhaps the leaf fragment scans a table and applies a filter. Drill then runs many copies of this fragment in parallel; these instances are called *minor fragments*.

Let's focus on minor fragment 1. The scan operator in that fragment begins to read a file and discovers the schema for that file (schema-on-read). Drill gathers records into batches. The scan operator sends the batches downstream to the filter operator. How does the filter operator learn the schema? By looking at the schema of the first batch of data. For all operators except scans, Drill uses code generation to create custom code that does the work for the operator. In this case, the filter operator in fragment 1 uses the schema of the first batch to generate its code and then processes the batch.

Suppose that, for some reason, the scan operator in fragment 1 encounters a later record with a new schema (as can happen for, say, a JSON file). The scan operator passes the new batch of records along with a flag that says, "Hey, the schema for this batch is different than for the previous ones." This is called a *schema change*. Although some operators in Drill can handle a schema change, others cannot. We discuss these cases shortly.

Meanwhile, over on another node, in fragment 2, the exact same process occurs for a different file or block in the same file. Because Drill uses a shared-nothing distribution architecture, the two fragments do not communicate directly; they make their own independent schema decisions. In a pathological case, fragment 1 will happily read a file with the schema (`a, b`), whereas fragment 2 reads a file with schema (`c, d`).

Eventually, the two schemas must be merged, which happens after a network exchange. Fragments 1 and 2 both send their rows (actually, batches of rows called *record batches*) to a common fragment, maybe the root or an intermediate fragment. Let's assume that they send their rows to a sort operator. The sort operator receives the schemas from the two leaf fragments. If the schemas are identical (the typical case), all is fine. But, if they differ (as in our pathological example), the sort will fail with a *schema change exception* because it does not know how to combine mismatched schemas.

On the other hand, if there is no sort (or other schema-sensitive operator), the record batches will be sent all the way back to the client. The native Drill client handles these cases: it tells you the schema for each batch of data as it arrives. You can then apply your own rules to work with the data. The native Drill client is thus very powerful, having been designed to handle varying schemas.

However, you will most likely use the JDBC or ODBC clients, which cannot handle schema changes. In this case, the driver itself will detect the schema change and throw an error if it cannot handle the change.

The conclusion is that Drill as a whole is very flexible in dealing with multiple schemas per table, but various operators (such as the sort operator discussed earlier) and clients (such as JDBC and ODBC) have inherent restrictions that limit your ability to exploit divergent schemas. If your tables have a single, consistent schema, everything just works—but if your schema varies or is ambiguous, you need to know some tricks to make things work. We explore those tricks a bit later.

At the time of this writing, the Drill community was beginning to discuss adding a schema mechanism to Drill. If such a mechanism becomes available, you might be able to work around some of the schema-on-read issues by declaring a schema up front so that Drill knows how to resolve schema conflicts when they occur. Drill also supports Hive metastore, which does much the same thing.

Distributed File Scans

Let's take a deeper look at how Drill scans files and decodes records. As we said earlier, Drill is a distributed query engine, meaning that it tries to spread file scanning work as widely as possible across your cluster. If you have a single machine, such as when running Drill on your laptop, your "cluster" is just one node. Regardless of cluster size, Drill runs multiple scans per Drillbit; by default, the number of scans is about 70% of the number of CPU cores on the node. It is helpful to know how Drill divides up the scanning work.

If your query references a directory, Drill creates a separate scan task for each file. If you use the local filesystem (the file:// protocol), this is the maximum parallelism Drill can achieve.

In Drill, leaf minor fragments are those that directly scan data files. Each leaf fragment contains one or more readers, each of which scans a single block of the file for splittable files on HDFS, or the entire file for nonsplittable or local files.

As discussed in the previous section, Drill divides a query into a set of major fragments, each of which is parallelized into a set of minor fragments. Each minor fragment contains one or more operators and an exchange. Drill distributes minor fragments symmetrically across Drillbits. Leaf fragments are those that read data. Drill creates leaf fragments on each data node. The number of leaf fragments per node depends on the number of CPUs on that node. (Drill assumes nodes are symmetric; all nodes have the same number of CPUs.) In the preceding example, if the nodes have eight CPUs, Drill will run something like six minor fragments per node. If you query the entire file, with 32 blocks per node, then each minor fragment will read 5 or 6 blocks.

The Drill web console provides a tool to visualize these concepts: you will see major fragments or stages visualized graphically. Then, in the associated tables, you see the worker tasks, or minor fragments for each stage. At least one set of minor fragments will be for the scan. What might not be apparent from the UI is that each scan minor fragment actually runs one or more individual readers, each of which scans a single block of an HDFS file.

Consider the following query which sorts a large file, then throws away the results (which provides a non-trivial plan without overloading our query tool):

```
SELECT t.a, t.b FROM (
  SELECT a, b
  FROM `dfs`.`/user/test/sample.csvh`
  ORDER BY b) t
WHERE t.a < 0
```

The resulting visualized plan is shown in Figure 8-1.

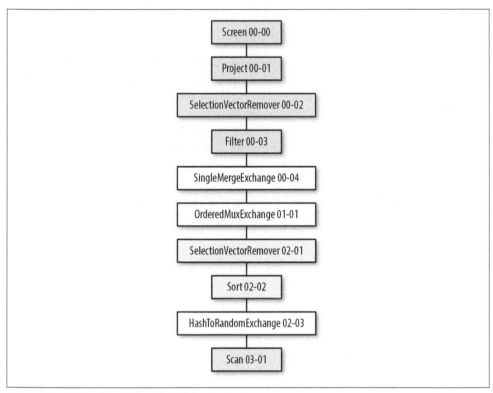

Figure 8-1. Visualized plan for the sample query

Because data is replicated, Drill has a great deal of flexibility in how to assign scan operators to nodes. In general, Drill tries to run a scan operator on a node that contains the block to be scanned, but also tries to avoid skew by ensuring that all nodes have the same number of scan operators ±1. In extreme cases, Drill will perform remote reads (running the scan on a node remote from the data and transferring the data over the network) when necessary to avoid skew.

From this description, we can learn two things:

- We get better performance from Drill when data is stored in a splittable file format such as Parquet, most versions of CSV, and so on. By contrast, JSON is not splittable: even if we have a 1 GB JSON file, Drill must read that entire file in a single scan operator, which causes skew and very likely requires remote reads.

- Much of Drill's internal work entails moving data across the network from scan nodes, to internal worker tasks, to the Foreman node (the one that runs the query), and finally back to the client (such as JDBC, ODBC, SQLLine, etc.).

Schema Inference for Delimited Data

Schema inference is the process of creating a relational schema for each file, or file block, as Drill reads it. Schema inference is only as good as the data itself. If the data contains sufficient hints, Drill can do an excellent job of inferring the schema. But certain data patterns that we will encounter later in the chapter can run into the limitations of schema inference. The general rule of thumb is that schema inference cannot predict the future; it can only react to data as it is read.

As noted earlier, Drill infers schemas in two main ways:

- From the data itself (specifically, from the first record of the file or file block)
- From metadata stored in the same file as the data, as in Parquet

We will explore schema inference from the simplest to the most complex cases using some of the file formats most commonly used with Drill.

All of the sample files used here reside in the book's GitHub repository. We begin by setting the GitHub repository's *data* folder as the default schema:

```
USE `local`.`data`;
```

CSV with header

The simplest file format for Drill is CSV. Drill supports a wide variety of text file formats, but CSV is the most widely used. A CSV file can have a header, or it can exclude the header. In Drill, this option is configured in the format plug-in configuration, as described in "Format Plug-ins and Format Configuration" on page 140.

You indicate to Drill that your CSV file has a schema via the format configuration. The default dfs storage configuration defines a csvh (CSV with header) format:

```
"csvh": {
    "type": "text",
    "extensions": [
    "csvh"
    ],
    "extractHeader": true,
    "delimiter": ","
}
```

You can copy this into the `local` storage configuration you created earlier. Because Drill considers CSV files with headers to be a different format than CSV files without headers, we must use a distinct file suffix for our examples with headers: *.csvh*. By default Drill uses *.csv* for files without headers and *.csvh* for files with headers, but you are free to assign suffixes as you want as long as each format has a distinct suffix or they are declared in distinct storage configurations.

For files with a header, every reader starts by reading the header line, which must be the first line of the file. Even if the CSV file is large enough to be split into blocks, each of which is read by a different reader, all readers start by reading the header line.

For example, suppose we have the file *csvh/cust.csvh*:

```
custId,name,balance,status
123,Fred,456.78
125,Betty,98.76,VIP
128,Barney,1.23,PAST DUE,30
```

What is the schema of this file? As a human, we might know that this is a simple customer list with customer ID, name, balance, and status. We might know that the `customerID` is an `INT` and the balance is a `FLOAT`.

But all Drill knows is that this is a CSV file: a file consisting of comma-separated values. We use the query to impose types beyond that inferred from the file. For example, run this query:

```
SELECT * FROM `csvh/cust.csvh`;
```

```
+---------+---------+---------+----------+
| custId  |  name   | balance |  status  |
+---------+---------+---------+----------+
| 123     | Fred    | 456.78  |          |
| 125     | Betty   | 98.76   | VIP      |
| 128     | Barney  | 1.23    | PAST DUE |
+---------+---------+---------+----------+
```

Drill's CSV schema inference has determined two things from our file:

- The file contains four columns
- The names of each column

The format plug-in creates each column as type (non-nullable) `VARCHAR`. The fields are all `VARCHAR` because Drill does not attempt to guess column types. This might be surprising, because some tools, such as Excel, will sample the data to infer column type. However, Drill does not do type inference for CSV files.

The first record of our file omitted the `status` field. Drill knows the type of the missing field must be `VARCHAR` and that CSV columns are required; that is, they are not nullable. So, recent versions of Drill simply fill the missing field with an empty string, as if the line were the following:

```
123,Fred,456.78,
```

The third record had an extra fifth field at the end (the number of days past due). Drill ignored this field because the header declared only four fields.

Explicit projection

Explicit projection describes the case in which the query specifies the columns to read from a table. By contrast, *implicit projection*, or *wildcard projection*, occurs when we use SELECT *.

Suppose we use the same CSV file as in the previous example but with the following query:

```
SELECT CustId, Name, Address FROM `csvh/cust.csvh`;
```

```
+---------+---------+---------+
| CustId  |  Name   | Address |
+---------+---------+---------+
| 123     | Fred    |         |
| 125     | Betty   |         |
| 128     | Barney  |         |
+---------+---------+---------+
```

Note that the Address column does not actually appear in the file. Because Drill uses schema-on-read, it cannot know that Address is missing until it actually reads the file. After Drill realizes that the field is missing, it will create a dummy column. Often Drill creates the column as nullable INT. But because Drill knows that all CSV columns are always of type VARCHAR, it creates Address as non-nullable VARCHAR and fills the column with empty strings.

Notice that we have subtly renamed the columns. The customer ID column is shown as custID in the CSV file and when using a wildcard query. But, because we referenced the name as the capitalized CustId in the explicit project list, that is how Drill returned the column. Here is the general rule:

- Drill uses the name as it appears in the projection list, if listed explicitly.
- Drill uses the name as it appears in the table for wildcard queries.

TypeOf functions

We can determine part of the field type using Drill's typeof() function, as demonstrated here:

```
SELECT typeof(custId) AS custId_type FROM `csvh/cust.csvh` LIMIT 1;

+--------------+
| custId_type  |
+--------------+
| VARCHAR      |
+--------------+
```

This function has a couple of limitations, however. First, it won't show if the column is nullable, non-nullable, or repeated (an array). Second, if the column contains a NULL value, typeof() reports the type as NULL even though Drill does not actually have a NULL type. This makes it difficult to illustrate some of the issues described here using the current Drill version.

Further, typeof() usually but not always reports Drill's internal type names, not the type names you use in SQL statements.

We can use typeof() to spy on column types to see what Drill thinks the type is within the aforementioned limitations:

```
SELECT typeof(custId) as custId_type, typeof(address) AS addr_type
FROM `csvh/cust.csvh` LIMIT 1;

+--------------+-----------+
| custId_type  | addr_type |
+--------------+-----------+
| VARCHAR      | VARCHAR   |
+--------------+-----------+
```

To work around these limitations, we contributed two new functions to Drill for inclusion in Drill 1.14. If you are using an earlier version of Drill, only typeof() is available.

The first function, sqlTypeOf(), returns the actual SQL type name for a column, whether that column is NULL or not. The SQL type name is the name that you can use in a CAST (discussed later) to force a column to that type.

Second, modeOf(), returns the cardinality of the column, which Drill calls the *mode*: NULLABLE, NOT NULL, or ARRAY.

We use these new functions next to get a clearer view of Drill's internal data types.

Casts to specify types

We as humans can use our extra knowledge of the columns to see that custId is really an INT and balance is a FLOAT. Or, said another way, we might choose to represent those columns as those types for some purposes. In Drill, we impose the types by forcing a data conversion using a CAST. We can apply a CAST only with explicit projection; that is, when we name columns, as demonstrated in the following example:

```
SELECT CAST(custID AS INT) AS custId, name,
    CAST(balance AS FLOAT) AS balance
FROM `csvh/cust.csvh`;

+---------+---------+---------+
| custId  |  name   | balance |
+---------+---------+---------+
| 123     | Fred    | 456.78  |
| 125     | Betty   | 98.76   |
| 128     | Barney  | 1.23    |
+---------+---------+---------+
```

We can use the type functions to ensure that the types were converted correctly:

```
SELECT sqlTypeOf(custId) As custId_type,
       modeOf(custId) AS custId_mode,
       sqlTypeOf(balance) AS bal_type,
       modeOf(balance) AS bal_mode
FROM (
  SELECT CAST(custID AS INT) AS custId,
         name, CAST(balance AS FLOAT) AS balance
  FROM `csvh/cust.csvh`)
LIMIT 1;

+-------------+-------------+----------+----------+
| custId_type | custId_mode | bal_type | bal_mode |
+-------------+-------------+----------+----------+
| INTEGER     | NOT NULL    | FLOAT    | NOT NULL |
+-------------+-------------+----------+----------+
```

The columns retain the NOT NULL cardinality from the original VARCHAR column.

We can now apply numeric operations to the numeric values. It is often handy to express this as a nested query, here using nonsensical operations:

```
SELECT AVG(custId) AS avgId, SUM(balance) totalBal
FROM (
  SELECT CAST(custID AS INT) AS custId,
         name, CAST(balance AS FLOAT) AS balance
  FROM `csvh/cust.csvh`)

+--------------------+--------------------+
|       avgId        |      totalBal      |
+--------------------+--------------------+
| 125.33333333333333 | 556.7700009346008  |
+--------------------+--------------------+
```

The key thing to remember, however, is that we treated the two fields as numbers only because we wanted to for this query: we could also keep them as VARCHARs if that were more convenient for some other operation.

CSV Summary

In summary, for a CSV file with headers:

- The number of columns and the column names are specified by the headers in the first line of the file. If any name repeats, Drill will create a unique field name by appending a number. If a name is blank, Drill uses EXPR$0 and so on.
- The type of every column is non-nullable VARCHAR.
- Extra columns past those described in the header are ignored.
- Columns declared in the file header but missing from a row are set to a blank VARCHAR.
- Columns referenced in the SELECT clause but missing from the file are set to a blank VARCHAR and filled with empty (not NULL) values.
- Columns are read as VARCHAR. Use a CAST to convert a column to a different type.

CSV without a header row

When a CSV file does not provide a header row, Drill uses a different rule to infer the schema as you saw in Chapter 4. Consider a simple example (*csv/fred.csv*):

```
123,Fred,456.78
```

We discussed CSV files with headers, for which Drill can determine the column count and names. Without headers, Drill does not know the names of the columns. Without names, Drill is not even sure of the column count that the next record could well have. Maybe some customer records have an additional loyalty level—Betty turns out to be very loyal:

```
125,Betty,98.76,VIP
```

To handle this case, Drill supports array (so-called *repeated*) types. So, Drill will represent each row using the special columns column.

```
SELECT * FROM `csv/cust.csv`;

+------------------------------+
|            columns           |
+------------------------------+
| ["123","Fred","456.78"]      |
| ["125","Betty","98.76","VIP"]|
+------------------------------+
```

Although this file has three or four columns, Drill stores each record in a single columns column as an array of VARCHAR. As it turns out, CSV is the only file format that uses the columns approach.

Again, you can use the type functions to see this in action:

```
SELECT sqlTypeOf(columns) AS cols_type,
       modeOf(columns) AS cols_mode
FROM `csv/cust.csv` LIMIT 1;

+---------------------+------------+
|      cols_type      | cols_mode  |
+---------------------+------------+
| CHARACTER VARYING   | ARRAY      |
+---------------------+------------+
```

Explicit projection

Sometimes, the array of values is all you need. But neither JDBC nor ODBC handles arrays very well, so most often you'll want to "parse" the array into named columns. Notice that indexing starts at 0:

```
SELECT columns[0] AS custId,
    columns[1] AS custName,
    columns[2] AS balance,
    columns[3] AS loyalty
FROM `csv/cust.csv`;

+---------+-----------+----------+----------+
| custId  | custName  | balance  | loyalty  |
+---------+-----------+----------+----------+
| 123     | Fred      | 456.78   | null     |
| 125     | Betty     | 98.76    | VIP      |
+---------+-----------+----------+----------+
```

Notice also that Fred's missing loyalty value is shown as NULL. This is different from the CSV-with-headers case, in which missing values are returned as empty VARCHARs. Although Drill provides no way to visualize the fact, the columns we created here are nullable VARCHAR, unlike the CSV-with-headers case in which the columns are non-nullable VARCHAR.

If you want a blank value to be consistent with the CSV-with-headers case, you can manipulate the data:

```
SELECT custId, custName, balance,
    CASE WHEN loyalty IS NULL THEN '' ELSE loyalty END
FROM (
  SELECT columns[0] AS custId,
      columns[1] AS custName,
      columns[2] AS balance,
      columns[3] AS loyalty
  FROM `csv/cust.csv`);
```

And of course, as in the previous section, you can use CAST statements to convert the text data to some other type when needed.

In summary, for CSV files without headers:

- All columns are represented by the special `columns` array of type repeated VAR CHAR.

- The length of the array depends on the number of fields on a given line and will differ across records if the number of fields differs across lines in the CSV file.

- If a value is not available in the `columns` array, you can still request it, but the value returned is NULL.

Schema Inference for JSON

The Drill project website notes that Drill uses JSON as its native data model. That is, Drill can support (a subset of) the same structures that JSON does:

- Scalar types
- Null values (unlike JSON, Drill's nulls are typed)
- Lists
- Maps

In practice JSON is much more expressive than Drill, for the simple reason that JSON can express arbitrary tree-structured data, but Drill must coerce all input into an extended relational structure.

Limitations of JSON Data

An inherent limitation of JSON is that no matter how large your JSON file is, Drill cannot parallelize the scan of a single file. This is a limitation of the JSON format itself. Splittable formats require a clear "end-of-record" marker (such as a newline); however, JSON provides no such marker. Still, if your query reads multiple JSON files, Drill will read the files in parallel.

JSON column names

Drill infers column names from the names of JSON map elements:

```
{"column1": 10, "column2": "foo"}
```

Here's a simple query:

```
SELECT * from `json/quoted.json`;

+---------+---------+
| column1 | column2 |
+---------+---------+
| 10      | foo     |
+---------+---------+
```

As a harmless extension to JSON, Drill does not require column names to be enclosed in quotes, so the following is also valid:

```
{column1: 10, column2: "foo"}

SELECT * from `json/unquoted.json`;

+----------+----------+
| column1  | column2  |
+----------+----------+
| 10       | foo      |
+----------+----------+
```

In JSON, column names are case sensitive. So, the following has two columns:

```
{a: 10, A: 20}
```

Drill, however, follows the SQL standard in which column names are case insensitive. Drill treats the preceding example as a single column; the first field provides the name, but the second value overwrites the first:

```
SELECT * FROM `json/ambig.json`;

+-----+
|  a  |
+-----+
| 20  |
+-----+
```

JSON scalar types

JSON supports a small set of scalar types: number, string, null, true, and false. Drill maps the JSON types to Drill types, which you can see listed in Table 8-1.

Table 8-1. Drill versus JSON data types

JSON type	Drill data type
number	Nullable DOUBLE if the number contains a decimal point; nullable BIGINT otherwise
string	Nullable VARCHAR
true, false	Nullable BOOLEAN (a single-byte, unsigned integer with true = 1 and false = 0)
null	A NULL value for a column type previously inferred

Limitations on Schema Inference

Recall the key rule about Drill's schema inference: *Drill cannot pre-dict the future*. Drill infers column type using the first row only. (Actually, Drill infers column type from the first appearance of each column, which is often, but not necessarily, in the first row.)

We use the term *schema ambiguity* to refer to the case in which information in the first row is insufficient for Drill to select the proper column type. You can often resolve the ambiguity using a set of session options and with the clever use of query features.

Of course, if your JSON files are well structured, you may not run into the schema ambiguity issues. On the other hand, in a data lake, you often don't have control over the format of JSON files created by others. If a file contains nulls or missing values, is sloppily writ-ten, or has a schema that has changed over time, you might run into schema ambiguity issues and can resolve them as described here. Converting such files to Parquet is your best production solu-tion; use the solutions here to explore the files prior to conversion.

Ambiguous Numeric Schemas

JSON has only one numeric type: number. But Drill has multiple numeric types, and chooses a type for the field based on the first record. In general, if the first value con-tains a decimal point, Drill chooses DOUBLE; otherwise, it chooses BIGINT.

Because Drill is more strict than JSON, the "can't predict the future" rule can surprise the unwary. Suppose we have the following JSON file (*json/int-float.json*):

```
{a: 10}
{a: 10.1}
```

A query against this table fails:

```
SELECT * FROM `json/int-float.json`;
Error: INTERNAL_ERROR ERROR: You tried to write a Float8 type when
    you are using a ValueWriter of type NullableBigIntWriterImpl.
```

The problem is that Drill infers the type BIGINT from the first value and then fails because the second value is not a valid BIGINT. You cannot fix this problem in the query because the problem occurs during read, long before your query statements take effect.

Drill provides a solution, albeit one that's a bit awkward. Like many SQL engines, Drill lets you customize various settings at runtime. You can make a change for just the current login session using ALTER SESSION. Or, if you have admin rights, you can change the setting for all users in all sessions using ALTER SYSTEM. Because changing a system setting might cause queries to behave differently, be very cautious before making such system-level changes. Here, we'll make all the changes for just the one session; the options will go back to their default values in the next session.

If your file has pathological cases like this, you can read all numbers as DOUBLE:

```
ALTER SESSION SET `store.json.read_numbers_as_double` = true;
```

The query will now work fine because Drill is given a hint to use the DOUBLE type for numbers, so there is no conflict. The awkward bit is that you must remember to set the option before each query of the troublesome file, and you must remember to reset it afterward:

```
ALTER SESSION RESET `store.json.read_numbers_as_double`;
```

Some query tools don't provide a convenient way to issue such statements. Further, you cannot encapsulate such statements in a view. As a result, it is much better to avoid creating such ambiguous files in the first place.

 The session options must be set in each connection session before querying the file. You must reset them before querying the next file. This means that the users of Drill must know which options to set for each file. This is a good motivation to convert troublesome files to Parquet, as explained later in the chapter.

Mixed string and number types

A similar issue occurs if you mix string and number types that are distinct JSON types. Mixing of types can occur if the JSON schema evolves. Perhaps a product number starts as a number but is later changed to a string to allow codes such as 104A. Or perhaps a sloppy script writes numbers as strings and is later corrected, as in this case (*json/int-str.json*):

```
{a: 10}
{a: "20"}
```

Try to query this file:

```
SELECT * FROM `json/int-str.json`;
Error: INTERNAL_ERROR ERROR: You tried to write a VARCHAR type when you are using
a ValueWriter of type NullableFloat8WriterImpl.
```

Here you can use an even more general solution, *all-text mode*, which instructs JSON to read all scalar fields as nullable VARCHAR:

```
ALTER SESSION SET `store.json.all_text_mode` = true;
SELECT * FROM `json/int-str.json`;

+-----+
|  a  |
+-----+
| 10  |
| 20  |
+-----+
```

It is not clear from the SQLLine output, but the type of the preceding fields is VARCHAR, which you can verify as follows:

```
SELECT typeof(a) AS a_type FROM `json/int-str.json` LIMIT 1;

+----------+
|  a_type  |
+----------+
| VARCHAR  |
+----------+
```

If you meant for the field to be a number, you can add a CAST:

```
SELECT CAST(a AS BIGINT) AS a FROM `json/int-str.json`;
+-----+
|  a  |
+-----+
| 10  |
| 20  |
+-----+
```

Missing values

JSON is very flexible, allowing you to simply omit values if they are not needed. That is, the following is perfectly valid (*json/missing2.json*):

```
{custId: 123, name: "Fred", balance: 123.45}
{custId: 125, name: "Barney"}
```

When Drill encounters this, it simply fills in a NULL for the missing value:

```
SELECT * FROM `json/missing2.json`;

+---------+---------+----------+
| custId  |  name   | balance  |
+---------+---------+----------+
| 123     | Fred    | 123.45   |
| 125     | Barney  | null     |
+---------+---------+----------+
```

The "can't predict the future" rule can trip you up if the file contains too many missing fields at the beginning. Consider the following file (*json/missing3.json*):

```
{a: 0}
{a: 1}
{a: 2, b: "hello there!"}
```

Now consider this query:

```
SELECT a, b FROM `json/missing3.json` WHERE b IS NOT NULL ORDER BY a;

+----+---------------+
| a  |       b       |
+----+---------------+
| 2  | hello there!  |
+----+---------------+
```

Do the same but with 70,000 of the a-only records (*gen/70kmissing.json*). This time you get:

```
SELECT a, b FROM `gen/70kmissing.json`
WHERE b IS NOT NULL ORDER BY a;

Error: UNSUPPORTED_OPERATION ERROR:
  Schema changes not supported in External Sort.
  Please enable Union type.
Previous schema BatchSchema [fields=[[`a` (BIGINT:OPTIONAL)],
  [`b` (INT:OPTIONAL)]], selectionVector=NONE]
Incoming schema BatchSchema [fields=[[`a` (BIGINT:OPTIONAL)],
  [`b` (FLOAT8:OPTIONAL)]], selectionVector=NONE]
```

The reason is that Drill breaks data into batches of 65,536 or fewer records. The 70,000 records are enough to cause Drill to split the data into at least two batches. The first has only one column, but the second has two. Because you requested a column b, even in batches in which b does not exist, Drill invents a dummy column of type nullable INT. This change in schema confuses the sort operator. In Drill terminology, the preceding situation is a schema change.

Sometimes schema changes are benign, as you can see by running this query in SQLLine:

```
SELECT a, b,
       sqlTypeOf(b) AS b_type, modeof(b) AS b_mode
FROM `gen/70kmissing.json`
WHERE mod(a, 70000) = 1;

+--------+-------+----------+-----------+
|   a    |   b   |  b_type  |  b_mode   |
+--------+-------+----------+-----------+
| 1      | null  | INTEGER  | NULLABLE  |
| 70001  | 10.5  | DOUBLE   | NULLABLE  |
+--------+-------+----------+-----------+
```

The schema change is present, but because of the way SQLLine works, the change is harmless. Specifically, SQLLine converts all columns to string, regardless of type.

Because both `DOUBLE` and `INT` columns can be converted to a string, SQLLine does not complain.

You can be surprised when you get an error when using a tool or Drill operator that is stricter about types. For example, the sort operation failed because it is such a strict operator. The error message says that the sort operator does not know how to combine a `DOUBLE` (called `FLOAT8` internally) and an `INT` into the same column. Use the `sqltypeof()` function, as shown in the prior example, to see the type conflict if you run into this kid of error.

All-text mode should work to force the missing fields to `VARCHAR`, but a bug in Drill 1.13 (DRILL-6359 (*https://issues.apache.org/jira/browse/DRILL-6359*)) prevents that from happening. You can work around this by doing the conversion yourself:

```
SELECT a, CAST(b AS DOUBLE) AS b
FROM `gen/70kmissing.json`
WHERE b IS NOT NULL ORDER BY a;

+--------+-------+
|   a    |   b   |
+--------+-------+
| 70001  | 10.5  |
+--------+-------+
```

The general rule is that, with JSON, leading nulls can cause issues because Drill cannot predict the type that will eventually appear. Similarly, if a column is missing at the beginning of the file, Drill has no way to predict that the column will appear (or its eventual type). As a result, JSON works best with Drill when all columns are present with non-null values or if you add query logic to resolve the ambiguity.

Leading null values

We noted earlier that Drill treats missing JSON values as if the column were present, but contains nulls. As a result, the discussion about missing values applies to null values, as well.

JSON treats `null` as a type separate from all other types. However, in Drill (as in SQL), NULL is a state of a value, and that value must be of some type. That is, despite what the `typeof()` function seems to say, Drill has no NULL type, only null values.

Drill's behavior with JSON nulls is a bit different from how it treats missing values in one way: when Drill gets to the end of the first batch, it must guess a type for the all-null column, and Drill guesses nullable INT. This is, in fact, an odd guess given that no JSON value is ever treated as INT, and so this Drill behavior might change in future releases. For example, given this file:

```
{a: null}
{a: null}
```

we get these query results:

```
SELECT a FROM `json/all-null.json`;

+-------+
|   a   |
+-------+
| null  |
| null  |
+-------+
```

You can see the type using new functions added in Drill 1.14:

```
SELECT sqlTypeOf(a) AS a_type, modeOf(a) AS a_mode
FROM `json/all-null.json` LIMIT 1;

+----------+----------+
|  a_type  |  a_mode  |
+----------+----------+
| INTEGER  | NULLABLE |
+----------+----------+
```

The general rule is that you should include a non-null value somewhere in the first hundred records or so.

Null versus missing values in JSON output

As just noted, Drill internally represents JSON null and empty values in the same way: as a NULL value of some type. If you were to use a CREATE TABLE statement in Drill to copy your input JSON to an output JSON file, you would see that Drill omits columns with NULL values:

```
ALTER SESSION SET `store.format` = 'json';
CREATE TABLE `out/json-null` AS SELECT * FROM `json/null2.json`;
```

The output is:

```
{
  "custId" : 123,
  "name" : "Fred",
  "balance" : 123.45
} {
  "custId" : 125,
  "name" : "Barney"
}
```

The general rule is this: although a null and a missing value are different in JSON, Drill's mapping of JSON into SQL equates them.

Aligning Schemas Across Files

Drill can query multiple files, and these are read in distinct threads or on distinct nodes, as explained earlier. As a result, the reader on one node cannot predict what another node will read. Because the JSON reader decides on a schema based on the first record in each file, the readers can settle on different schemas because of the aforementioned ambiguities. In this case, Drill will detect the problem only when the query attempts to combine the data from the various readers.

This behavior can lead to issues similar to those described earlier if you query multiple files and column b occurs in some files but not others:

```
json/missing/
  file1.json:
    {a: 1}
  file2.json:
    {a: 2, b: "foo"}
```

If Drill reads the preceding in the same minor fragment, this example might work if Drill happens to read *file2* before *file1* (the order in which Drill reads files is random). But the query will fail if Drill reads *file1* before *file2*. How it fails depends on the query.

For example, in one test, the following query works:

```
SELECT a, b FROM `json/missing` ORDER BY a;
```

But if you rename *file1.json* to *file3.json*, the same query now produces an error:

```
Error: UNSUPPORTED_OPERATION ERROR:
  Schema changes not supported in External Sort.
  Please enable Union type.

Previous schema BatchSchema [fields=[[`a` (BIGINT:OPTIONAL)]],
  selectionVector=NONE]
Incoming schema BatchSchema [fields=[[`a` (BIGINT:OPTIONAL)],
  [`b` (VARCHAR:OPTIONAL)]], selectionVector=NONE]
```

You can use the sqlTypeOf() function to visualize the problem:

```
SELECT sqlTypeOf(b) AS b_type FROM `json/missing`;

+--------------------+
|       b_type       |
+--------------------+
| INTEGER            |
| CHARACTER VARYING  |
+--------------------+
```

You can apply the same workaround as earlier, including an explicit cast:

```
SELECT a, CAST(b AS VARCHAR) AS b FROM `json/missing` ORDER BY a;

+----+-------+
| a  |   b   |
+----+-------+
| 1  | null  |
```

```
| 2  | foo  |
+----+------+
```

Again, the general lesson is this: ensure identical schemas across all of the JSON files to be read by a query. This means that if your schema evolves, you must go back and update any existing files so that they have a matching schema.

JSON Objects

JSON allows tree-structured data such as the following for a customer (*json/nested.json*):

```
{custId: 101, name: {first: "John", last: "Smith"}}
```

Try querying the file:

```
SELECT * FROM `json/nested.json`;

+----------+---------------------------------+
| custId   |               name              |
+----------+---------------------------------+
| 101      | {"first":"John","last":"Smith"} |
+----------+---------------------------------+
```

In JSON, both the outer and inner groupings are objects. Drill converts the outer object to a record, and it converts the inner structure to a Drill MAP. Although Drill uses the name MAP for this data type, it is more like a Hive STRUCT: it is actually a nested record with its own set of named columns. It is not, as you might suspect from the name, a collection of name/value pairs. Chapter 5 discusses how to work with MAP columns.

Maps in JDBC

The MAP type is very useful, but should be used only within the query itself. Convert the map to a set of top-level columns when you use the JDBC or ODBC clients. JDBC does not support the idea of a nested tuple. JDBC does support, however, the idea of a column returned as a generic Java object. SQLLine uses JDBC to connect to Drill. SQLLine uses a special trick to make it look like JDBC does support the MAP type. The SQLLine tool retrieves the Java object value for each column and displays the data by calling the Java toString() method on that object. To ensure that the toString() method produces the nice formatting shown in the previous example, the Drill JDBC driver returns the MAP as the Java implementation of a JSON object. You can use this same trick in your own Java code that uses the Drill JDBC driver.

You can use the `sqltypeof()` function to verify that the column is actually a Drill MAP:

```
SELECT sqlTypeOf(`name`) AS name_type FROM `json/nested.json`;

+------------+
| name_type  |
+------------+
| MAP        |
+------------+
```

You can also peek inside the `MAP` to determine the type of the map's members:

```
SELECT sqlTypeOf(`t`.`name`.`first`) AS name_type
FROM `json/nested.json` AS t;

+--------------------+
|      name_type     |
+--------------------+
| CHARACTER VARYING  |
+--------------------+
```

Since neither JDBC nor ODBC support `MAP` columns, you usually don't want to return the `MAP` to the client. Instead, you want to flatten `MAP` columns using the Drill functions provided, or manually:

```
SELECT custId,
       `t`.`name`.`first` AS `first`,
       `t`.`name`.`last` AS `last`
FROM `json/nested.json` AS `t`;

+---------+--------+--------+
| custId  | first  | last   |
+---------+--------+--------+
| 101     | John   | Smith  |
+---------+--------+--------+
```

Note the format required:

- When referencing a `MAP`, you must prefix the entire name by a table name, or the SQL parser will think that the map name refers to a table.
- Because Drill table names are complex, it is handy to give the table an alias as we did with `t`.

JSON allows fields to contain dots in their names. To identify that you want the name of a map followed by its member, you must enclose each name part in backticks, and separate the parts by dots outside the backticks.

Because the inner map is a separate structure, names in one map (including the top-level record) can be the same as those in another:

```
{a: {c: 10}, b: {c: 20}}
```

The names are unique in their full path names, however: `a`.`c` and `b`.`c`.

JSON itself places no restrictions on the contents of objects. Two records can have completely different object schemas (*json/disjoint-nest.json*):

```
{a: {b: 10}}
{a: {c: "foo"}}
```

If Drill encounters objects such as those in the preceding example, it simply adds each column to a compound map. That is, Drill treats the previous example as if it were the following:

```
{a: {b: 10, c: null}}
{a: {b: null, c: "foo"}}
```

This is, in fact, really just the same rule that we saw applied to the top-level record itself. So, the same caveats apply.

However, when displayed in SQLLine, it appears that Drill has treated the maps as separate schemas due to the "omit null columns" rule for SQLLine output:

```
SELECT * FROM `json/disjoint-nest.json`;

+--------------+
|      a       |
+--------------+
| {"b":10}     |
| {"c":"foo"}  |
+--------------+
```

Despite this convenient formating, both columns are present in both maps. As we saw earlier, when Drill renders a row (or MAP) as JSON it omits null values, giving the output shown in the preceding example.

JSON Lists in Drill

JSON provides a list type (*json/int-list.json*):

```
{a: [10, 20, 30]}
```

Querying this data produces the following results:

```
SELECT * FROM `json/int-list.json`;

+--------------+
|      a       |
+--------------+
| [10,20,30]   |
+--------------+

SELECT sqlTypeOf(a) AS a_type, modeOf(a) AS a_mode
FROM `json/int-list.json`;

+----------+----------+
| a_type   | a_mode   |
```

```
+---------+---------+
| BIGINT  | ARRAY   |
+---------+---------+
```

In JSON, a list is not a list of numbers or list of strings, it is simply a list of values, and the values can be of any type. That is, the following is perfectly fine JSON (*json/mixed-list.json*):

```
{a: [10, "foo", {b: 30}, ["fred", "barney"]]}
```

Again, Drill must pull a relational structure out of the JSON data, and it cannot do so for heterogeneous lists.[1]

Sometimes, clever programmers use JSON arrays as a record format: just list the values in order without the overhead of name/value pairs when using objects. However, Drill cannot read a JSON array that contains mixed scalar types (*json/scalar-list.json*):

```
{a: [ 123, "Fred", 123.45 ] }
```

Here's what happens when you query the file:

```
SELECT * FROM `json/scalar-list.json`;
Error: UNSUPPORTED_OPERATION ERROR: In a list of type BIGINT,
 encountered a value of type VARCHAR. Drill does not support lists of different types.
```

The workaround is to use `all_text_mode`:

```
ALTER SESSION SET `store.json.all_text_mode` = true;
SELECT * FROM `json/scalar-list.json`;

+--------------------------+
|            a             |
+--------------------------+
| ["123","Fred","123.45"]  |
+--------------------------+
```

Now you can pull out the fields and cast them to the proper type:

```
SELECT * FROM (
  SELECT CAST(a[0] AS INT) AS custId,
         a[1] AS name,
         CAST(a[2] AS DOUBLE) AS balance
  FROM `json/scalar-list.json`);

+---------+-------+----------+
| custId  | name  | balance  |
+---------+-------+----------+
| 123     | Fred  | 123.45   |
+---------+-------+----------+

ALTER SESSION RESET `store.json.all_text_mode`;
```

---

1 Drill does have a LIST data type originally designed to represent heterogeneous lists. However, at the time of this writing, the type is still experimental and not fully implemented.

The general rule in Drill is that if a column is represented by a JSON list, all the values in the list must be of the same type. This allows Drill to infer the type of the list as one of the types discussed earlier, but with repeated cardinality. Using `all_text_mode` is a workaround, but it has the fiddly issues discussed earlier.

JSON lists can include null values (*json/int-null-list.json*):

```
{a: [10, null, 30]}
```

However, Drill does not allow null values in lists. JSON data with nulls in lists will cause the query to fail:

```
SELECT * FROM `json/int-null-list.json`;
Error: UNSUPPORTED_OPERATION ERROR:
  Null values are not supported in lists by default.
  Please set `store.json.all_text_mode` to true
  to read lists containing nulls. Be advised that this will treat
  JSON null values as a string containing the word 'null'.
```

Here, the message helpfully explains the workaround:

```
ALTER SESSION SET `store.json.all_text_mode` = true;
SELECT * FROM `json/int-null-list.json`;

+---------------------+
|          a          |
+---------------------+
| ["10","null","30"]  |
+---------------------+

ALTER SESSION RESET `store.json.all_text_mode`;
```

In this case, there is no good way to convert the text fields to numbers short of turning them into top-level fields.

JSON allows a list to be null. Just as Drill does not differentiate between missing and null scalar values in JSON, it does not differentiate between missing, empty, and null lists. Consider this file (*json/null-list.json*):

```
{a: 1, b: [10, 20]}
{a: 2, b: null}
{a: 3, b: []}
{a: 4}
```

If you query the file, you get these results:

```
SELECT * FROM `json/null-list.json`;

+----+----------+
| a  |    b     |
+----+----------+
| 1  | [10,20]  |
| 2  | []       |
| 3  | []       |
```

```
| 4  | []       |
+----+----------+
```

The "can't predict the future" rule applies to lists too. Here's another example (*json/empty-str-list.json*):

```
{a: []}
{a: ["Fred", "Barney"]}
```

A query on this file will work if all of the data fits into one batch. But if the empty array fills one batch, Drill must guess a type for that batch. It will guess array of INT and then will fail when the second batch tries to convert VARCHAR values to INT values. For example:

```
SELECT * FROM `gen/70Kempty.json`;
Error: UNSUPPORTED_OPERATION ERROR: In a list of type INT,
encountered a value of type VARCHAR.
Drill does not support lists of different types.
```

The workaround is our old friend, all text mode:

```
ALTER SESSION SET `store.json.all_text_mode` = true;
SELECT * FROM `gen/70Kempty.json` WHERE a=70001;

+--------+--------------------+
|   a    |          b         |
+--------+--------------------+
| 70001  | ["Fred","Barney"]  |
+--------+--------------------+
```

Drill allows lists to contain other lists, a so-called *repeated list*. A list can also contain maps, which is a *repeated map*. In these cases, the use of all-text mode will not work to handle long runs of empty lists. Drill will guess text, but when the first non-null value appears and is an array or a map, Drill reports an error. The rule is that if the array is nonscalar, it must begin with a non-null value, or Drill will be unable to resolve the ambiguity. Another alternative is to do an ETL of the data into Parquet, which provides metadata to resolve the ambiguity.

JSON Summary

In summary, the following rules apply to JSON:

- JSON keys become Drill column names.
- JSON types map to specific Drill types.
- Drill can handle columns with list or object values, with certain restrictions.
- JSON object keys are case sensitive, but Drill column names are case insensitive.

To get the best results with Drill, take care to produce JSON that maps cleanly to a relational representation by doing the following:

- Avoid null values in the first record.
- For each column, avoid missing values early in the file.
- Lists must be homogeneous with no null values.
- Avoid empty lists in the first record.
- Ensure that floating-point numbers always include a decimal point.
- Avoid including some column in one set of files, but excluding it from another set.

A workaround for some but not all of these issues is to enable all text mode for the JSON table in the JSON format plug-in configuration, which will read all scalar columns as nullable VARCHAR and all scalar arrays as repeated VARCHAR. The query can then perform its own type conversions as demonstrated earlier.

 As mentioned in Chapter 5, Drill provides a Union type that might help to resolve these issues. However, this feature is still considered experimental.

Using Drill with the Parquet File Format

Apache Parquet (*https://parquet.apache.org/*) has become Drill's preferred file format, for many reasons. Drill developers have heavily optimized the Parquet reader. It has the best read performance across all data file formats and is the ultimate answer to the schema issues described for text files.

Parquet provides optimal performance because of the following:

- Parquet is a columnar file format that allows Drill to read only those columns that are needed for a query. You see the maximum benefit when you project a subset of the available columns.
- Parquet is compressed, minimizing the amount of input/output (I/O) needed to read data from disk at the cost of extra CPU to decode the data.
- Parquet files contain schema metadata, which avoids the need for Drill to infer the schema from the data.
- Parquet files often contain additional metadata, such as data ranges, which Drill can use to skip unneeded blocks of data.

Parquet has many of the benefits of a database's own storage format, but in the form of a file that usable by many tools, including Drill. Parquet is not, however, a source file format: data often arrives in text or JSON formats. You then use an ETL process to create the Parquet files.

Some people use Drill for ETL, which works fine as long as the source files are well structured to ensure that Drill's schema inference rules pick the right types, or you can apply the data manipulation techniques described earlier. If you encounter a file that requires Drill to predict the future in order to correctly infer types, Drill will be a poor choice for ETL for that file. Instead, you can use some other tool for ETL: Hive and Spark are popular options. Many commercial options are also available. ETL is also a good option when converting from file formats that Drill does not support.

The ETL process often writes the converted Parquet files into a partitioned structure, as discussed shortly.

Parquet is an evolving format, as is Drill's support for Parquet. Although Drill should read most Parquet files written by other tools, and other tools can usually read Parquet written by Drill, there are exceptions. See the Drill documentation (*http:// drill.apache.org/docs/parquet-format/*), or you can discuss it with the Drill community (*http://drill.apache.org/mailinglists/*), to understand limitations in current Drill versions.

Schema Evolution in Parquet

Suppose that we have a directory, *parquetDir*, that contains two Parquet files: *file1* and *file2*. *file1* has a single column a of type Integer. *file2* has two columns: the same column a, but also column b of type String.

As explained for JSON, if we do an explicit SELECT:

```
SELECT a, b FROM `parquetDir` ORDER BY b
```

Drill will fail for the same reasons explained earlier. From this we can see that we have to plan schema evolution carefully, even for Parquet. After we have a collection of Parquet files, we must plan how to handle the situation when columns are added to or removed from the files from which we create our Parquet files. Our ETL process that creates Parquet files should be rerun to re-create older files when we find the need to insert or remove columns with a type other than nullable INT. (Or, we should reprocess the older files to add or remove the columns in question.)

Partitioning Data Directories

Suppose that your data lake contains Parquet files that record the details of sales for each retail store per day, with data accumulated over the past three years. How might you store this data?

On the one hand, you could write the data for each store for each day into a separate file. Although this strategy is fine for small datasets, in this case you would create 100,000 files. If all the files reside in one large *sales* directory, Drill must scan all of them to answer each query. For example, suppose that you want only one month of data. Drill must still scan all the files to read the `year` column needed in the query:

```
SELECT ... FROM `sales` WHERE `year` = 2017
```

If you stored the data in a relational database, you would define indexes on the table, perhaps for date, store, product, and so on. With a date index, the database could quickly ignore all years except 2017.

However, indexes don't work very well in the big data world. Instead, we use a related concept: *partitioning*. With partitioning, you divide data into subdirectories based on some key. Although a database can index on multiple columns (called "dimensions" in a data warehouse), partitioning works along only a single dimension. We then give Drill the information it needs to scan a subset of our partition subdirectories.

Typically, if your data is large enough to be considered "big data," you have time series data: few other datasets grow to such large scales. In this example case, you have a time series of sales. Most queries will include a date range: "sales for stores in the Western region for product *X* over the last four quarters" or "sales by store for the last week." Because most queries include dates, the `date` column is the natural one to use for your partitions:

```
sales
|- ...
|- 2017
   |- 01
   |- ...
   |- 12
      |- 01
      |- ...
      |- 31
         |- store001.parquet
         |- ...
         |- store100.parquet
```

Suppose that you want to query the sales over a month period that spans from December 15, 2017 to January 14, 2018. Let's see how to do that.

Because Drill uses the directory structure as its own schema, we'll write a query to work with our directory structure. We'll write our query against the *sales* folder. We need to know that `dir0` is the first level of subdirectory (*year*), `dir1` is the second (*month*), and `dir2` is the third (*day*). Even though we can include these implicit columns in the `SELECT` clause, they are most useful in the `WHERE` clause. We can now write the query like this:

```
SELECT ... FROM `sales`
WHERE (dir0 = '2017' AND dir1 = '12' AND dir2 >= '15')
   OR (dir0 = '2018' AND dir1 = '01' AND dir2 < '15')
```

This works, but it is not pleasant to use. A better strategy is to use a single level of directories using an ISO-encoded date as the directory name. For example, directories might be named *2016-04-21, 2016-04-22, … 2018-04-22*. We would have a about 1,000 directories, each containing 100 files, one for each store on that date. For example:

```
sales
|- ...
|- 2017-12-31
   |- store001.parquet
   |- ...
   |- store100.parquet
```

With this structure, the preceding query becomes much easier to write:

```
SELECT ... FROM `sales`
WHERE dir0 BETWEEN '2017-12-15' AND '2018-01-14'
```

Although you could parse the date out from the dir0 value, it is more convenient to repeat the date within the file itself. For something like sales, the file will probably actually contain the full timestamp of the sale.

If the history were much larger, say 10 years of data, you might be forced to choose the multilevel structure. Unfortunately, if you do that, you must rewrite all the queries because the queries encode the directory structure. This is a case in which you want to get the structure right the first time.

Sometimes you can use the directory structure directly as part of the table name rather than in the WHERE clause. For example, if you want only sales for 2017:

```
SELECT ... FROM `sales/2017`
```

You can also use wildcards in directory or filenames. Suppose that you want only sales for the month of July using the one-level structure:

```
SELECT ... FROM `sales/*-07-*`
```

You can also use the same trick to pick out specific files across directories. For example, if you want only 2017 sales data for store 123:

```
SELECT ... FROM `sales/2017-*/store123.parquet`
```

Choose a structure that works for your data. The goal is to look at typical queries and group data so that most queries hit just a single partition at the leaf or higher level, and the query does not scan unnecessary data. Further, choose a partition structure that reflects the dimensions (columns) most likely to appear in the WHERE clause.

Although this section focused on Parquet files, partitioning works for all file formats and can be useful if your data arrives from a data source that partitions data as it arrives (typically by time).

In this example, if you know that most analysis is done by date across all stores, the partition-by-day format might be best. If, on the other hand, most analysis was done by store and then by date, perhaps a better partitioning structure would be to first partition by store and then by date.

Although we've focused on using partitions with Drill, partitions are a common big data structure used by many tools. For example, partitions in Drill are similar to those in Hive and serve the same purpose. The main difference is that Hive explicitly attaches a schema to a directory hierarchy, whereas Drill does not. Also, Hive encodes partition information in directory names, whereas Drill does not. Drill handles manual partitions as well as partitions created by Hive in identical fashion with no loss of functionality or performance.

If you use Drill for your ETL tasks, Drill itself can create the partitions using the `PARTITION BY`clause (*http://drill.apache.org/docs/partition-by-clause/*) of the `CREATE TABLE AS` (CTAS) statement.

Defining a Table Workspace

The partition directories and files within the directories are essentially a table. Hive, in fact, defines the entire structure as a table and automatically works out how to scan the data. Because it uses no external schema, Drill is not aware of the table concept. The closest we can get in Drill is to simulate tables using directory structures. Suppose that you want to define multiple partitioned tables: `sales`, `returns`, `promotions`, and so on. You begin by defining a top-level directory with subdirectories for each table:

```
retail
|- sales
|- returns
|- promotions
```

Each of the child directories is partitioned, say by date. Next, you declare a workspace, and then you can reference your tables within that schema:

```
SELECT * FROM `retail`.`sales` LIMIT 10
```

When you use a directory name (only) in a query, Drill assumes that you want to scan all files in that directory and all its children. If you use a directory pattern (with wildcards), Drill assumes that you want all files in the selected directories.

Drill requires that all files in a single `FROM` element be of the same type and have the same suffix. In this case, perhaps all the sales files are in Parquet format.

If the directories contain multiple file types, you can use wildcards to pick out a single type.

Working with Queries in Production

In the previous section, you saw many ways that Drill can work with schema-free source data, and the inherent limitations and ambiguities that you might encounter in these situations. We also discussed how to avoid most issues by converting your data from its source format into Parquet.

Finally, in this section, we discuss how to apply these rules to production queries.

Capturing Schema Mapping in Views

You have seen various ways in which you can use session options and query constructs to work around ambiguities in various kinds of data files. After you work out the proper solutions, it makes sense that you would like to reuse them for future queries. Views are Drill's solution to such reuse.

You will have noticed that several of the examples are written in such a way that the grunt work is handled by a subquery. This is not an accident: the subquery can be reused as a view.

Unfortunately, Drill cannot also encapsulate session options in a view. This means that if you must use all text mode, say, to handle schema ambiguities, the users of your view must also set all text mode before using the view and remember to reset the mode afterward.

This is important if you want to run such queries in a business intelligence tool such as Tableau. In such a tool, you might not have the luxury of turning session options on and off around each query, especially if the queries are automated as part of a dashboard or other structure. Your best bet in such cases is to convert the data to Parquet and then query the converted data.

Running Challenging Queries in Scripts

Another handy approach is to run challenging queries (those that require specific session options) in a script. You can then use SQLLine to run the script, which sets up the required session options and then runs the query.

SQLLine has a number of command-line options that you can see using the -h option:

```
$DRILL_HOME/bin/sqlline -h
```

Here's the partial output:

```
Usage: java sqlline.SqlLine
...
 --showHeader=[true/false]     show column names in query results
 --numberFormat=[pattern]      format numbers using DecimalFormat
                               pattern
 --maxWidth=MAXWIDTH           the maximum width of the terminal
 --silent=[true/false]         be more silent
 --outputformat=[table/vertical/csv/tsv]
                               format mode for result display
 --run=/path/to/file           run one script and then exit
```

What if you wanted to run a single query to sum the sales for 2017? You might create a script file such as the following:

```
USE `local`.`data`;
SELECT SUM(CAST(amount AS DOUBLE)) FROM `sales/2017-*`;
```

You would do so like this (assuming a single Drillbit on localhost):

```
$DRILL_HOME/bin/sqlline \
   -u jdbc:drill:drillbit=localhost \
   --run=/full/path/to/countSales.sql \
   --silent=true \
   --outputformat=csv \
   --numberFormat=##,###.00
```

Here's what the results look like:

```
'ok','summary'
'true','Default schema changed to [local.data]'
'EXPR$0'
'10,914.00'
```

Although not perfect, you could apply a bit of text editing to pull out the lines that you want, ignoring the unwanted output from the USE command. You can extend this technique to add ALTER SESSION commands and to use scripting to pass parameters into the query. You can do something similar in Java using the Drill JDBC driver, or in Python as shown in Chapter 7.

Conclusion

You now have a deep understanding of how to apply Drill to your most challenging data file formats as well as how to diagnose problems when they occur. Drill is very powerful, but it cannot predict the future, meaning that certain data patterns are difficult for Drill to understand. You now have the tools to identify such situations and to work around them. You also now have a deeper appreciation for the many benefits of Parquet as the preferred data format for Drill.

CHAPTER 9

Deploying Drill in Production

The two most common usage patterns for Drill are a single (often embedded) instance used to learn Drill, and a fully distributed, multinode setup used in production. This chapter explains the issues to consider when moving from personal usage to a production cluster. This chapter does not explain the basics of setting up a distributed Hadoop or Amazon Web Services (AWS) cluster; we assume that you already have that knowledge.

Installing Drill

This section walks you through the steps required to get the Drill software on your nodes. Later sections explain how to configure Drill.

You have several options for how to install Drill on your servers:

Vendor-provided installer
> If you are a MapR customer, the easiest solution is to use the MapR installer. Note that the MapR configuration does not use the site directory (see "Creating a Site Directory" on page 177); if you upgrade Drill, be sure to follow the manual steps in the MapR documentation to save your configuration and JAR files before upgrading.

Casual installation
> If you are trying Drill on a server but are not quite ready for production use, you can install Drill much as you would on your laptop: just download Drill into your home directory and then follow the steps listed in Chapter 2.

Production installation
> This is a more structured way to install Drill onto your system; see "Production Installation" on page 176.

Regardless of how you do the installation, there are three common deployment patterns, as explained in earlier chapters:

Single-node
> This is handy for learning Drill, developing plug-ins and user-defined functions (UDFs), and simple tasks. Data generally resides on your local disk.

HDFS-style cluster
> Drill runs on each data node to ensure that data is read from the local HDFS. This is called *data locality*.

Cloud-style cluster
> Drill runs on a set of, say, AWS instances, but the data itself resides in the cloud vendor's object store (such as Amazon S3). This is called *separation of compute and storage*.

Drill runs fine in all of these configurations. After you become familiar with Drill, you can also experiment with hybrid configurations (run on a subset of your HDFS nodes, say, or use a caching layer such as Alluxio (*https://www.alluxio.org/*) with cloud storage.) Because Drill makes minimal assumptions about storage, it will run fine in many configurations.

Prerequisites

Drill has only two prerequisites:

- Java 8
- ZooKeeper

Install the version of Java 8 appropriate for your operating system. Drill works with both the Oracle and OpenJDK versions. Install the JDK (development) package, not the JRE (runtime) package; Drill uses the Java compiler, which is available only in the JDK. Be sure to install Java on all your nodes.

Drill uses Apache ZooKeeper to coordinate the Drill cluster. Follow the standard ZooKeeper installation procedures to set up a ZooKeeper quorum (typically three or five nodes). See the ZooKeeper documentation (*https://zookeeper.apache.org/doc/r3.1.2/zookeeperStarted.html?*) for installation instructions.

Production Installation

In this section we describe one way to set up Drill on a production server, using a site directory to separate your configuration from Drill files to ease upgrades.

First, use `wget` to download Drill. To find a mirror, and the latest version, visit the Drill download page (*http://drill.apache.org/download/*) and click the "Find an Apache Mirror" button. Pass the resulting link into a `wget` command:

```
wget download link
```

Then, expand the archive:

```
tar xzf apache-drill-1.XX.0.tar.gz
```

Move the resulting directory to */opt/drill*:

```
mv apache-drill-1.XX.0 /opt/drill
```

Creating a Site Directory

By default, Drill expects its configuration files to appear in *$DRILL_HOME/conf* and its plug-ins to appear in *$DRILL_HOME/jars*. Many users, when first deploying Drill, continue to follow this model. Although convenient, the model becomes a nuisance when it is time to upgrade. You must copy your own files from the old distribution to the new one. This requires that you remember to save the old distribution before overwriting it with the new one. Then, you must remember which files you edited (or compare the file lists between the new and old distributions and sort out which are new in Drill and which are those that you added). Clearly, this is not a reliable way to maintain your system.

The alternative is to completely separate your own files from the Drill distribution files by using a *site directory*, which is simply a directory, located anywhere on your system outside the Drill directories, in which you place your configuration. In the following example, $DRILL_SITE points to the site directory:

```
$DRILL_SITE
|- drill-env.sh
|- drill-override.conf
|- logback.xml
|- jars/
   |- Your custom JARs (UDFs, plug-ins, etc.)
|- lib/
   |- Your custom native libraries (PAM modules, etc.)
```

Then, you simply instruct Drill to use your site directory instead of the default location:

```
drillbit.sh --site $DRILL_SITE start
```

If you set the $DRILL_SITE variable, Drill will use that location without you specifying the `--site` option.

When it is time to upgrade, replace the Drill distribution and restart Drill. There's no need to copy or merge files, and so on.

Let's put the site directory adjacent to *opt/drill*:

```
mkdir /opt/drill-site
```

Drill must have at least the *drill-override.conf* file. You can create this from the example provided in Drill:

```
cp /opt/drill/conf/drill-override.conf /opt/drill-site
cp /opt/drill/conf/drill-env.sh /opt/drill-site
cp /opt/drill/conf/logback.xml /opt/drill-site
```

Next, create a custom launch command by creating the file */opt/drill-site/drill.sh*:

```
#! /bin/bash
export DRILL_SITE=`basename "${BASH_SOURCE-$0}"`
export DRILL_HOME=/opt/drill
$DRILL_HOME/bin/drillbit.sh --site $DRILL_SITE $@
```

You'll use this to launch Drill instead of the usual `drillbit.sh` command so you can set the site directory. Finally, make the script executable:

```
chmod +x drill.sh
```

Configuring ZooKeeper

The next step is to configure Drill. We'll assume that you are using the production installation.

In the most basic Drill configuration, ZooKeeper is all you need to configure in */opt/drill-site/drill-override.conf*:

```
drill.exec: {
  cluster-id: "drillbits1",
  zk.connect: "zkHost1:2181;zkHost2:2181;zkHost3:2181"
}
```

In this example, zkHost1 is the name of your first ZooKeeper host, and so on. Replace these names with your actual host names. Port 2181 is the default ZooKeeper port; replace this with your custom port if you changed the port number.

Advanced ZooKeeper configuration

The `cluster-id` is used as part of the path to Drill's znodes. The default path is as follows:

```
drill/drillbits1
```

Normally, you just use the defaults. However, if you ever have the need to run two separate Drill clusters on the same set of nodes, you have two options:

- The Drill clusters share the same configuration (storage configurations, system options, etc.).

- The Drill clusters are completely independent.

To create clusters that share state, change just the `cluster-id`. To create distinct shared-nothing Drill clusters, change the `zk.root`; for example:

```
drill.exec: {
  cluster-id: "drillbits2",
  zk.root: "mySecondDrill",
  zk.connect: "zkHost1:2181;zkHost2:2181;zkHost3:2181"
}
```

Configuring Memory

Drill uses three types of memory:

- Heap
- Direct memory (off-heap)
- Code Cache

Drill is an in-memory query engine and benefits from ample direct memory. When your query contains an operation such as a sort or hash join, Drill must accumulate rows in memory to do the operation. The amount of memory depends on the total number of rows your query selects, the width of each row, and the number of Drill-bits you run in your cluster. The more rows, or the wider the row, the more memory is needed. Adding Drillbits spreads that memory need across multiple nodes.

For small, trial queries, the default memory is probably sufficient. But as you go into production, with large datasets, you must consider how much memory Drill needs to process your queries.

Memory tuning is a fine art. By default, Drill uses 8 GB of direct memory, 4 GB of heap, and 1 GB of code cache setting. You will likely not need to change the code cache. The other two memory settings depend entirely on your workload and the available memory on your nodes.

When running Drill in distributed mode (multiple Drillbits), each Drillbit must be configured with the same memory settings because Drill assumes that the Drillbits are symmetric.

Recent versions of Drill have added spill-to-disk capabilities for most operators so that if Drill encounters memory pressure, it will write temporary results to disk. Although this avoids out-of-memory errors, it does slow query performance consid-erably. (To gain maximum benefit, you will want to enable query queueing, as described in a moment.)

The best rule of thumb is to give Drill as much memory as you can. Ideally, Drill will run on a dedicated node. If you run on a cloud provider such as AWS, reading data from the cloud provider's storage (such as Amazon S3), the simplest solution is to run Drill on its own instance, with Drill using all available memory on that instance. As your queries grow larger and you need more memory, simply upgrade to a larger instance, adjusting the Drill memory settings accordingly.

If you run Drill on-premises on an HDFS cluster, you will want to run Drill colocated with your HDFS data nodes (more on this shortly). In this case, try to give Drill a large share of memory.

Next, run sample queries, especially those that include sorts and joins. Examine the query profiles to determine the amount of memory actually used. Then, determine the expected number of concurrent queries and adjust the direct memory accordingly.

Drill tends to need much less heap memory than direct, and the relationship between the two is not linear. You can adjust heap via trial and error (increase it if you hit Java out-of-memory errors), or you can use a Java monitoring tool to watch the heap. Frequent garbage collection events mean that Java has insufficient heap memory.

You set memory in the *drill-env.sh* file. The file starts with a large number of commented-out options along with descriptions. Suppose that you want to set direct memory to 20 GB and heap to 5 GB. Find the lines in the snippet that follows. First remove the leading comment characters, and then set the desired values:

```
export DRILL_HEAP=${DRILL_HEAP:-"5G"}
export DRILL_MAX_DIRECT_MEMORY=${DRILL_MAX_DIRECT_MEMORY:-"20G"}
```

The funny syntax allows you to override these values using environment variables. If the environment variables are already set, they are used, and if not your values are used. (This feature is used in the Drill-on-YARN integration, described later.)

Configuring Logging

Like most servers, Drill creates log files to inform you as to what is happening. Drill places logs in *$DRILL_HOME/log* by default. Although this is fine for experimenting with Drill, it is not good practice in production where logs can grow quite large. Let's put the logs in */var/log/drill*, instead. Edit *drill-env.sh* as described in the previous section:

```
export DRILL_LOG_DIR=${DRILL_LOG_DIR:-/var/log/drill}
```

Then create the log directory:

```
sudo mkdir /var/log/drill
```

Drill uses Logback for logging, which is configured by the *logback.xml* file. By default, Drill uses rotating log files with each file growing to 100 MB, and retaining up to 10 old log files. You can change this by editing the *logback.xml* file in your site directory.

Suppose that you want your files to be no more than 50 MB and you want to keep up to 20 files:

```
<appender name="FILE" class="ch.qos.logback.core.rolling.RollingFileAppender">
  <file>${log.path}</file>
  <rollingPolicy class="ch.qos.logback.core.rolling.FixedWindowRollingPolicy">
    <fileNamePattern>${log.path}.%i</fileNamePattern>
    <minIndex>1</minIndex>
    <maxIndex>20</maxIndex>
  </rollingPolicy>
  <triggeringPolicy
      class="ch.qos.logback.core.rolling.SizeBasedTriggeringPolicy">
    <maxFileSize>50MB</maxFileSize>
  </triggeringPolicy>
```

Drill sets the log level to info by default. This level is really needed only if you are trying to track down problems. Otherwise, you can reduce log output by setting the level to error, as shown here:

```
<logger name="org.apache.drill" additivity="false">
  <level value="error" />
  <appender-ref ref="FILE" />
</logger>
```

Testing the Installation

Drill should now be ready to run on your single node. Let's try it using the script created earlier:

```
/opt/drill/drill.sh start
```

Verify that the Drillbit started:

```
/opt/drill/drill.sh status
<node-name>: drillbit is running.
```

Verify that Drill has indeed started by pointing your browser to the following URL:

```
http://<node-ip>:8047
```

If the Drill Web Console appears, click the Query tab and run the suggested sample query:

```
SELECT * FROM cp.`employee.json` LIMIT 20
```

If the query works, congratulations! You have a working one-node Drill cluster. If the connection times out, Drill has failed. Double-check the preceding instructions and examine the log files, which should be in */var/log/drill*. Common mistakes include the following:

- Misconfiguring ZooKeeper
- ZooKeeper not running

- No Java installed

- Installing the Java JRE instead of the JDK

- Making a typo somewhere along the way

Stop Drill to prepare for the next step:

```
/opt/drill/drill.sh stop
```

Distributing Drill Binaries and Configuration

Every system administrator must choose a way to distribute software on a cluster. If you run Hadoop, you very likely already have a solution: one provided by your Hadoop vendor or one preferred by your shop.

If you are learning, a very simple solution is *clush* (*http://bit.ly/2SyaN58*) (CLUster SHell), which is easy to install on any Linux system. The big advantage of *clush* is that it makes no assumptions about your system and is completely standalone. Of course, that is its primary weakness as well, and why it is useful only in simple development or test environments. Still, we use it here to avoid depending on more advanced production tools such as Ambari, Puppet, Chef, or others.

Installing clush

On CentOS and the like, type the following:

```
yum --enablerepo=extras install epel-release
yum install clustershell
```

Check the *clush* documentation for installation instructions for other Linux flavors.

clush depends on passwordless Secure Shell (SSH) between nodes. Many online articles exist to explain how to do the setup.

clush provides shortcut syntax to reference your nodes if your nodes follow a simple numbering convention. For our examples, let's assume that we have three nodes: drill-1, drill-2, and drill-3. We further assume that we've done the setup thus far on drill-1 and so must push changes to drill-2 and drill-3.

Distributing Drill files

We created three directories in our installation that we must now re-create on each node: the Drill distribution, the site directory, and the log directory.

The log directory is created only once at install time (Drill will fail if the directory does not exist):

```
clush -w drill-[2-3] mkdir -p /var/log/drill
```

You must copy the Drill distribution only on first install, and then again when you upgrade to a new version:

```
clush -w drill-[2-3] --copy /opt/drill --dest /opt/drill
```

However, you must copy the site directory each time you make a configuration change:

```
clush -w drill-[2-3] --copy /opt/drill-site --dest /opt/drill-site
```

It is essential that all nodes see the same configuration; obscure errors will result otherwise. To help ensure consistency, you should make it a habit to change configuration only on a single node (drill-1 here) and to immediately push the configuration out to your other nodes.

Starting the Drill Cluster

You are now ready to start your full Drill cluster:

```
clush -w drill-[1-3] /opt/drill/drill.sh start
```

Next, verify that the Drillbits started:

```
clush -w drill-[1-3] /opt/drill/drill.sh status
```

You should see:

```
drill-1: drillbit is running.
drill-2: drillbit is running.
drill-3: drillbit is running.
```

Open the Drill web console as before, pointing to any of the nodes:

```
http://drill-1:8047
```

Now you should see all your nodes listed on the main web page.

Again run a test query. If it succeeds, congratulations; you have a working Drill cluster. The next step will be to configure access to your distributed filesystem.

If, however, you get error messages from *clush*, or you do not see all the nodes in the Drill web console, it is time to do a bit of debugging. Identify which nodes work and which failed. Look in the logs (in */var/log/drill*) on those nodes for errors. Common mistakes include the following:

- Wrong host name for ZooKeeper (use the internal name as known by your nodes, not the public name, or use IP addresses, but use the internal IP addresses in the cloud, such as on AWS)
- Forgetting to copy some of the files (particularly any changes to configuration files)
- Forgetting to install Java on all nodes

- Forgetting to create the */var/log/drill* directory on all nodes

If all else fails, post to the Drill user mailing list for help; signup information is available on the Drill website (*http://drill.apache.org/mailinglists/*).

Configuring Storage

Drill is a distributed query engine. As soon as you move past a single node, Drill requires a distributed filesystem to hold the data. On-premises, the standard solution is HDFS or an HDFS-compatible filesystem such as MapR (*http://mapr.com*), Alluxio (*http://www.alluxio.org*), and so on. In the cloud, Drill supports data stored in Amazon S3. Here, we discuss generic Apache Hadoop HDFS (*http://hadoop.apache.org*) and Amazon S3. If you are a MapR customer, the MapR installer will set up the MapR filesystem for you.

Working with Apache Hadoop HDFS

Drill can work with data stored in Hadoop HDFS as well as many other formats. Drill is designed to be independent of Hadoop, but you can integrate it with Hadoop when needed, such as to read data from HDFS.

There are two ways to do the integration: the simple way and with full integration.

Simple HDFS integration

If your HDFS configuration does not enable security and uses mostly default settings, you can probably access HDFS with the simple configuration described in Chapter 6:

1. Open the Drill web console.
2. Click the Storage tab.
3. Find the `dfs` storage configuration, and then click Update.
4. Add the HDFS URL to the `connection` field, as follows:

        "connection": "hdfs://name-node:port",

5. Click Update.

Because the configuration is stored in ZooKeeper, it is immediately available for Drill to use. Try a simple query to verify the setup.

Full HDFS integration

If you are familiar with HDFS, you know that you configure it using a set of configuration files within */etc/hadoop* or a similar location.

By default, however, Drill ignores these files. There is often an ambiguity in Hadoop configuration files: are options meant for the server or client? What if tool A needs one option, but Drill needs a different option? Drill works around this by storing Hadoop configuration in the storage configuration rather than getting it from Hadoop configuration. If you need extra configuration settings, you can provide them in the "config" property, as shown in the next section for Amazon S3.

In a secure system, however, configuration becomes complex quickly, and you do not want to duplicate settings between Drill and Hadoop. In this case, you can use tighter HDFS integration by adding Hadoop's configuration directory to the Drill class path. You do this by editing /opt/drill-site/drill-env.sh as follows:

```
EXTN_CLASSPATH=/etc/hadoop
```

Use the actual path to your Hadoop configuration files, which must exist on all nodes on which Drill runs.

If you're using MapR-FS, configuration is even simpler because it is done automatically by the MapR storage system driver.

Crash Error in Drill 1.13

In Drill 1.13, if you set the value of the fs.defaultFS property (the most important one!), Drill will fail to start. The workaround is to create a "hadoop" directory in your /opt/drill-site directory, copy the configurations there, remove fs.defaultFS, and use clush to push your updated configuration to all your nodes, as shown earlier. See DRILL-6520 (http://bit.ly/2SteoB9).

Must Duplicate the HDFS Name Node URL

Ideally, if given an HDFS configuration in the core-site.xml file, you would not need to specify the same information in Drill's storage plug-in configuration. But, Drill will fail to save your configuration if you omit the connection. So, you must duplicate the HDFS name node URL from your HDFS configuration into the plug-in configuration. See DRILL-6521 (http://bit.ly/2AxeL74).

Working with Amazon S3

Chapter 6 and the Drill documentation (http://drill.apache.org/docs/s3-storage-plugin/) provides a good overview of working with Amazon S3. Here is one way to set up Amazon S3 access on a distributed Drill cluster. We assume that you've created an Amazon S3 bucket and have obtained the required access keys. We also assume you are familiar with Amazon S3.

Drill uses the Hadoop HDFS s3a connector (*http://bit.ly/2x1YLb7*) for Amazon S3. As of Drill 1.13, Drill uses the 2.x version of HDFS. The s3a library in that version does not support Amazon's newer temporary access keys; you must use the regular access keys.

The example Amazon S3 storage configuration that ships with Drill suggests you put your keys in the storage plug-in configuration. However, the configuration is stored in ZooKeeper. Unless you have secured ZooKeeper, keys configured that way will be visible to prying eyes. Here, we'll store the keys in files in a way that depends on whether you've already configured Hadoop for Amazon S3.

Access keys with Hadoop

If you already use Hadoop, you have likely configured it to access Amazon S3 as described in the Hadoop documentation. You only need to point Drill at that configuration by adding a line to */opt/drill-site/drill-env.sh*:

```
export EXTN_CLASSPATH=/etc/hadoop
```

Standalone Drill

If Drill runs on a server with no other components, you can create just the one Hadoop configuration file: *core-site.xml*.

Create the *core-site.xml* file:

```
cp /opt/drill/conf/core-site-example.xml \
    /opt/drill-site/core-site.xml
```

Edit the file to include your keys and add your endpoint:

```
<configuration>
    <property>
        <name>fs.s3a.access.key</name>
        <value>ACCESS-KEY</value>
    </property>
    <property>
        <name>fs.s3a.secret.key</name>
        <value>SECRET-KEY</value>
    </property>
    <property>
        <name>fs.s3a.endpoint</name>
        <value>s3.REGION.amazonaws.com</value>
    </property>
</configuration>
```

In the preceding example, replace ACCESS-KEY, SECRET-KEY, and REGION with your values.

Distributing the configuration

Each time you change any of your configuration files, you must push the updates to all of your nodes using the same command we used earlier:

```
clush -w drill-[2-3] --copy /opt/drill-site --dest /opt/drill-site
```

If Drill was running, be sure to restart it using the `stop` and `start` commands. Or, use the handy `restart` command to do the restart in a single step:

```
clush -w drill-[1-3] /opt/drill/drill.sh restart
```

Defining the Amazon S3 storage configuration

After you've configured Drill to work with Amazon S3, you must create a storage configuration to bind a Drill namespace to your Amazon S3 bucket. If you have multiple buckets, you can create multiple storage configurations. This setup is a bit different than the one in Chapter 6 because we're using an external *core-site.xml* file.

1. Start Drill if it is not yet running.
2. Navigate to the web console.
3. Click the Storage tab.
4. In the Disabled Storage Plugins section, locate the `s3` configuration, and then click Update.
5. Remove the `config` section (if present), because you want to take the configuration from the *core-site.xml* file:

   ```
   "config": {},
   ```

6. Revise the `connection` to the proper format:

   ```
   "connection": "s3a://your-bucket/",
   ```

   Use your actual bucket name in place of *your-bucket*.
7. Click Update.
8. Click Enable.

The storage configuration is stored in ZooKeeper and so is immediately available to all your running Drillbits.

Troubleshooting

Try a sample query to verify that the configuration works. If so, you're good to go. Otherwise, here are some things to try:

- If you're using the Hadoop integration, be sure that the EXTN_CLASSPATH environment variable in *drill-env.sh* points to the Hadoop configuration directory: the one that contains *core-site.xml*.

- If you're using a Drill-specific file, be sure that the file is called *core-site.xml* and is in your site directory.

- Double-check the credentials and the endpoint.

- On the Storage tab in the Drill web console, verify that your s3 configuration is enabled.

- Be sure that you removed the default config section. If the key properties are left in the storage configuration, they will override the credentials in *core-site.xml*.

For hints about the problem, look at the Error tab in the query profile for the query that failed.

You can also look in the Drill logs: */var/drill/logs/drillbit.log*. (Looking in the Drill logs is generally a good practice anytime something goes awry.)

Admission Control

Drill is a shared, distributed query engine intended to run many queries concurrently. It can be quite difficult to understand how to size a query engine for your load or how much load a given configuration can support. Further, because queries differ in resource needs, it can be surprising why a given number of queries works fine sometimes but causes Drill to run out of memory at other times.

If you use Drill for "casual" usage, simply sizing memory as described earlier is often sufficient. But if you subject Drill to heavy load and occasionally hit out-of-memory issues, you might want to consider enabling Drill's admission control features.

At the time of this writing (Drill 1.13), admission control is good, but basic. Check back to see how the story might have evolved if you use a newer version. Here's how to turn on admission control:

```
ALTER SESSION SET `exec.queue.enable` = true
```

Perhaps the easiest way to set and review the options is to use the Options tab at the top of the Drill web console page.

Admission control uses two queues: one for "small" queries and another for "large" queries. The idea is that you might want to run a number of small interactive queries concurrently but allow only one large, slow query. The dividing line is a query cost number as computed by the Drill query planner and shown in the query profile. To set this number, sample a few of your smaller queries and a few larger queries. Because query plan numbers tend to grow exponentially, it is often not too difficult to pick a dividing line. Specify your selected number in the `exec.queue.threshold` property.

Then, determine how much bigger the larger queries are than the small ones by consulting your query profiles. You might find, say, that large queries generally want 5 or 10 times the memory of a small query. Use this to set `exec.queue.memory_ratio` to the ratio between query memory sizes.

Next, specify the maximum number of concurrent small queries using `exec.queue.small` and then do the same for large queries with `exec.queue.large`. This then lets you determine the amount of memory given to each query:

```
memory units = exec.queue.small +
               exec.queue.large * exec.queue.memory_ratio
```

Suppose that Drill is given M bytes of memory. Then, each small query gets:

```
small query memory = M / memory units
```

And each large query gets:

```
large query memory = M * exec.queue.memory_ratio / memory units
```

You can use these formulas to choose values for queue size if you know the available Drill memory and the desired memory for each query. Or, you can work out how much memory to give Drill in order to run some number of queries with a certain amount of memory each.

After you've enabled admission control, Drill automatically enforces the memory limits by limiting the data stored in memory by buffering operators such as sort, hash aggregate, and hash join. As of Drill 1.11, both the sort and hash aggregate operators will spill to disk to stay under the memory limit; Drill 1.14 adds support for the hash join operator.

If you hit a peak load where more queries arrive than the maximum you have set, Drill will automatically queue those queries to wait for one of the running queries to complete. Queries wait in the queue for up to `exec.queue.timeout_millis` milliseconds, after which they fail due to a timeout.

Admission control works best when the system is tuned to handle your peak workload over the timeout period, with the queue smoothing out spikes that exceed the limits by using otherwise spare capacity during valleys in activity.

See the Drill documentation (*http://drill.apache.org/docs/enabling-query-queuing/*) for additional details.

Additional Configuration

You have now completed the basis of configuring Drill. Depending on your needs, you may need to configure one or more optional features.

User-Defined Functions and Custom Plug-ins

Later chapters explain how to write user-defined functions and custom format plug-ins. To use these with a production Drill installation, the code (and sources, for UDFs) must be available on all Drill nodes. The Drill documentation suggests putting the files into the Drill product directory, but we've already explained that doing so is an awkward choice for a production cluster. The simplest solution is simply to copy your JAR files into the */opt/drill-site/jars* directory and then use *clush* to push the files to all nodes and restart Drill.

You can also use the Dynamic UDF (*http://drill.apache.org/docs/dynamic-udfs/*) feature to distribute new UDFs without restarting Drill. Even here, after your UDF is solid and ready to go into production, you should move it into the site directory to minimize runtime overhead.

Security

When using Drill for development and evaluation, it is easiest to run it as some specific user (such as your login user on a Mac) or as *root* (such as on AWS). As you go into production, you'll want to define a user specifically for Drill, such as *drill*, that is given only the permissions needed to do the work required.

When multiple users start using Drill, you must configure Drill to "impersonate" each user using various forms of authentication and impersonation.

Drill provides multiple ways to implement security in a secure cluster. Drill security is a complex, specialized, and evolving topic that very much depends on the type of system to which you want to integrate. For example, MapR security is different from Kerberos security, which differs from Pluggable Authentication Module (PAM) security. Drill provides multiple kinds of security, such as (but not limited to) the following:

- Kerberos
- Basic security using Linux users (PAM integration)
- Encryption for each of the communication paths
- User impersonation (the Drillbit can access distributed filesystem files as the session user instead of as the user running Drill)

- Restricting administration access (such as the ability to alter storage plug-in configurations)

We recommend that you consult the Drill documentation (*http://drill.apache.org/docs/securing-drill-introduction/*) and the user mailing list (*http://drill.apache.org/mailinglists/*) for up-to-date information.

Logging Levels

Drill uses Logback (*https://logback.qos.ch*) for logging, which you configure via the *logback.xml* file in your site directory. You copied over the *logback.xml* file when you created the site directory earlier.

Logging in Drill, as in most software, is used primarily to diagnose problems such as these:

- Startup failures
- Failed queries
- Unusually slow performance
- Data source errors

This was reworked directly in the files to merge this with the prior logging section:

```
<logger name="org.apache.drill" additivity="false">
  <level value="info" />
  <appender-ref ref="FILE" />
</logger>
```

As with all Java loggers, you can turn on detailed logging just for one part of Drill. However, it can be difficult to know which class or package name to use unless you are familiar with Drill internals. If you work with other Drill users to resolve an issue, they might be able to suggest a limited set of additional logging to enable.

Logging at the info level provides a wealth of detailed information about Drill internals added by Drill developers to help tune each bit of code. The information does require a deep knowledge of the code. If you want to better understand how Drill works, "info" logging, along with reading the code, will give you solid understanding of how operators work, the flow of record batches up the operator directed acyclic graph (DAG), and so on.

If you run Drill in production, it will produce a large volume of log messages. Drill uses Logback's rolling log feature to cap each log file at a certain size. The default size is 50 MB, as shown here:

```
<triggeringPolicy class="ch.qos.logback.core.rolling.SizeBasedTriggeringPolicy">
  <maxFileSize>50MB</maxFileSize>
</triggeringPolicy>
```

Each time the size limit is reached, Logback creates a new file. It also begins to delete old files when the number of those files exceeds a configured limit. The default maximum is 20 files, as demonstrated here:

```
<rollingPolicy class="ch.qos.logback.core.rolling.FixedWindowRollingPolicy">
  <fileNamePattern>${log.path}.%i</fileNamePattern>
  <minIndex>1</minIndex>
  <maxIndex>20</maxIndex>
</rollingPolicy>
```

Controlling CPU Usage

Drill is designed as a massively parallel query engine and aggressively consumes CPU resources to do its work. Drill converts your SQL query into an operator DAG that you see in the Drill web console. Operators are grouped into major fragments: each major fragment contains a string of operators up to a network exchange (shuffle).

 This section includes a discussion on fragments. For a more detailed look at how Drill creates and uses fragments, refer to Chapter 3.

Drill parallelizes each major fragment into a set of minor fragments, each of which runs as a thread on your Drillbits. Multiple minor fragments run on each node. In fact, the number of minor fragments per node defaults to 70% of the number of cores on your node, so if your node has 24 cores, Drill will create 16 minor fragments (threads) per node.

If you run multiple concurrent queries, each query is also parallelized. If you run 10 queries on your 24-core node, Drill will run 160 concurrent threads, or about 7 threads per core.

For most queries, each thread spends much of its time waiting for I/O (either from the data source or for network shuffles). Thus, running a thread number larger than the core count helps Drill achieve better parallelization across queries.

If, however, your queries tend to be compute-bound (as can occur with aggregations, joins, and so on), you might want to reduce the number of threads to avoid excessive context switches.

You can do so by adjusting a session option: `planner.cpu_load_average`. Adjusting this to, say, `0.25` means that Drill will create one minor fragment per major fragment for each four cores on the system.

As of Drill 1.13, there are few automated ways to limit the overall number of slices per query; thus, highly complex queries can, by themselves, create a large number of fragments, even if you limit the per-fragment parallelization factor.

Drill was originally designed to dominate the node on which it runs. Drill assumes that it will be given all of the memory on the node (so it can efficiently do in-memory processing) and that it is free to use all CPU resources on that node, hence, the aggressive CPU scheduling.

If you run Drill in the cloud, the simplest and most effective design is simply to choose an instance size that fits your workload and then run Drill as the only process on that instance.

There are times when you might want to limit the amount of CPU that Drill can use. This is especially useful if Drill is placed on the same node as your data storage and must share that node with other components, such as YARN.

Drill 1.14 added support to use Linux cgroups to limit the amount of CPU that Drill will consume. Because this is a new and evolving feature, you should check the Drill documentation (*http://bit.ly/2StBs34*) for details.

Note that cgroups does not limit the number of threads that Drill runs; it limits only the amount of CPU time that those threads can consume. If you put Drill under heavy load, limiting CPU will cause queries to run slower than without a limit and can lead to increased thread context switches. Monitor your system if you suspect that you are hitting these limitations. We discuss how to do this next.

Monitoring

Monitoring of Drill is divided into three distinct tasks:

- Monitoring the Drill process
- Monitoring Drill JMX metrics
- Monitoring queries

Monitoring the Drill Process

The two most important metrics for Drill are CPU and memory. CPU is the easiest to monitor: you can get an instantaneous view using the Linux top command or you can use your favorite Linux tools to get a time series view. You should expect to see Drill using a large percentage of CPU while queries are active (see the previous section for details), with usage dropping to near zero between queries. Enabling admission control will help to smooth out peaks by shifting some queries to run when Drill would otherwise be idle.

A related metric is the number of context switches. As the number of concurrent queries increases, the number of threads per Drillbit will increase. If context switches become excessive, you will want to limit parallelism or use admission control to throttle queries, both of which were described earlier.

The other key metric is memory. Here, it is important to understand how memory works in Drill and Java. As Drill runs, it will request more memory from the operating system, but it will never release it. You will see a chart that stair-steps upward. Some people interpret such a chart as a memory leak, but this is simply how Java manages memory. The memory is not leaked; it is simply held in Java's (heap) and Drill's (direct) memory free pools, waiting to be used by the next query. When memory allocated to Drill reaches the configured maximum, subsequent requests will be satisfied only by the free list.

One other metric of interest is I/O; however, this is much more difficult to measure and understand. If Drill runs on a MapR cluster, the MapR tools will tell you the performance of Drill's reads against the MapR filesystem. If your data is stored on Amazon S3, all reads are network reads and you must measure network performance, but you must tease apart traffic to the data hosts from other network traffic.

When Drill spills to disk, it uses local disk but only during spill reads and writes. You can see this activity by monitoring local I/O.

When Drill does an exchange (shuffle), it serializes potentially large amounts of data across the network between Drillbits.

Monitoring JMX Metrics

Process monitoring provides information about the Drill process in a generic way. To get more detail, you can use JMX monitoring via JConsole or a similar JMX tool. The standard metrics (CPU, threads, memory) are useful.

Drill publishes a number of metrics available as MBeans with the prefix `drill`. For example, `drill.fragments.running` will show you the number of fragments currently running, which is a good way to judge Drillbit load. See the documentation (*http://drill.apache.org/docs/monitoring-metrics/*) for details.

Monitoring Queries

The aforementioned tools allow you to monitor the Drill process as a whole. The tools indicate Drill's overall load level, but not why that load occurs. To understand the specifics of load, there is no better tool than the Drill query profiles, which are available in the web console. The profile provides a large amount of information, including:

- Runtimes, memory, and record counts for each operator

- The number of operators, major fragments (groups of operators), and minor fragments
- Operator-specific metrics such as the amount of data spilled to disk

If a query is slow, you can determine whether one of the following is the cause:

- Reading a large amount of data from disk
- An ineffective filter that accepts more rows than you intended
- Excessive data exchanges
- Insufficient file splits (which can occur when reading nonsplittable files such as JSON)
- Excessive disk spilling because the sort, hash aggregate, or hash join operators had too little memory to hold query data

Other Deployment Options

Thus far, this chapter has primarily discussed deploying Drill using the most basic of tools: clush. Experienced admins will use this information to automate the processes with their favorite tools such as Chef or Puppet. In this section, we discuss three other techniques.

MapR Installer

MapR, which developed Drill and contributed it to the Apache Software Foundation, includes Drill in its MapR Ecosystem Package (MEP) releases. If you are a MapR customer, the MapR installer is the easiest way to deploy Drill, but you still need to configure Drill as described earlier in this chapter. As of this writing, MapR does not, however, support the site directory concept; the various configuration files mentioned earlier must go into the Drill distribution directory, and you must manually copy those files across from your old to new installations each time you upgrade. (Check the MapR documentation to see if this changes in some future release.)

Drill-on-YARN

Drill 1.13 added the ability to deploy Drill on your cluster using YARN as a cluster manager. You launch a YARN application master (AM) using the tool provided and then interact with the AM to add or remove nodes. YARN takes care of copying the Drill software and configuration files from your master copy onto the target nodes.

With Drill-on-YARN, you can create multiple Drill clusters, which is sometimes helpful when different organizations want to separate their resources (or need different configurations). You simply give each Drill cluster a unique ZooKeeper "root," as described earlier, and then configure each cluster with distinct port numbers (*http:// drill.apache.org/docs/ports-used-by-drill/*). Clients will pick up this configuration from ZooKeeper.

See the Drill-on-YARN documentation (*http://drill.apache.org/docs/drill-on-yarn-introduction/*) for details.

Docker

Drill primarily runs on Hadoop clusters, which have traditionally used "bare-metal" or YARN deployment models. It can, however, sometimes be useful to deploy Drill on Docker, especially for testing and development, or on Amazon S3, where there is less need to run in the classic Hadoop formats.

Drill 1.14 provides a Dockerfile to build the Docker container for Drill running in embedded mode. Future releases promise to add support for running in server mode (a Drillbit) in a Docker container. Check the Drill website and the dev list for the latest information.

Conclusion

Drill is a very flexible tool: it works just as well on your laptop as in a large distributed Hadoop cluster. This section discussed many of the most common tasks involved in scaling Drill to run on a production cluster. The details will vary depending on whether you run on a MapR cluster, a classic Hadoop cluster, in AWS, or other variations. The way you perform the specific tasks will vary depending on whether you do the tasks manually (as described here) or take advantage of the MapR installer or your favorite administration tool.

This chapter could not hope to cover every issue that might arise, so we concentrated on the most common factors. The Drill user mailing list (*http://drill.apache.org/ mailinglists/*) is a great place to discuss advanced deployment needs and to learn how others have deployed Drill.

After you've mastered the deployment steps, you'll find that Drill makes a solid addition to your big data toolkit, complementing Hive and Spark and allowing your users to query big data using their favorite BI tools.

CHAPTER 10

Setting Up Your Development Environment

If you plan to develop code for Drill, you will need to set up a Java development environment. You will find it convenient to create two kinds of projects. The first is a clone of the Drill source code. Often you will need to reference Drill code to find how to accomplish a task.

The next two chapters describe how to create user-defined functions and format plug-ins. It is often easiest to debug your custom code as part of the Drill build so that you can get rapid edit-compile-debug cycles, create unit tests, and so on. Later, when your code is stable, you have the option to package the code into the second kind of project: an extension project separate from Drill.

Drill makes use of Maven for the build-and-test process. A detailed description of Maven operations is beyond the scope of this book, but we do cover how to install it for Drill development.

Installing Maven

To develop Drill extensions, you need JDK version 1.8 (as of Drill 1.13) installed on your computer. For information on how to install this, see Chapter 2. In addition to the JDK, you will also need to install Maven version 3.3.1 or greater. On Linux machines, you can easily install Maven using yum or apt-get, and on Macs, you can install it using brew.

On Windows, installation is a little more complex. You first must download Maven from the Apache Software Foundation page (*https://maven.apache.org/download.cgi*) and unzip it. After you've unzipped it, move the uncompressed file to *C:\Program Files\Apache\Maven*. Next, you need to add two environment variables to your environment: M2_HOME and MAVEN_HOME. These variables should be set to the folder in which you unzipped Maven (in our example, *C:\Program Files\Apache\Maven*).

Finally, you will also need to update the PATH variable to include the Maven binaries. To do this, add %M2_HOME%\bin to the PATH variable.

On either system, verify that you have successfully installed Maven by entering mvn --version at the command line. You should a result similar to this:

```
$ mvn --version
Apache Maven 3.5.0 (...
Maven home: /usr/local/Cellar/maven/3.5.0/libexec
Java version: 1.8.0_65, vendor: Oracle Corporation
Java home: /Library/Java/JavaVirtualMachines/jdk1.8.0_65.jdk/Contents/Home/jre
Default locale: en_US, platform encoding: UTF-8
OS name: "mac os x", version: "10.12.5", arch: "x86_64", family: "mac"
```

Developing for Drill is complex, and you will save yourself a lot of headaches by using a Java integrated development environment (IDE). Although IntelliJ is the most popular IDE for use with Drill, many developers successfully use Eclipse.

Creating the Drill Build Environment

For this project, you will need a clone of the Apache Drill project and a Java IDE.

Begin by cloning Apache Drill from the Apache GitHub repo (*https://github.com/apache/drill*) into your own private GitHub repository. This step is not strictly necessary (you can clone directly to your laptop), but it is convenient. Plus, you will need your own GitHub repository if you choose to offer your plug-in to Apache Drill in the form of a pull request.[1]

Setting Up Git and Getting the Source Code

First, if you have not done so already, fork the Apache Drill source code into your own GitHub repo by clicking the Fork button shown in Figure 10-1.

Figure 10-1. Forking the Drill repo

---

1 We are both committers to the Drill project, and we strongly encourage you to think about contributing to the project, as well.

When you have forked the repository, open a terminal, navigate to where you want to store your files, and clone your fork with the following command, replacing *user name* with your GitHub user account:

```
git clone https://github.com/username/drill
```

Building Drill from Source

At this point, you should have the source code downloaded on your machine. Navigate to that folder and enter the following Maven command to build Drill:

```
mvn clean install -DskipTests
```

After this command is complete, there will be a tarball in the *distribution/target* folder. Copy that to where you want Drill to reside and unzip it; you now have a working installation of Drill.

Don't Forget to Test Drill

After you have built Drill, make sure to start it and run a few queries to verify that everything is in fact working properly. You can also run the complete Drill unit tests (though this takes a while):

```
mvn clean install
```

Installing the IDE

The final step is installing the IDE. As indicated earlier, we strongly recommend that you use either IntelliJ or Eclipse to develop Drill. Installing either of these tools is straightforward and simply involves downloading the installer from the tool's website and running it. After you have done that, you can import the project by opening the *pom.xml* file in your Drill fork root directory.

Using the Drill Source Style Templates

If you intend to develop code to share with the Drill community, you should download the Drill IDE formatters, which will format your code according to the Drill community standards:

- Eclipse (*http://bit.ly/2O6zwdW*)
- IntelliJ (*http://bit.ly/2x2Kvyy*)

Eclipse is able to compile Java code, but it is not able to do other tasks in Maven, such as code generation. A good practice after each update from Git is to rebuild Drill using Maven (mvn `clean install -DskipTests`) and then refresh all files in Eclipse by selecting Refresh from the context for the `drill-root` project in the Package Explorer view.

Also, in Eclipse, it is convenient to group all Drill projects into a Drill working set using the File → New → Java Working Set command.

Finally, we encourage you to review the Drill developer guidelines (*http://bit.ly/2O5NqNE*) to become familiar with developer resources.

Conclusion

With your development environment set up, you are now ready to develop extensions for Drill.

CHAPTER 11

Writing Drill User-Defined Functions

In the previous chapters, you learned about Drill's powerful analytic capabilities. There are many situations in which you might want to perform a transformation on some data and Drill simply does not have the capability readily at hand. However, it is quite possible to extend Drill's capabilities by writing your own user-defined functions (UDFs).

Drill supports two different types of UDFs: simple and aggregate. A *simple UDF* accepts a column or expression as input and returns a single result. The result can be a complex type such as an array or map. An *aggregate UDF* is different in that it accepts as input all the values for a group as defined in a GROUP BY or similar clause and returns a single result. The SUM( ) function is a good example: it accepts a column or expression, adds up all the values, and returns a single result. You can use an aggregate UDF in conjunction with the GROUP BY statement as well, and it will perform aggregate operations on a section of the data.

Use Case: Finding and Filtering Valid Credit Card Numbers

Suppose you are conducting security research and you find a large list of what appear to be credit card numbers. You want to determine whether these are valid credit card numbers and, if so, notify the appropriate banks.

A credit card number is not simply a random sequence of digits. Indeed, these numbers are quite specific and can be validated by an algorithm known as the *Luhn algorithm* (*https://en.wikipedia.org/wiki/Luhn_algorithm*). Although Drill does not have the Luhn algorithm built in, if you are analyzing log files that contain credit card numbers this would be very useful to have, and you can write a UDF to filter the data so that you could quickly determine whether the numbers are valid or not.

Additionally, you can extract several other pieces of metadata from a credit card number, including the issuing bank and what kind of credit card it is (e.g., Master-Card or Visa). Using Drill, you can quickly write some UDFs to extract these pieces of metadata from the numbers. The query might look something like this:

```
SELECT `card_number`,
    issuing_bank_code(`card_number`) AS issuing_bank_code,
    card_type(`card_number`) AS card_type
FROM <data>
WHERE is_valid_credit_card(`card_number`)
```

Table 11-1 presents the results.

Table 11-1. Query results with UDF

card_number	issuing_bank_code	card_type
4xxxxxxxxxxxxx	012345	Visa
5xxxxxxxxxxxxx	234567	MasterCard

When you have this data, you can write more advanced queries to aggregate and summarize the data, such as the following:

```
SELECT card_type(`card_number`) AS card_type,
    COUNT(*) AS card_count
FROM <data>
WHERE is_valid_credit_card(`card_number`)
GROUP BY card_type(`card_number`)
ORDER BY card_count DESC
```

This query counts the number of valid credit cards of each type. It will return something similar to that shown in Table 11-2.

Table 11-2. Counts of valid credit cards by type

card_type	card_count
MasterCard	315
Visa	212
Discover	200
American Express	

However, to perform this kind of analysis, you must write a few UDFs.

How User-Defined Functions Work in Drill

Nearly all modern programming languages employ the concept of a *function*—a section of code that takes input, performs some operation on it, and returns a value, as demonstrated here:

```
function addTwo(n) {
    result = n + 2
    return n
}

//Call the function
x = addTwo(4)
print(x)

>> 6
```

This pseudocode is an example of a simple function that takes a number as input, adds two to it, and then returns the result. The biggest conceptual difference between a regular function and *a Drill UDF is that a Drill UDF is always executed against a column of data instead of a single value.*[1] Additionally, the code for Drill UDFs is generated inline in Drill's own generated code.

Structure of a Simple Drill UDF

Drill UDFs are implemented in Java, and if you are not a Java developer, some aspects of writing a Drill UDF can seem a little complex—once you get past the boiler-plate code, you will find it is not much more difficult than writing a function in any language.

Let's take a look at the structure of a Drill UDF. In this section, we'll walk through the process of creating a few simple UDFs.

In the GitHub repository for this book you will find a folder called *udf_templates/simple*, which contains all the files you will need to create your own simple Drill UDF. Our first UDF will validate credit card numbers using the Luhn algorithm described earlier.

The pom.xml File

In the root directory of *udf_templates/simple* you will find *pom.xml*, which contains instructions that Maven uses to build the UDF. There is a section at the top of the *pom.xml* file that looks like this:

```
<groupId>org.apache.drill.contrib.function</groupId>
<artifactId>udf_template</artifactId>
<version>1.0</version>
<name>Drill Function Template</name>
```

---

1 OK, this isn't technically true. Drill functions are executed against one value at a time, but from a high level, it is helpful to think of a Drill UDF as operating against a column of data.

You can change the name of the project and the version here, although it does not affect the functionality of the function.

Don't Forget the Source JAR!

Though typically not needed in other projects, for Drill UDFs, Maven *must* be configured to produce a source JAR file as well as the executable. To accomplish this, you must include the following in your *pom.xml* file:

```
<build>
  <plugins>
    <plugin>
      <groupId>org.apache.maven.plugins</groupId>
      <artifactId>maven-source-plugin</artifactId>
      <version>2.4</version>
      <executions>
        <execution>
          <id>attach-sources</id>
          <phase>package</phase>
          <goals>
            <goal>jar-no-fork</goal>
          </goals>
        </execution>
      </executions>
    </plugin>
    <plugin>
      <artifactId>maven-compiler-plugin</artifactId>
      <version>3.0</version>
      <configuration>
        <verbose>true</verbose>
        <compilerVersion>1.7</compilerVersion>
        <source>1.7</source>
        <target>1.7</target>
      </configuration>
    </plugin>
  </plugins>
</build>
```

Including dependencies

When you start building Drill UDFs, you will find that it can be very useful to include other libraries from Maven Central. In this example, there is a pre-existing library in Apache Commons (`commons-validator`) that performs all kinds of credit card validations, including the Luhn algorithm. To use this library in your Drill UDF, you need to add the dependency to the *pom.xml* file. Make sure that the version of Drill in the *pom.xml* file matches the version of Drill that you are using:

```
<dependencies>
  <dependency>
    <groupId>org.apache.drill.exec</groupId>
```

```
      <artifactId>drill-java-exec</artifactId>
      <version>1.14.0</version>
      <scope>provided</scope>
    </dependency>
    <dependency>
      <groupId>commons-validator</groupId>
      <artifactId>commons-validator</artifactId>
      <version>1.6</version>
      <scope>provided</scope>
    </dependency>
  </dependencies>
</dependencies>
```

The Function File

The actual functionality of the UDF is implemented in a file called *UDFTemplate.java*, which you can find in */src/main/org/apache/drill/contrib/function*. This file contains a template for a simple UDF with a lot of the boilerplate code, but it is important to understand that Drill doesn't directly execute this code. This code is a template that Drill uses to implement the method directly in Drill's generated code—that's why Drill also needs your function's source code.

The first part of the UDF is the function template, which looks like the following snippet:

```
@FunctionTemplate(
    name = "is_valid_credit_card",  //Your function name here
    scope = FunctionTemplate.FunctionScope.SIMPLE,
    nulls = FunctionTemplate.NullHandling.NULL_IF_NULL
)
public static class ValidCreditCardFunction implements DrillSimpleFunc {

    @Param
    VarCharHolder creditCardNumber;

    @Output
    BitHolder isValid;

    @Override
    public void setup() {
    }

    @Override
    public void eval() {
        //Your function logic here
    }
}
```

In the class that implements `DrillSimpleFunc`, there are three elements in your function template annotation that must be set for your UDF to work properly. The first, name, is the name that will be used to call your function in a Drill query. Drill function names may not be Drill reserved words, nor may they start with a digit. If you have multiple versions of the same function that accept different inputs, you may use the same name for multiple functions. For instance, suppose that you have a Drill function that converts pounds to kilograms. You might want one version of your function to accept an INT as an input and another to accept a FLOAT, and so on. (One note about data types: in Drill, JSON always generates BIGINT and DOUBLE types, so UDFs that work with numbers should at least provide these data types.)

If you would like to define aliases for your function, you can also do this as shown here:

```
names = {"name_1", "name_2"}
```

The scope variable specifies to Drill whether the function is a simple or aggregate function. For this example, this needs to be set to SIMPLE.

The nulls variable defines how the function will deal with null values. Setting this to NULL_IF_NULL configures Drill to skip null rows, instead of having to handle them in the function body. In this case, query results will contain NULL for null rows.

After you've defined these variables, the next step is to actually begin writing the function body.

Defining input parameters

In most programming languages, the input parameters for a function are defined in the function declaration. For instance, in Java, you would define the input parameters to a function as follows:

```
public int foo(int x, int y)
```

In this example, both the input parameters—x and y—as well as their data types are defined in the function definition.

Due to Drill's UDF templating system, Drill requires you to use holder objects to define input parameters. Table 11-3 lists some common Holders.

Table 11-3. Drill holders and corresponding Java data types

Data type	Drill holder object
INT	IntHolder
FLOAT	Float4Holder
DECIMAL9	Decimal9Holder
DOUBLE	Float8Holder
BIGINT	BigIntHolder
VARCHAR	VarCharHolder
DATE	DateHolder

Data type	Drill holder object
BOOLEAN	BitHolder
TIMESTAMP	TimeStampHolder
VARBINARY	VarBinaryHolder
TIME	TimeHolder

For every input parameter you would like your function to accept, you must define a `@Param` with the appropriate holder object in the order that they will appear when you call the function, as shown in the code snippet that follows. Drill defines both nullable and non-nullable holders. The preceding list shows the non-nullable holders. Use this if you have Drill do NULL handling:

```
nulls = FunctionTemplate.NullHandling.NULL_IF_NULL
```

If your function handles nulls, use the Nullable holder, which is the same name but with "Nullable" prepended (for example, `NullableIntHolder`).

```
@Param
VarCharHolder rawCardNumber;
```

In this example, the function would accept a single VARCHAR as an input parameter. This example has only one parameter, but if you wanted to have multiple parameters, you could just define them as follows:

```
@Param
VarCharHolder inputTextA;

@Param
IntHolder integer_parameter;

@Param
Float8Holder float_parameter;
```

Setting the output value

After you've defined the input parameters, you also must define the output value. In a conventional Java function, the return value is specified in the function body with the `return` keyword and the data type is defined in the function declaration. For instance, if you wanted to define a function that returned an integer, the function might look something like this:

```
public int foo(int x) {
    int result;
    // Do something
    return result;
}
```

In this example, the function accepts an integer as input and returns an integer as output. In a Drill UDF, you do not have a `return` statement; rather, you define a member variable, annotated with @OUTPUT, defined as a holder object of the appropriate data type. For example:

```
@Output
BitHolder isValid;
```

Accessing data in holder objects

Before you actually write the function, you need to know how to access the data that is contained in the holder objects, both for reading and writing. Numeric holder objects are the easiest; they have a property called value. To read or set the value of a numeric holder object, simply access or set the value property, as shown in this snippet:

```
//Read integer holder
int myInt = intParam1.value;

//Set integer output
outputInteger.value = myInt;
```

VARCHAR and complex types (MAP, arrays) are more complicated to access and write. Drill provides a helper function to access the contents of a VarCharHolder object. The following code snippet demonstrates how to access text contained in a VarChar Holder named rawCardNumber:

```
String creditCardNumber = org.apache.drill.exec.expr.fn.impl.
    StringFunctionHelpers.toStringFromUTF8(rawCardNumber.start,
    rawCardNumber.end, rawCardNumber.buffer);
```

Drill Requires Absolute Class References in UDFs

As shown in the previous example, if you reference any class other than those in java.lang, or java.util, Drill requires you to include an absolute reference to the class. When Drill copies your UDF code into Drill's own generated code, it does not copy imports. For the code to compile in Drill's generated code, you must instead use fully qualified class references.

Writing to a VarCharHolder for output is more complex as well, and requires you to convert the String you are placing in the holder into a byte array. You then need to assign a buffer to the VarCharHolder, define the start and end points for the String, and, finally set the bytes in the buffer. The following snippet demonstrates how to assign a string named outputValue to the output VarCharHolder called output:

```
byte outBytes[] = outputValue.getBytes(com.google.common.base.Charsets.UTF_8);
outputBuf = outputBuf.reallocIfNeeded(outBytes.length);
outputBuf.setBytes(0, outBytes);
output.buffer = outputBuf;
```

```
output.start = 0;
output.end = outBytes.length;
```

This code demonstrates how to write a string as a UDF output. The first line converts the `String outputValue` into a byte array called `outBytes`. Next, we reallocate the buffer for the output `VarCharHolder` by calling the `reallocIfNeeded()` method. In the next line we call the `setBytes()` method, which writes the byte array to the output buffer. Finally, we set the start and stop positions in the output buffer.

The Simple Function API

Now that you have defined your input parameters, the next step is to implement the `DrillSimpleFunc` interface, which consists of two void functions: `setup()` and `eval()`. In some instances, you might have variables or objects that you want to initialize at the beginning of the function's execution and reuse in every function call. If that is the case, you can initialize these variables in the `setup()` function. If you do not have any variables like this, you can simply leave the `setup()` function blank, but you must include it because it is part of the `DrillSimpleFunc` interface.

The `eval()` function is where you actually implement the function's logic and where you assign a value to the holder for your output. The `eval()` function itself is a void function, meaning that it does not return anything.

The pseudocode for our example function might look something like this:

```
function is_valid_credit_card (credit_card_number) {
    return luhn(credit_card_number);
}
```

Putting It All Together

To put this all together, the following code demonstrates how to convert the simple function into a Drill UDF:

```
@FunctionTemplate(
  name = "is_valid_credit_card",
  scope = FunctionTemplate.FunctionScope.SIMPLE,
  nulls = FunctionTemplate.NullHandling.NULL_IF_NULL)

public class IsValidCreditCardFunction implements DrillSimpleFunc {

  @Param
  VarCharHolder rawCardNumber;

  @Workspace
  org.apache.commons.validator.routines.CreditCardValidator ccv;

  @Output
  BitHolder out;
```

```
public void setup() {
    org.apache.commons.validator.routines.CreditCardValidator ccv =
        new org.apache.commons.validator.routines.CreditCardValidator();
}

public void eval() {
    String creditCardNumber = org.apache.drill.exec.expr.fn.impl
        .StringFunctionHelpers
        .toStringFromUTF8(rawCardNumber.start,
                          rawCardNumber.end,
                          rawCardNumber.buffer);
    if (ccv.isValid(creditCardNumber)) {
        out.value = 1;
    } else {
        out.value = 0;
    }
}
}
```

Use the Workspace for Variables Carried Over Between Iterations

In the preceding example, the variable ccv is the validator object
that is used in every function iteration. To maximize performance,
the UDF stores the validator object in the @Workspace and initializes it in the setup() function.

The previous UDF uses a BitHolder as the output value, where 1 is true and 0 is
false. This UDF also has a dependency on the Apache commons-validator package,
which you need to include in the dependencies section of the *pom.xml* file, as shown
in the following snippet:

```
<dependencies>
  <dependency>
    <groupId>org.apache.drill.exec</groupId>
    <artifactId>drill-java-exec</artifactId>
    <version>1.13.0</version>
  </dependency>
  <dependency>
    <groupId>commons-validator</groupId>
    <artifactId>commons-validator</artifactId>
    <version>1.6</version>
  </dependency>
</dependencies>
```

There is one additional file that you will need in order for Drill to recognize your
UDF. In your function package, in the */src/main/resources* folder, you will need to create a file called *drill-module.conf*, which contains the following:

```
drill.classpath.scanning.packages += "org.apache.drill.contrib.function"
```

You might need to adjust the package name to reflect your UDF.

Building and Installing Your UDF

After you have implemented your Drill UDF, the next step is to build and install it. Open a command-line prompt and navigate to the root folder of your UDF. You can then build your UDF with Maven by entering `mvn clean package -DskipTests`. If all goes according to plan, Maven will generate a JAR file of your UDF in the *target/* folder of the UDF as well as the JAR file containing the source code.

You can either install the UDF *statically* or *dynamically*. Regardless of which approach you take, there are three components that you need in order to install the UDF:

- The JAR file for the UDF. You can find this in the *target/* folder after you build the UDF.

- The JAR file containing the source code of the UDF. Again, you can find this in the *target/* folder after you build the UDF.

- The JAR files for any dependencies your UDF has. You can download these from Maven Central or configure Maven via your *pom.xml* file to copy them into the *target/* folder.

Statically Installing a UDF

Let's look at static installation first. If you are using Drill in embedded mode in a non-shared environment, simply copy the aforementioned files into your Drill installation in the *$DRILL_HOME/jars/3rdparty/* folder. If you are using Drill in a cluster, copy the JAR files into the *jars* folder in your site directory.[2]

Dynamically Installing a UDF

As of Drill version 1.9, you can also register and unregister UDFs dynamically without having to restart Drillbits. To do this, you need to first configure a few directories. Because these directories must be visible to all Drillbits, they must be in a distributed filesystem such as HDFS:

Staging directory
    This is where you will copy the JAR files before they are registered.

---

2 See Chapter 9 for instructions on setting up and using the site directory.

Local directory
> This is a temporary directory for dynamic UDF JAR files. This directory is cleaned out when Drill is closed.

Registry directory
> This is where the JAR files are copied after they are registered.

tmp directory
> This contains the backup JAR files.

You can set the locations of all these directories in *$DRILL_HOME/conf/drill-override.conf*, however usually you just set the base and let Drill define the UDF directories as subdirectories under the base directory.

```
drill.exec.udf: {
   retry-attempts: 5,
   directory: {
      # Override this property if custom file system should be used to create
      # remote directories
      # instead of default taken from Hadoop configuration
      fs: "hdfs:///",
      # Set this property if custom absolute root should be used for remote
      # directories
      root: "/app/drill"

   }
}
```

After configuring the filesystem and base directory, you are ready to dynamically register a UDF. First copy the JAR files to the staging directory. After that, you can register the UDF by running the following command:

```
CREATE FUNCTION USING JAR 'jar_file';
```

If you want to unregister a UDF, you can do so with the following command:

```
DROP FUNCTION USING JAR 'jar_file';
```

After you have installed your UDF, you can use it in queries just as you would any other Drill built-in function.

Complex Functions: UDFs That Return Maps or Arrays

As you have seen in previous chapters, Drill supports two complex data types: arary and MAP. These are analogous to arrays and key–value pairs in other languages and enable Drill to analyze and query complex, nested data. It can be useful to write Drill UDFs that return these complex data types.

Example: Extracting User Agent Metadata

Often, you will encounter data artifacts from which you can extract many different pieces of metadata. For instance, user agent strings are strings of text that are sent to a web server when a user requests a web page. These strings are very useful for web servers because they can determine what version of a website a user receives. They're also useful for analyzing the type of traffic that is hitting a website. Although user agent strings are extremely useful, they are difficult to parse, and it is not really possible to simply split them by some delimiter. The example user agent string that follows illustrates why this is the case:

```
Mozilla/5.0 (Windows NT 5.1; rv:35.0) Gecko/20100101 Firefox/35.0
```

From this user agent string, it is possible to extract the following metadata:

```
{
"DeviceClass":"Desktop",
"DeviceName":"Desktop",
"DeviceBrand":"Unknown",
"DeviceCpuBits":"32",
"OperatingSystemClass":"Desktop",
"OperatingSystemName":"Windows NT",
"OperatingSystemVersion":"Windows XP",
"OperatingSystemNameVersion":"Windows XP",
"LayoutEngineClass":"Browser",
"LayoutEngineName":"Gecko",
"LayoutEngineVersion":"35.0",
"LayoutEngineVersionMajor":"35",
"LayoutEngineNameVersion":"Gecko 35.0",
"LayoutEngineNameVersionMajor":"Gecko 35",
"LayoutEngineBuild":"20100101",
"AgentClass":"Browser",
"AgentName":"Firefox",
"AgentVersion":"35.0",
"AgentVersionMajor":"35",
"AgentNameVersion":"Firefox 35.0",
"AgentNameVersionMajor":"Firefox 35"
}
```

Instead of writing a function to extract each piece of metadata individually, you might find it convenient to write a function that extracts all this metadata all at once and returns a map of these fields, and then extract the individual fields of interest. But to do that, you need to write a UDF that returns a map of all the fields.

The ComplexWriter

The ComplexWriter object enables you to write maps and arrays and return them as output from your Drill UDF. The first step in writing a UDF that returns a complex result is setting the ComplexWriter as the output parameter, as shown in the snippet that follows:

```
@Output
BaseWriter.ComplexWriter out Writer;
```

Fundamentally, functions that return complex results are no different from the simple UDFs that you have already written, with the exception of the output parameter. In the example here, we are setting the output parameter of the UDF to be a Complex Writer called outWriter. The next step is to access either a MapWriter or ListWriter object—depending on whether you want to create a map or an array—from the Com plexWriter object by calling the rootAsMap() or rootAsList() function:

```
public void eval() {
  MapWriter queryMapWriter = outWriter.rootAsMap();
  ...
}
```

In regular Drill UDFs, the output is contained in holder variables. In a UDF that returns a complex data type, the MapWriter created in the previous snippet[3] will contain holder objects for the various fields that will populate the result. You can create a holder separately or you can use the various writer functions to indirectly create a field, as shown in the following snippets:

```
//Write a floating-point field
queryMapWriter.float4("field_name")
            .writeFloat8(floating_point_value);
queryMapWriter.float8("field_name")
            .writeFloat8(floating_point_value);

//Write an integer field
queryMapWriter.bigInt("field_name").writeInt(int_value);
queryMapWriter.integer("field_name").writeInt(int_value);

//Write a date field
queryMapWriter.date("field_name").writeDate(long_date);
```

Adding a string to a map is a little more complicated, but the essential process is the same. It is a little clearer if you create the holder object outside of the MapWriter object and then pass the MapWriter object the holder. This code snippet demonstrates how to write a string to a MAP:

```
VarCharHolder rowHolder = new VarCharHolder();
String field = <text>;

byte[] rowStringBytes = field.getBytes(com.google.common.base.Charsets.UTF_8)
outBuffer.reallocIfNeeded(rowStringBytes.length);
outBuffer.setBytes(0, rowStringBytes);
```

---

3 For spacing, the snippet omits the full package name; however, when writing UDFs you must include the full package names (in this case, org.apache.drill.exec.vector.complex.writer.BaseWriter.MapWriter).

```
    rowHolder.start = 0;
    rowHolder.end = rowStringBytes.length;
    rowHolder.buffer = outBuffer;

    queryMapWriter.varChar(field_name).write(rowHolder);
```

Here is the complete code for the function to parse user agent strings:

```
public void eval() {

  org.apache.drill.exec.vector.complex.writer.BaseWriter.MapWriter
      queryMapWriter = outWriter.rootAsMap();
  String userAgentString =
   org.apache.drill.exec.expr.fn.impl
   .StringFunctionHelpers
   .toStringFromUTF8(input.start, input.end, input.buffer);

  if (userAgentString.isEmpty() || userAgentString.equals("null")) {
    userAgentString = "";
  }

  nl.basjes.parse.useragent.UserAgent agent = uaa.parse(userAgentString);

  for (String fieldName : agent.getAvailableFieldNamesSorted()) {

   org.apache.drill.exec.expr.holders.VarCharHolder rowHolder =
      new org.apache.drill.exec.expr.holders.VarCharHolder();
   String field = agent.getValue(fieldName);

   byte[] rowStringBytes = field.getBytes(com.google.common.base.Charsets.UTF_8);
   outBuffer.reallocIfNeeded(rowStringBytes.length);
   outBuffer.setBytes(0, rowStringBytes);

   rowHolder.start = 0;
   rowHolder.end = rowStringBytes.length;
   rowHolder.buffer = outBuffer;

   queryMapWriter.varChar(fieldName).write(rowHolder);
  }
}
```

Writing Aggregate User-Defined Functions

Now that you have written a simple UDF, you will find that writing an aggregate UDF
is not much more difficult; however, before you begin to write one, you should
understand that there are several significant limitations for custom aggregate functions:

- Drill aggregate functions cannot have complex variables in the @Workspace.

- You cannot use any kind of variable-length or complex variable in the `@Output` or `@Workspace`.

- All `@Workspace` variables must be contained in holders.

These are significant limitations and effectively restrict aggregate functions to numeric calculations. If you want to use any kind of nonnumeric holder in the `@Work space`, you can use the `ObjectHolder`; however, this is a bit of a hack in that at the time of writing, the `ObjectHolder` class has been deprecated. If your UDF uses the `ObjectHolder`, it will still work, but your queries will fail if your datasets are large enough that Drill's hash aggregate operator must spill to disk. One workaround is to disable the hash aggregate operator using the following query:[4]

```
ALTER SESSION SET `planner.enable_hashagg` = false
```

Much like simple Drill functions, aggregate functions perform operations on collections of data; however, instead of returning a single result for every input, aggregate functions iterate through all the data but return only a single result. You can use aggregate functions with the `GROUP BY` clause to segment the data into smaller segments.

The function declaration is slightly different from a simple Drill function in that the scope must be set to `POINT_AGGREGATE`. Additionally, aggregate functions *must* handle null values internally and therefore the `nulls` variable must be set to `FunctionTemplate.NullHandling.INTERNAL`. Following is the complete function template:

```
@FunctionTemplate(
    name = "kendall_correlation",
    scope = FunctionTemplate.FunctionScope.POINT_AGGREGATE,
    nulls = FunctionTemplate.NullHandling.INTERNAL
)
```

The Aggregate Function API

Writing an aggregate function is not significantly different than a simple Drill UDF; however, there are four additional functions that you must implement:

setup()
:   This function is executed once when the function is first called and is where you initialize any variables that will be used throughout the function iterations.

---

[4] For more information, check out the GitHub page (*https://github.com/paul-rogers/drill/wiki/Aggregate-UDFs*).

```
add()
```
This function processes every record and is roughly equivalent to the `eval()` function in a simple Drill UDF. This is where the actual logic of the function will be implemented.

```
output()
```
This function is where the final output will be calculated and output. This is executed at the end of every segment of data that the function encounters.

```
reset()
```
This function is similar to the `setup()` function and is called at the beginning of each new section of data or when a column changes from one data type to another. You should reset your counters or totals in this method.

Example Aggregate UDF: Kendall's Rank Correlation Coefficient

To demonstrate an aggregate UDF, let's write a UDF that implements the *Kendall's rank correlation coefficient*, otherwise known as *Kendall's tau*. Kendall's tau (*https://en.wikipedia.org/wiki/Kendall_rank_correlation_coefficient*) is a measurement of correlation between two vectors that ranges from 1, which indicates perfect correlation, to –1, which indicates perfect negative correlation.

Kendall's tau is calculated by comparing pairs of numbers in the two vectors; if both pairs of numbers share the same Boolean relationship, they are considered a *concordant pair*, and if not, they are a *discordant pair*:

$$\tau = \frac{(number\ of\ concordant\ pairs)\ -\ (number\ of\ discordant\ pairs)}{n(n-1)/2}$$

To implement this as a Drill function, you need to first initialize a counter of concordant and discordant pairs as well as a counter of the number of items. You initialize these variables in the `reset()` function. The `add()` function will compare the rows, make the determination as to whether the pair is concordant or discordant, and increment the appropriate counter as well as the row counter. Finally, the `output()` function will perform the calculation and output the result.

The code snippet that follows demonstrates how to write an aggregate UDF in Drill:

```
@Param
Float8Holder xInput;

@Param
Float8Holder yInput;

@Workspace
Float8Holder prevXValue;
```

```
@Workspace
Float8Holder prevYValue;

@Workspace
IntHolder concordantPairs;

@Workspace
IntHolder discordantPairs;

@Workspace
IntHolder n;

@Output
Float8Holder tau;
```

In the first part of this UDF, we define the input parameters, the workspace variables, and the output variable. This function needs two input variables, xInput and yInput, which are both floating-point numbers. For these, the UDF uses Float8Holders. Next, the UDF defines several @Workspace variables. The prevXValue and prevY Value variables hold the values from the previous iteration, and the concordantPairs and discordantPairs holders contain the running totals of pairs. Finally, n contains the number of pairs in the grouping. Notice that the pair holders and n are integers and the others are all double holders. The last parameter is the output parameter tau, which also uses a Float8Holder.

Now that the inputs and outputs are all defined, as well as several workspace variables, the next steps are to implement the four functions of the aggregate function API. The first function is the add() function, which performs the bulk of the calculations. This function is called on every row, and for each row, it compares the current pair with the previous pair that it saw and increments the appropriate counter based on whether the pair is concordant or discordant:

```
@Override
public void add() {
  double xValue = xInput.value;
  double yValue = yInput.value;

  if (n.value > 0) {
    if ((xValue > prevXValue.value
        && yValue > prevYValue.value)
      || (xValue < prevXValue.value
        && yValue < prevYValue.value)) {
      concordantPairs.value = concordantPairs.value + 1;
      prevXValue.value = xInput.value;
      prevYValue.value = yInput.value;
      n.value = n.value + 1;
    } else if ((xValue > prevXValue.value
              && yValue < prevYValue.value)
              || (xValue < prevXValue.value
```

```
                && yValue > prevYValue.value)) {
        discordantPairs.value = discordantPairs.value + 1;
        prevXValue.value = xInput.value;
        prevYValue.value = yInput.value;
        n.value = n.value + 1;
      } else {
        //Tie...
        prevXValue.value = xInput.value;
        prevYValue.value = yInput.value;
      }

    } else if (n.value == 0) {
      prevXValue.value = xValue;
      prevYValue.value = yValue;
      n.value = 1;
    }
  }
}
```

The next function in the API is the setup() function, which in this case is not needed and left blank:

```
@Override
public void setup() {
}
```

The reset() function is called before each group's execution. In this snippet, we use the reset() function to initialize all the variables and counters to zero:

```
@Override
public void reset() {
  prevXValue.value = 0;
  prevYValue.value = 0;
  concordantPairs.value = 0;
  discordantPairs.value = 0;
  n.value = 0;
}
```

The last function in the API that we must implement is the output() function, which calculates the difference between the pairs, divides it by (n * n - 1) / 2, and sets the value of the output holder, tau:

```
@Override
public void output() {
  double result = 0.0;
  result = (concordantPairs.value - discordantPairs.value) /
      (0.5 * n.value * (n.value - 1));
  tau.value = result;
}
```

Conclusion

One of Drill's biggest strong points is its extensibility and ease of customization. In this chapter, you learned how to perform more sophisticated analyses by extending the functionality of Drill by implementing your own simple and aggregate custom UDFs. In Chapter 12, you will learn how to further extend Drill's functionality by writing format plug-ins that enable you to get Drill to read additional file types.

Writing a Format Plug-in

As described in Chapter 8, Apache Drill uses storage and format plug-ins to read data. The storage plug-in connects to a storage system such as Kafka, a database, or a distributed filesystem. The DFS interface is based on the HDFS client libraries and can obtain data from HDFS, Amazon S3, MapR, and so on.

A distributed filesystem contains a wide variety of files (Parquet, CSV, JSON, and so on.) The dfs storage plug-in uses format plug-ins to read data from these files. In this chapter, we explore how to create custom format plug-ins for file formats that Drill does not yet support.

Format plug-ins integrate tightly with Drill's internal mechanisms for configuration, memory allocation, column projection, filename resolution, and data representation. Writing plug-ins is therefore an "advanced" task that requires Java experience, patience, frequent consultation of existing code, and posting questions on the "dev" mailing list.

Drill provides two ways to structure your plug-in. Here we focus on the "Easy" format plug-in, useful for most file formats, that handles much of the boilerplate for you. It is also possible to write a plug-in without the Easy framework, but it is unlikely you will need to do so.

The Example Regex Format Plug-in

As an example, we're going to create a format plug-in for any text file format that can be described as a regular expression, or regex. The regex defines how to parse columns from an input record and is defined as part of the format configuration. The query can then select all or a subset of the columns. (This plug-in is a simplified version of the one that was added to Drill 1.14.)

You can find the full code for this plug-in in the GitHub repository for this book, in the *format-plugin* directory.

The plug-in configuration defines the file format using three pieces of information:

- The file extension used to identify the file
- The regex pattern used to match each line
- The list of column names that correspond to the patterns

For example, consider Drill's own log file, *drillbit.log*, which contains entries like this:

```
2017-12-21 10:52:42,045 [main] ERROR
  o.apache.drill.exec.server.Drillbit -
  Failure during initial startup of Drillbit.
```

(In the actual file, all the above text is on one line.) This format does not match any of Drill's built-in readers, but is typical of the ad hoc format produced by applications. Rather than build a plug-in for each such format, we will build a generalized plug-in using regexes. (Although regular expressions might be slow in production, they save a huge amount of development time for occasional work.)

For Drill's format we might define our regex as follows:

```
(\\d{4})-(\\d\\d)-(\\d\\d) (\\d\\d):(\\d\\d):(\\d\\d),\\d+
\\[([^]]*)] (\\w+)\\s+(\\S+) - (.*)
```

 This example is shown on two lines for clarity due to the physical size restrictions of the printed book; however, it must be on a single line in the configuration.

We define our fields as follows:

```
year, month, day, hour, minute, second,
thread, level, module, message
```

Drill logs often contain multiline messages. To keep things simple, we'll simply ignore input lines that do not match the pattern.

Creating the "Easy" Format Plug-in

To create a file format plug-in using the Easy framework, you must implement a number of code features:

- Plan-time hints
- Hints for the filename resolution mechanism

- Scan operator creation
- Projection resolution, including creating null columns
- Vector allocation
- Writing to value vectors
- Managing input files
- Managing file chunks

It can be tricky to get all the parts to work correctly. The secret is to find a good existing example and then adapt that for your use. This example is designed to provide most of the basic functionality you will need. We point to other good examples as we proceed.

Drill format plug-ins are difficult to write outside of the Drill source tree. Instead, a format plug-in is generally created as a subproject within Drill itself. Doing so allows rapid development and debugging. Later, we'll move the plug-in to its own project.

You begin by creating a local copy of the Drill source project, as described in Chapter 10. Then, create a new Git branch for your code:

```
cd /path/to/drill/source
git checkout -b regex-plugin
```

The example code on GitHub contains just the regex plug-in code; if you want to follow along without typing in the code, you'll need to drop this into an existing Drill project to build it.

Iterative development is vital in a system as complex as Drill. Let's begin with a simple single-field regex pattern so that we can focus on the required plumbing. Our goal is to create a starter plug-in that does the following:

- Reads only text columns
- Handles both wildcard (SELECT *) and explicit queries (SELECT a, b, c)
- Loads data into vectors

This provides a foundation on which to build more advanced features.

Creating the Maven pom.xml File

Chapter 11 explained how to create a Maven *pom.xml* file for a UDF. The process for the format plug-in is similar.

Custom plug-ins should reside in the contrib module. Examples include Hive, Kafka, Kudu, and others. Format plug-in names typically start with "format-". This example is called format-regex.

Create a new directory called *drill/contrib/format-regex* to hold your code. Then, add a *pom.xml* file in this directory:

```xml
<project xsi:schemaLocation="http://maven.apache.org/POM/4.0.0
    http://maven.apache.org/xsd/maven-4.0.0.xsd"
    xmlns="http://maven.apache.org/POM/4.0.0"
    xmlns:xsi="http://www.w3.org/2001/XMLSchema-instance">
  <modelVersion>4.0.0</modelVersion>

  <parent>
    <artifactId>drill-contrib-parent</artifactId>
    <groupId>org.apache.drill.contrib</groupId>
    <version>1.15.0-SNAPSHOT</version>
  </parent>

  <artifactId>drill-format-regex</artifactId>
  <name>contrib/regex-format-plugin</name>

  <dependencies>
    <dependency>
      <groupId>org.apache.drill.exec</groupId>
      <artifactId>drill-java-exec</artifactId>
      <version>${project.version}</version>
    </dependency>
    <dependency>
      <groupId>org.apache.drill</groupId>
      <artifactId>drill-common</artifactId>
      <version>${project.version}</version>
    </dependency>

    <!-- Test dependencies -->
    <dependency>
      <groupId>org.apache.drill.exec</groupId>
      <artifactId>drill-java-exec</artifactId>
      <version>${project.version}</version>
      <classifier>tests</classifier>
      <scope>test</scope>
    </dependency>
    <dependency>
      <groupId>org.apache.drill</groupId>
      <artifactId>drill-common</artifactId>
      <version>${project.version}</version>
      <classifier>tests</classifier>
      <scope>test</scope>
    </dependency>
  </dependencies>
</project>
```

Adjust the Drill version to match the version you are using.

The first two dependencies provide the code you need to implement your format plug-in. The second two provide test classes you will need for unit tests.

Next you must tell Drill to include this plug-in in the Drill build. Add the following to the `<modules>` section of the *pom.xml* file in the parent *drill/contrib* directory:

```
<module>format-regex</module>
```

Each Drill module, including this plug-in, creates a Java JAR file. You must tell Drill to copy the JAR file into the final product directory. In *drill/distribution/src/assemble/bin.xml*, find the following block of code and add the last `<include>` line shown here:

```
<dependencySet>
  <includes>
    <include>org.apache.drill.exec:drill-jdbc:jar</include>
    <include>org.apache.drill:drill-protocol:jar</include>
    ...
    <include>org.apache.drill.contrib:format-regex</include>
  </includes>
```

Change `format-regex` to the name of your plug-in.

Finally, you must add a dependency in the distribution *pom.xml* file to force Maven to build your plug-in before the distribution module.

Add the following just before the </dependencies> tag in the *pom.xml* file:

```
<dependency>
  <groupId>org.apache.drill.contrib</groupId>
  <artifactId>drill-format-regex</artifactId>
  <version>${project.version}</version>
</dependency>
```

Creating the Plug-in Package

If you create an Easy file format extension, as shown here, your code must reside in the core `java-exec` package. (The Easy plug-ins rely on dependencies that are visible only when your code resides within Drill's `java-exec` package.) For an Easy format plug-in, your code should live in the `org.apache.drill.exec.store.easy` package. We'll use `org.apache.drill.exec.store.easy.regex`. You can create that package in your IDE.

Drill Module Configuration

Drill uses the Lightbend (originally Typesafe) HOCON configuration system (*https://github.com/lightbend/config/blob/master/HOCON.md*), via the Typesafe library (*https://github.com/lightbend/config*), to express design-time configuration. The configuration is in the *src/main/resources/drill-module.conf* file in your plug-in directory; in this case, *contrib/format-regex/src/main/resources/drill-module.conf*:

```
drill: {
  classpath.scanning: {
    packages += "org.apache.drill.exec.store.easy.regex"
```

```
    }
  }
```

Format Plug-in Configuration

Drill terminology can be a bit complex given that the same terms are used for multiple things. So, let's begin by defining three common items:

Format plug-in
> The actual class that implements your format plug-in. (This name is often used for the JSON configuration, as you'll see shortly.)

Format plug-in configuration class
> A Jackson serialized class that stores the JSON configuration for a plug-in. (Often just called the "format config.")

Format plug-in configuration
> The JSON configuration for a plug-in as well as the Java class that stores that configuration. (Abbreviated to "format configuration" elsewhere in this book.)

The confusion is that "format plug-in" is used both for the class *and* the JSON configuration. Similarly, the term "format config" is used for the both the JSON configuration and the Java class that stores that configuration. To avoid confusion, we will use the terms we just listed.

Cautions Before Getting Started

Before we begin making changes, let's make sure we don't break anything important. When you edit storage or format configurations using the Drill Web Console, Drill stores those configurations in ZooKeeper. If you make a mistake while creating the configuration (such as a bug in the code), your existing `dfs` configuration will be permanently lost. If you have configurations of value, make a copy of your existing configuration before proceeding!

The easiest way to proceed is to work on your laptop, assuming that anything stored in ZooKeeper is disposable.

Also, it turns out that Drill provides no versioning of format plug-in configurations. Each time you make a breaking change, Drill will fail to start because it will be unable to read any configurations stored in ZooKeeper using the old schema. (We discuss later how to recover.) So, a general rule is that you can change the format configuration schema during development, but after the plug-in is in production, the configuration schema is pretty much frozen for all time.

Creating the Regex Plug-in Configuration Class

Let's begin by creating the format plug-in configuration class. A good reference example is TextFormatPlugin.TextFormatConfig.

You must implement a number of items:

- This is a Jackson serialized (*https://github.com/FasterXML/*) class, so give it a (unique) name using the @JsonTypeName annotation (*http://bit.ly/2yI5gAx*).
- Implement the equals() and hashCode() methods.

You need three properties:

- The regular expression
- A list of properties
- The file extension that this plug-in configuration supports

Jackson handles all the boilerplate for you if you choose good names, make the members public, and follow JavaBeans naming conventions (*http://bit.ly/2qgmoJ5*). So, go ahead and do so.

Next, create the plug-in class, RegexFormatPlugin, which extends EasyFormatPlugin:

```
package org.apache.drill.exec.store.easy.regex;

import org.apache.drill.common.logical.FormatPluginConfig;
import com.fasterxml.jackson.annotation.JsonInclude;
import com.fasterxml.jackson.annotation.JsonInclude.Include;
import com.fasterxml.jackson.annotation.JsonTypeName;
import com.google.common.base.Objects;

@JsonTypeName("regex")
@JsonInclude(Include.NON_DEFAULT)
public class RegexFormatConfig implements FormatPluginConfig {

  public String regex;
  public String fields;
  public String extension;

  public String getRegex() { return regex; }
  public String getFields() { return fields; }
  public String getExtension() { return extension; }

  @Override
  public boolean equals(Object obj) {
    if (this == obj) { return true; }
    if (obj == null || getClass() != obj.getClass()) {
      return false;
    }
```

```
    final RegexFormatConfig other = (RegexFormatConfig) obj;
    return Objects.equals(regex, other.regex) &&
           Objects.equals(fields, other.fields) &&
           Objects.equals(extension, other.extension);
  }

  @Override
  public int hashCode() {
    return Arrays.hashCode(new Object[] {regex, fields, extension});
  }
}
```

Format Configuration Limitations

This class might strike you as a bit odd. We would prefer to store the list of fields as a Java list. We'd also prefer to make the class immutable, with `private final` fields and a constructor that takes all of the field values. (Jackson provides the `@JsonProperty` annotation to help.)

This regex plug-in is a perfect candidate to use Drill's table functions, as you'll see in the tests. However, as of this writing, the table function code has a number of limitations that influence this class:

- DRILL-6169 (*http://bit.ly/2Azh3Tj*) specifies that we can't use Java lists.

- DRILL-6672 (*http://bit.ly/2qjzLbf*) specifies that we can't use setters (for example, `setExtension()`).

- DRILL-6673 (*http://bit.ly/2Q1ANEf*) specifies that we can't use a nondefault constructor.

Until these issues are fixed, making your fields public is the only available solution.

Copyright Headers and Code Format

To compile your code with Drill, you must include the Apache license agreement at the top of your file: simply copy one from another file. If your plug-in is proprietary, you can modify the Maven *pom.xml* file to remove the "rat" check for your files.

The code format is the preferred Drill formatting described in Chapter 10.

Testing the Configuration

You now have enough that you can test the configuration, so go ahead and build Drill (assuming that it is located in *~/drill*):

```
cd ~/drill
mvn clean install
```

For convenience, create an environment variable for the distribution directory:

```
export DRILL_HOME=~/drill/distribution/target/\
  apache-drill-1.xx.0-SNAPSHOT/apache-drill-1.xx.0-SNAPSHOT
```

Replace *xx* with the current release number, such as 14.

Start Drill:

```
cd $DRILL_HOME/bin
```

Then:

```
./drillbit.sh start
```

Connect to the Web Console (*http://drill.apache.org/docs/starting-the-web-console/*) using your browser:

```
http://localhost:8047
```

Click the Storage tab and edit the `dfs` plug-in. You need to add a sample configuration for the plug-in that includes just the date fields, to keep things simple to start. Add the following to the end of the file, just before the closing bracket:

```
"sample": {
  "type": "regex",
  "regex": "(\\d\\d\\d\\d)-(\\d\\d)-(\\d\\d) .*",
  "fields": "year, month, day",
  "extension": "samp"
}
```

The quoted name is yours to choose. In this example, we define a format called `"sample"` with a pattern, three columns, and a *.samp* file extension. The value of the `type` key must match that defined in the `@JsonTypeName` annotation of our format class. The other three keys provide values compatible with our format properties.

Save the configuration. If Drill reports "success" and displays the configuration with your changes, congratulations, everything works so far!

Fixing Configuration Problems

We noted earlier that bugs in your code can corrupt Drill's state in ZooKeeper. If you experience this problem, you can stop Drill and clear the ZooKeeper state, assuming that you have ZooKeeper installed in $ZK_HOME:

```
$ $DRILL_HOME/drillbit.sh stop
$ $ZK_HOME/bin/bin/zkCli.sh  -server localhost:2181

[zk: localhost:2181(CONNECTED) 0] ls /
[zookeeper, drill, hbase]
[zk: localhost:2181(CONNECTED) 1] ls /drill
[running, sys.storage_plugins, drillbits1]
[zk: localhost:2181(CONNECTED) 2] rmr /drill
```

```
[zk: localhost:2181(CONNECTED) 3] ls /
[zookeeper, hbase]
[zk: localhost:2181(CONNECTED) 6] quit
```

$ $DRILL_HOME/bin/drillbit.sh start

Note that if you're running Drill 1.12 and it won't start, see DRILL-6064 (*https://issues.apache.org/jira/browse/DRILL-6064*).

Plug-in Configurations Are Not Versioned

Drill plug-in configurations are not versioned. If you change the configuration class and ship your code to a user that has a JSON configuration for an earlier version, Drill might fail to start, displaying a very cryptic error. To fix the error, you must manually remove the old configuration from ZooKeeper before restarting Drill. (On a secure system, this can be quite difficult, so it is best to do your testing on your laptop without enabling Drill security.)

As noted earlier, the general rule for production systems is to never change the plug-in configuration class after you use it in production. This is an area where we want to get it right the first time!

Troubleshooting

If things don't work, look at the *$DRILL_HOME/log/drillbit.log* file. For example, suppose that you mistakenly named your get method for extensions as `getFileSuffix()`:

```
org.apache.drill.common.exceptions.DrillRuntimeException:
  unable to deserialize value at dfs
...
Caused by: com.fasterxml.jackson.databind.exc.
  UnrecognizedPropertyException:
  Unrecognized field "fileSuffix"
   (class org.apache.drill.exec.store.easy.regex.RegexFormatConfig),
  not marked as ignorable (2 known properties: "columnCount",
   "extension"])
```

Creating the Format Plug-in Class

With the configuration class working, you can now create the format plug-in class itself. First you create the basic shell and then you add the required methods, one by one.

To begin, create a class that extends the `EasyFormatPlugin`, using your configuration class as a parameter:

```
package org.apache.drill.exec.store.easy.regex;
...
```

```
public class RegexFormatPlugin extends
            EasyFormatPlugin<RegexFormatConfig> {
  ...
}
```

Add a default name and a field to store the plug-in configuration, and then add a constructor to pass configuration information to the base class:

```
public static final String DEFAULT_NAME = "regex";
private final RegexFormatConfig formatConfig;

public RegexFormatPlugin(String name, DrillbitContext context,
    Configuration fsConf, StoragePluginConfig storageConfig,
    RegexFormatConfig formatConfig) {

  super(name, context, fsConf, storageConfig, formatConfig,
    true,  // readable
    false, // writable
    false, // blockSplittable
    true,  // compressible
    Lists.newArrayList(formatConfig.extension),
    DEFAULT_NAME);
  this.formatConfig = formatConfig;
}
```

The constructor accomplishes a number of tasks:

- Accepts the plug-in configuration name that you set previously in the Drill Web Console.
- Accepts a number of configuration objects that give you access to Drill internals and to the filesystem.
- Accepts an instance of your deserialized format plug-in configuration.
- Passes to the parent class constructor a number of properties that define the behavior of your plug-in. (It is the ability to specify these options in the constructor that, in large part, makes this an Easy plug-in.)
- Defines the file extensions to be associated with this plug-in. In this case, you get the extension from the format plug-in configuration so the user can change it.

The gist of the code is that your plug-in can read but not write files. The files are not block-splittable. (Adding this ability would be simple: more on this later.) You can compress the file as a *.zip* or *tar.gz* file. You take the extension from the configuration, and the default name from a constant.

Next, you can provide default implementations for several methods. The first says that your plug-in will support (projection) push-down:

```
@Override
public boolean supportsPushDown() { return true; }
```

A reader need not support projection push-down. But without such support, the reader will load all of the file's data into memory, only to have the Drill Project operator throw much of that data away. Since doing so is inefficient, this example will show how to implement projection push-down.

The next two are stubs because the plug-in does not support writing:

```
@Override
public RecordWriter getRecordWriter(FragmentContext context,
      EasyWriter writer) throws IOException {
  return null;
}
 @Override

 public int getWriterOperatorType()
{ return 0;}
```

Eventually, you can register your plug-in with the Drill operator registry so that it will appear nicely in query profiles. For now, just leave it as a stub:

```
@Override

public int getReaderOperatorType()
{ return 0; }
```

Finally, we need to create the actual record reader. Leave this as a stub for now:

```
@Override
public RecordReader getRecordReader(FragmentContext context,
    DrillFileSystem dfs, FileWork fileWork,
    List<SchemaPath> columns,
    String userName) throws ExecutionSetupException {

  // TODO Write me!
  return null;
}
```

Before we dive into the reader, let's use a unit test and the debugger to verify that your configuration is, in fact, being passed to the plug-in constructor. You'll use this test many times as you continue development.

Creating a Test File

First, you need to create a sample input file that you'll place in Drill's resource folder, */drill-java-exec/src/test/resources/regex/simple.samp*. Getting sample data is easy: just grab a few lines from your *drillbit.log* file:

```
2017-12-19 10:52:41,820 [main] INFO  o.a.d.e.e.f.FunctionImplementationRegist...
2017-12-19 10:52:37,652 [main] INFO  o.a.drill.common.config.DrillConfig - Con...
Base Configuration:
  - jar:file:/Users/paulrogers/git/drill/distribution/target/apache-drill...
2017-12-19 11:12:27,278 [main] ERROR o.apache.drill.exec.server.Drillbit - ...
```

We've included two different message types (`INFO` and `ERROR`), along with a multiline message. (Our code will ignore the nonmessage lines.)

Configuring RAT

We've added a new file type to our project, *.samp*. Drill uses Apache RAT to check that every file has a copyright header. Because we've added a data file, we don't want to include the header (for some files, the header cannot be provided). Configure RAT to ignore this file type by adding the following lines to the *contrib/format-regex/pom.xml* file:

```
<build>
  <plugins>
   <plugin>
     <groupId>org.apache.rat</groupId>
     <artifactId>apache-rat-plugin</artifactId>
     <inherited>true</inherited>
     <configuration>
       <excludes>
         <exclude>**/*.samp</exclude>
       </excludes>
     </configuration>
   </plugin>
  </plugins>
</build>
```

Efficient Debugging

The first test you did earlier required that you run a full five-minute Drill build, then start the Drill server, and then connect using the Web Console. For that first test, this was fine because it is the most convenient way to test the format configuration. But for the remaining tasks, you'll want to have much faster edit-compile-debug cycles.

You can do this by running Drill in your IDE using Drill's test fixtures. See the developer documentation (*https://github.com/apache/drill/tree/master/docs/dev*) for details. You can also find more information about the test fixtures in the class `org.apache.drill.test.ExampleTest`.

Here is how to create an ad hoc test program that starts the server, including the web server, and listens for connections:

- In the *java_exec/src/test* directory, create the *org.apache.drill.exec.store.easy.regex* project.
- Create an "ad hoc" test program that launches the server with selected options.
- Run your test program from your IDE.

The following section shows you how to build the most basic test program.

Creating the Unit Test

You want your test to be fast and self-contained. This is such a common pattern that a class exists to help you out: `ClusterTest`.

Start by creating a test that derives from `ClusterTest`:

```java
public class TestRegexReader extends ClusterTest {

  @ClassRule
  public static final BaseDirTestWatcher dirTestWatcher =
    new BaseDirTestWatcher();

  @BeforeClass
  public static void setup() throws Exception {
    ClusterTest.startCluster(ClusterFixture.builder(dirTestWatcher));

    // Define a regex format config for testing.
    defineRegexPlugin();
  }
}
```

This is mostly boilerplate except for the `defineRegexPlugin()` method. As it turns out, annoyingly, Drill provides no SQL syntax or API for defining plug-in configuration at runtime. Either you use the Web Console, or you must create your own, which is what we show here:

```java
@SuppressWarnings("resource")
private static void defineRegexPlugin() throws ExecutionSetupException {

  // Create an instance of the regex config.

  RegexFormatConfig config = new RegexFormatConfig();
  config.extension = "samp";
  config.regex = "(\\\\d\\\\d\\\\d\\\\d)-(\\\\d\\\\d)-(\\\\d\\\\d) .*";
  config.fields = Lists.newArrayList("year", "month", "day");

  // Define a temporary format plug-in for the "cp" storage plug-in.

  Drillbit drillbit = cluster.drillbit();
  final StoragePluginRegistry pluginRegistry =
      drillbit.getContext().getStorage();
  final FileSystemPlugin plugin =
      (FileSystemPlugin) pluginRegistry.getPlugin("cp");
  final FileSystemConfig pluginConfig = (FileSystemConfig) plugin.getConfig();
  pluginConfig.getFormats().put("sample", config);
  pluginRegistry.createOrUpdate("cp", pluginConfig, false);
}
```

The first block of code simply uses the format configuration class to define a simple test format: just the first three fields of a Drill log.

The second block is "black magic": it retrieves the existing classpath (cp) plug-in, retrieves the configuration object for that plug-in, adds your format plug-in to that storage configuration, and then redefines the cp storage plug-in with the new configuration. (The Drill test framework has methods to set up a plug-in, but only in the context of a workspace, and workspaces are not supported for the classpath plug-in.) In any event, with the preceding code, you can configure a test version of your plug-in without having to use the Web Console.

Next, define the simplest possible test—just run a query:

```
@Test
public void testWildcard() {
    String sql = "SELECT * FROM cp.`regex/simple.samp`";
    client.queryBuilder().sql(sql).printCsv();
}
```

Of course, this test won't work yet: you haven't implemented the reader. But you can at least test that Drill is able to find and instantiate your plug-in.

Set a breakpoint in the constructor of the plug-in and then run the test in the debugger. When the debugger hits the breakpoint, inspect the contents of the format plug-in provided to the constructor. If everything looks good, congratulations, another step completed! Go ahead and stop the debugger because we have no reader implemented.

How Drill Finds Your Plug-in

If something goes wrong, it helps to know where to look for problems. Drill uses the following mappings to find your plug-in:

1. The name "sample" was used to register the plug-in configuration with the storage plug-in in defineRegexPlugin().

2. The Drill class FormatCreator scans the classpath for all classes that derive from FormatPlugin (which yours does via EasyFormatPlugin).

3. FormatCreator scans the constructors for each plug-in class looking for those of the expected format. (If you had added or removed arguments, yours would not be found and the plug-in would be ignored.)

4. To find the plug-in class for a format configuration, Drill searches the constructors of the format plug-ins to find one in which the type of the fifth argument matches the class of the format configuration registered in step 1.

5. Drill invokes the matching constructor to create an instance of your format plug-in class.

6. The format plug-in creates the reader that reads data for your format plug-in.

If things go wrong, step through the code in `FormatCreator` to determine where it went off the rails.

The Record Reader

With the boilerplate taken care of and with a working test environment, we are now ready to tackle the heart of the problem: the *record reader*. In Drill, the record reader is responsible for a number of tasks:

- Defining value vectors for each column
- Populating value vectors for each batch of records
- Performing projection push-down (mapping from input to query columns)
- Translating errors into Drill format

Each of these tasks can be complex when you consider all the nuances and use cases. Let's work on them step by step, discussing the theory as we go.

In Drill, a single query can scan multiple files (or multiple blocks of a single large file). As we've discussed earlier in this book, Drill divides queries into *major fragments*, one of which will perform the scan operation. The scan's major fragment is distributed across a set of *minor fragments*, typically running multiple instances on each node in the Drill cluster. If the query scans a few files, each scan operator might read just one file. But if the query touches many files relative to the number of scan minor fragments, each scan operator will read multiple files.

To read about fragments in more detail, see Chapter 3.

The scan operator orchestrates the scan operation, but delegates actual reading to a record reader. There is one scan operator per minor fragment, but possibly many record readers for each scan operator. In particular, Drill creates one record reader for each file. Many files are splittable. In this case, Drill creates one record reader per file block.

Because Drill reads "big data," files are often large. Blocks are often 256 MB or 512 MB. Drill further divides each block into a series of *batches*: collections of records that fit comfortably into memory. Each batch is composed of a collection of value vectors, one per column.

So, your job in creating a reader is to create a class that reads data from a single file (or block) in the context of a scan operator that might read multiple files, and to read the data as one or more batches, filling the value vectors as you read each record.

Let's begin by creating the `RegexRecordReader` class:

```java
public class RegexRecordReader extends AbstractRecordReader {

    private final DrillFileSystem dfs;
    private final FileWork fileWork;
    private final RegexFormatConfig formatConfig;

    public RegexRecordReader(FragmentContext context, DrillFileSystem dfs,
        FileWork fileWork, List<SchemaPath> columns, String userName,
        RegexFormatConfig formatConfig) {
      this.dfs = dfs;
      this.fileWork = fileWork;
      this.formatConfig = formatConfig;

      // Ask the superclass to parse the projection list.
      setColumns(columns);
    }

    @Override
    public void setup(OperatorContext context, OutputMutator output)
        throws ExecutionSetupException { }

    @Override
    public int next() { }

    @Override
    public void close() throws Exception { }
}
```

The `RegexRecordReader` interface is pretty simple:

Constructor
Provides the five parameters that describe the file scan, plus the configuration of our regex format

`setup()`
Called to open the underlying file and start reading

`next()`
Called to read each batch of rows from the data source

`close()`
Called to release resources

The `AbstractRecordReader` class provides a few helper functions that you'll use later.

If you create a format plug-in without the Easy framework, or if you create a storage plug-in, you are responsible for creating the scan operator, the readers, and quite a bit of other boilerplate.

However, we are using the Easy framework, which does all of this for you (hence the name). The Easy framework creates the record readers at the time that the scan operator is created. Because of this, you want to avoid doing operations in the constructor that consume resources (such as memory allocation or opening a file). Save those for the setup() call.

Let's consider the constructor parameters:

FragmentContext
> Provides information about the (minor) fragment along with information about the Drill server itself. You most likely don't need this information.

DrillFileSystem
> Drill's version of the HDFS FileSystem class. Use this to open the input file.

FileWork
> Provides the filename along with the block offset and length (for block-aware files).

List<SchemaPath>
> The set of columns that the query requested from the data source.

String userName
> The name of the user running the query, for use in some security models.

RegexFormatConfig
> The regex format configuration that we created earlier.

You must also instruct Drill how to instantiate your reader by implementing the following method in your RegexFormatPlugin class:

```
@Override
public RecordReader getRecordReader(FragmentContext context,
    DrillFileSystem dfs, FileWork fileWork, List<SchemaPath> columns,
    String userName) throws ExecutionSetupException {
  return new RegexRecordReader(context, dfs, fileWork,
      columns, userName, formatConfig);
}
```

Testing the Reader Shell

As it turns out, you've now created enough structure that you can successfully run a query; however, it will produce no results. Rerun the previous SELECT * query using the test created earlier. Set breakpoints in the getRecordReader() method and examine the parameters to become familiar with their structure. (Not all Drill classes provide Javadoc comments, so this is a good alternative.) Then, step into your constructor to see how the columns are parsed.

If all goes well, the console should display something like this:

```
Running org.apache.drill.exec.store.easy.regex.TestRegexReader#testWildcard
Total rows returned: 0.  Returned in 1804ms.
```

You are now ready to build the actual reader.

Logging

Logging is the best way to monitor your plug-in in production or to report runtime errors. Define a logger as a `static final` class field:

```
private static final org.slf4j.Logger logger =
        org.slf4j.LoggerFactory.getLogger(RegexRecordReader.class);
```

Error Handling

Drill's error handling rules are a bit vague, but the following should stand you in good stead:

- If a failure occurs during construction or setup, log the error and throw an `ExecutionSetupException`.
- If a failure occurs elsewhere, throw a `UserException`, which will automatically log the error.

In both cases, the error message you provide will be sent back to the user running a query, so try to provide a clear message.

Error Display in the Drill Web Console

The SQLLine program will show your error message to the user. However, at present, the Web Console displays only a cryptic message, losing the message text. Because of this, you should use SQLLine if you want to test error messages. You can also check the query profile in the Web Console.

Drill's `UserException` class wraps exceptions that are meant to be returned to the user. The class uses a fluent builder syntax and requires you to identify the type of error. Here are two of the most common:

`dataReadError()`
    Indicates that something went wrong with opening or reading from a file.

```
validationException()
```
Indicates that something went wrong when validating a query. Because Drill does column validation at runtime, you can throw this if the projected columns are not valid for your data source.

See the `UserException` class for others. You can also search the source code to see how each error is used in practice.

The `UserException` class allows you to provide additional context information such as the file or column that triggered the error and other information to help the user understand the issue.

One odd aspect of `UserException` is that it is unchecked: you do not have to declare it in the method signature, and so you can throw it from anywhere. A good rule of thumb is that if the error might be due to a user action, the environment, or faulty configuration, throw a `UserException`. Be sure to include the filename and line number, if applicable. If the error is likely due to a code flaw (some invariant is invalid, for example), throw an unchecked Java exception such as `IllegalStateException`, `IllegalArgumentException`, or `UnsupportedOperationException`. Use good unit tests to ensure that these "something is wrong in the code" exceptions are never thrown when the code is in production.

Because the `UserException` allows us to provide additional context, we use it in this example, even in the setup stage.

Setup

In the `setup()` method, you need to set up the regex parser, define the needed projection, define vectors, and open the file:

```
@Override
public void setup(OperatorContext context, OutputMutator output) {
  setupPattern();
  setupColumns();
  setupProjection();
  openFile();
  defineVectors(output);
}
```

Regex Parsing

Because the purpose of this exercise is to illustrate Drill, the example uses the simplest possible regex parsing algorithm: just the Java `Pattern` and `Matcher` classes. (Production Drill readers tend to go to extremes to optimize the per-record path—which we leave as an exercise for you—and so the simple approach here would need optimization for production code.) Remember that we decided to simply ignore lines that don't match the pattern:

```
    private Pattern pattern;

    private void setupPattern() {
      try {
        pattern = Pattern.compile(formatConfig.getRegex());
      } catch (PatternSyntaxException e) {
        throw UserException
            .validationError(e)
            .message("Failed to parse regex: \"%s\"",
                    formatConfig.getRegex())
            .build(logger);
      }
    }
```

As is typical in a system as complex as Drill, error handling can consume a large fraction of your code. Because the user supplies the regex (as part of the plug-in configuration), we raise a `UserException` if the regex has errors, passing the original exception and an error message. The `build()` method automatically logs the error into Drill's log file to help with problem diagnosis.

Defining Column Names

Here is the simplest possible code to parse the list of columns:

```
    private List<String> columnNames;

    private void setupColumns() {
      String fieldStr = formatConfig.getFields();
      columnNames = Splitter.on(Pattern.compile(
                    "\\s*,\\s*")).splitToList(fieldStr);
    }
```

See the complete code in GitHub for the full set of error checks required. They are omitted here because they don't shed much light on Drill itself.

Projection

Projection is the process of picking some columns from the input, but not others. (In SQL, the projection list confusingly follows the `SELECT` keyword.) As explained earlier, the simplest reader just reads all columns, after which Drill will discard those that are not projected. Clearly this is inefficient; instead, each reader should do the projection itself. This is called *projection push-down* (the projection is pushed down into the reader).

We instructed Drill that our format plug-in supports projection push-down with the following method in the `RegexFormatPlugin` class:

```
    @Override
    public boolean supportsPushDown() { return true; }
```

To implement projection, you must handle three cases:

- An empty project list: SELECT COUNT(*)
- A wildcard query: SELECT *
- An explicit list: SELECT a, b, c

The base AbstractRecordReader class does some of the work for you when you call setColumns() from the constructor:

```
// Ask the superclass to parse the projection list.

setColumns(columns);
```

Here is the top-level method that identifies the cases:

```
private void setupProjection() {
  if (isSkipQuery()) {
    projectNone();
  } else if (isStarQuery()) {
    projectAll();
  } else {
    projectSubset();
  }
}
```

The isSkipQuery() and isStartQuery methods are provided by the superclass as a result of calling setColumns() in the example prior to this one.

Column Projection Accounting

Because the regex plug-in parses text files, we can assume that all of the columns will be nullable VARCHAR. You will need the column name later to create the value vector, which means that you need a data structure to keep track of this information:

```
private static class ColumnDefn {
  private final String name;
  private final int index;
  private NullableVarCharVector.Mutator mutator;

  public ColumnDefn(String name, int index) {
    this.name = name;
    this.index = index;
  }
}
```

The Mutator class is the mechanism Drill provides to write values into a value vector.

Project None

If Drill asks you to project no columns, you are still obligated to provide one dummy column because of an obscure limitation of Drill's internals. Drill will discard the column later:

```
private void projectNone() {
  columns = new ColumnDefn[] { new ColumnDefn("dummy", -1) };
}
```

Project All

When given a wildcard (SELECT COUNT(*)) query, SQL semantics specify that you should do the following:

- Include all columns from the data source.
- Use the names defined in the data source.
- Use them in the order in which they appear in the data source.

In this case, the "data source" is the set of columns defined in the plug-in configuration:

```
private void projectAll() {
  columns = new ColumnDefn[groupCount];
  for (int i = 0; i < columns.length; i++) {
    columns[i] = new ColumnDefn(columnNames.get(i), i);
  }
}
```

Project Some

The final case occurs when the user requests a specific set of columns; for example, SELECT a, b, c. Because Drill is schema-free, it cannot check at plan time which projected columns exist in the data source. Instead, that work is done at read time. The result is that Drill allows the user to project any column, even one that does not exist:

- A requested column matches one defined by the configuration, so we project that column to the output batch.
- A requested column does not match one defined by the configuration, so we must project a null column.

By convention, Drill creates a nullable (OPTIONAL) INT column for missing columns. In our plug-in, we only ever create VARCHAR values, so nullable INT can never be right. Instead, we create nullable VARCHAR columns for missing columns.

To keep the code simple, we will use nullable VARCHAR columns even for those columns that are available. (You might want to modify the example to use non-nullable [REQUIRED] columns, instead.)

As an aside, the typical Drill way to handle other data types is to read a text file (such as CSV, or, here, a log file) as VARCHAR, then perform conversions (CASTs) to other types within the query itself (or in a view). You could add functionality to allow the format configuration to specify the type, then do the conversion in your format plug-in code. In fact, this is exactly what the regex plug-in in Drill does. Review that code for the details.

Following are the rules for creating the output projection list:

- Include in the output rows only the columns from the project list (including missing columns).
- Use the names provided in the project list (which might differ in case from those in the data source).
- Include columns in the order in which they are defined in the project list.

Drill is case-insensitive, so you must use case-insensitive name mapping. But Drill labels columns using the case provided in the projection list, so for the project-some case, you want to use the name as specified in the project list.

For each projected name, you look up the name in the list of columns and record either the column (pattern) index, or –1 if the column is not found. (For simplicity we use a linear search; production code might use a hash map.)

The implementation handles all these details:

```
private void projectSubset() {

    // Ensure the projected columns are only simple columns;
    // no maps, no arrays.
    Collection<SchemaPath> project = this.getColumns();
    assert ! project.isEmpty();
    columns = new ColumnDefn[project.size()];
    int colIndex = 0;
    for (SchemaPath column : project) {
      if (column.getAsNamePart().hasChild()) {
        throw UserException
            .validationError()
            .message("The regex format plugin supports only" +
                    " simple columns")
            .addContext("Projected column", column.toString())
            .build(logger);
      }

      // Find a matching defined column, case-insensitive match.
```

```
      String name = column.getAsNamePart().getName();
      int patternIndex = -1;
      for (int i = 0; i < columnNames.size(); i++) {
        if (columnNames.get(i).equalsIgnoreCase(name)) {
          patternIndex = i;
          break;
        }
      }

      // Create the column. Index of -1 means column will be null.
      columns[colIndex++] = new ColumnDefn(name, patternIndex);
    }
  }
```

The cryptic check for hasChild() catches subtle errors. Drill allows two special kinds of columns to appear in the project list: arrays (columns[0]) and maps (a.b). Because our plug-in handles only simple columns, we reject requests for nonsimple columns.

Note what happens if a requested column does not match a column from that provided by the plug-in configuration: the patternIndex ends up as -1. We use that as our cue later to fill that column with null values.

Opening the File

Drill uses the DrillFileSystem class, which is a wrapper around the HDFS FileSystem class, to work with files. Here, we are concerned only with opening a file as an input stream, which is then, for convenience, wrapped in a BufferedReader:

```
private void openFile() {
  InputStream in;
  try {
    in = dfs.open(new Path(fileWork.getPath()));
  } catch (Exception e) {
    throw UserException
      .dataReadError(e)
      .message("Failed to open open input file: %s", fileWork.getPath())
      .addContext("User name", userName)
      .build(logger);
  }
  reader = new BufferedReader(
              new InputStreamReader(in, Charsets.UTF_8));
}
```

Here we see the use of the dataReadError form of the UserException, along with a method to add the username as context (in case the problem is related to permissions).

Notice that, after this call, we are holding a resource that we must free in close(), even if something fails.

Record Batches

Many query systems (such as MapReduce and Hive) are row-based: the record reader reads one row at a time. Drill, being columnar, works with groups of records called *record batches*. Each reader provides a batch of records on each call to next(). Drill has no standard for the number of records: some readers return 1,000, some 4,096; others return 65,536 (the maximum). For our plug-in, let's go with the standard size set in Drill's internals (4,096):

```
private static final int BATCH_SIZE =
        BaseValueVector.INITIAL_VALUE_ALLOCATION;
```

The best batch size depends strongly on the size of each record. At present, Drill simply assumes records are the proper size. For various reasons, it is best to choose a number that keeps the memory required per batch below a few megabytes in size.

Let's see how our size of 4,096 works out. We are scanning Drill log lines, which tend to be less than 100 characters long. 4,096 records * 100 characters/record = 409,600 bytes, which is fine.

Drill's Columnar Structure

As a columnar execution engine, Drill stores data per column in a structure called a *value vector* (*http://drill.apache.org/docs/value-vectors/*). Each vector stores values for a single column, one after another. To hold the complete set of columns that make up a row, we create multiple value vectors.

Drill defines a separate value vector class for each data type. Within each data type, there are also separate classes for each cardinality: non-nullable (called REQUIRED in Drill code), nullable (called OPTIONAL) and repeated.

We do not write to vectors directly. Instead, we write through a helper class called a (vector) Mutator. (There is also an Accessor to read values.) Just as each combination of *(type, cardinality)* has a separate class, each also has a separate Mutator and Accessor class (defined as part of the vector class).

To keep the example code simple, we use a single type and single cardinality: OPTIONAL VARCHAR. This makes sense: our regex pattern can only pull out strings, it does not have sufficient information to determine column types. However, if you are reading from a system that maps to other Drill types (INT, DOUBLE, etc.), you must deal with multiple vector classes, each needing type-specific code.

Drill 1.14 contains a new RowSet mechanism to greatly simplify the kind of work we explain here. At the time of writing, the code was not quite ready for full use, so we explain the current techniques. Watch the "dev" list for when the new mechanism becomes available.

Defining Vectors

With that background, it is now time to define value vectors. Drill provides the OutputMutator class to handle many of the details. Because we need only the mutator, and we need to use it for each column, let's store it in our column definition class for easy access:

```
private static class ColumnDefn {
  ...
  public NullableVarCharVector.Mutator mutator;
```

To create a vector, we just need to create metadata for each column (in the form of a MaterializedField) and then ask the output mutator to create the vector:

```
private void defineVectors(OutputMutator output) {
  for (int i = 0; i < columns.length; i++) {
    MaterializedField field =
        MaterializedField.create(columns[i].name,
                Types.optional(MinorType.VARCHAR));
    try {
      columns[i].mutator = output.addField(field,
                NullableVarCharVector.class).getMutator();
    } catch (SchemaChangeException e) {
      throw UserException
        .systemError(e)
        .message("Vector creation failed")
        .build(logger);
    }
  }
}
```

The code uses two convenience methods to define metadata: Materialized Field.create() and Types.optional().

The SchemaChangeException thrown by addField() seems odd: we are creating a vector, how could the schema change? As it turns out, Drill requires that the reader provide exactly the same value vector in each batch. In fact, if a scan operator reads multiple files, all readers must share the same vectors. If reader #2 asks to create column c as a nullable VARCHAR, but reader #1 has already created c as a REQUIRED INT, for example, the exception will be thrown. In this case, all readers use the same type, so the error should never actually occur.

Reading Data

With the setup completed, we are ready to actually read some data:

```
@Override
public int next() {
  rowIndex = 0;
  while (nextLine()) { }
  return rowIndex;
}
```

Here we read rows until we fill the batch. Because we skip some rows, we can't simply use a for loop: we want to count only matching lines (because those are the only ones loaded into Drill).

The work to do the pattern matching is straightforward:

```
private boolean nextLine() {
  String line;
  try {
    line = reader.readLine();
  } catch (IOException e) {
    throw UserException
      .dataReadError(e)
      .addContext("File", fileWork.getPath())
      .build(logger);
  }
  if (line == null) {
    return false;
  }
  Matcher m = pattern.matcher(line);
  if (m.matches()) {
    loadVectors(m);
  }
  return rowIndex < BATCH_SIZE;
}
```

Loading Data into Vectors

The next task is to load data into the vectors. The nullable VARCHAR Mutator class lets you set a value to null, or set a non-null value. You must tell it the row to write—the Mutator, oddly, does not keep track of this itself. In our case, if the column is "missing," we set it to null. If the pattern itself is null (the pattern is optional and was not found), we also set the value to null. Only if we have an actual match do we copy the value (as a string) into the vector (as an array of bytes). Recall that regex groups are 1-based:

```
private void loadVectors(Matcher m) {

  // Core work: write values into vectors for the current
  // row. If projected by name, some columns may be null.
```

```
        for (int i = 0; i < columns.length; i++) {
          NullableVarCharVector.Mutator mutator = columns[i].mutator;
          if (columns[i].index == -1) {
            // Not necessary; included just for clarity
            mutator.setNull(rowIndex);
          } else {
            String value = m.group(columns[i].index + 1);
            if (value == null) {
              // Not necessary; included just for clarity
              mutator.setNull(rowIndex);
            } else {
              mutator.set(rowIndex, value.getBytes());
            }
          }
        }
      }
      rowIndex++;
    }
```

In practice, we did not have to set values to null, because null is the default; it was done here just for clarity.

Filling Empty Values

Drill employs the concept of "fill empties." Suppose that your data source has a varying set of columns across records (think JSON or XML). If record 5, for example, is missing column c, how do you know to fill in the missing value?

For nullable values, Drill does it automatically. If record 4 has a value for c but you don't see another value again until record 10, Drill will automatically fill in nulls for records 5 through 9.

Note, however, that this works only for nullable values, not for REQUIRED or REPEATED values. Failure to write a value for each record for a REQUIRED type might leave garbage values for the empty rows. Omitting a value for a REPEATED vector can corrupt the internal vector structures.

Releasing Resources

The only remaining task is to implement close() to release resources. In our case, the only resource is the file reader. Here we use logging to report and then ignore any errors that occur on close:

```
@Override
public void close() {
  if (reader != null) {
    try {
      reader.close();
    } catch (IOException e) {
```

```
      logger.warn("Error when closing file: " + fileWork.getPath(), e);
    }
    reader = null;
  }
}
```

Testing the Reader

The final step is to test the reader. Although it can be tempting to build Drill, fire up SQLLine, and throw some queries at your code, you need to resist that temptation and instead do detailed unit testing. Doing so is easy with Drill's testing tools. Plus, you can use the test cases as a way to quickly rerun code in the unlikely event that the tests uncover some bugs in your code.

Testing the Wildcard Case

You can use your existing test to check the wildcard (SELECT *) case:

```
@Test
public void testWildcard() {
  String sql = "SELECT * FROM cp.`regex/simple.samp`";
  client.queryBuilder().sql(sql).printCsv();
}
```

When you run the test, you should see something like the following:

```
Running org.apache.drill.exec.store.easy.regex.TestRegexReader#testWildcard
3 row(s):
year<VARCHAR(OPTIONAL)>,month<VARCHAR(OPTIONAL)>,day<VARCHAR(OPTIONAL)>
2017,12,17
2017,12,18
2017,12,19
Total rows returned : 3.  Returned in 10221ms.
```

Congratulations, you have a working format plug-in! But we're not done yet. This is not much of a test given that it requires that a human review the output. Let's follow the examples in ExampleTest and actually validate the output:

```
@Test
public void testWildcard() throws RpcException {
  String sql = "SELECT * FROM cp.`regex/simple.log1`";
  RowSet results = client.queryBuilder().sql(sql).rowSet();

  BatchSchema expectedSchema = new SchemaBuilder()
      .addNullable("year", MinorType.VARCHAR)
      .addNullable("month", MinorType.VARCHAR)
      .addNullable("day", MinorType.VARCHAR)
      .build();

  RowSet expected = client.rowSetBuilder(expectedSchema)
      .addRow("2017", "12", "17")
```

```
      .addRow("2017", "12", "18")
      .addRow("2017", "12", "19")
      .build();

  RowSetUtilities.verify(expected, results);
}
```

We use three test tools. `SchemaBuilder` lets us define the schema we expect. The row set builder lets us build a row set (really, just a collection of vectors) that holds the expected values. Finally the `RowSetUtilities.verify()` function compares the two row sets: both the schemas and the values. The result is that we can easily create many tests for our plug-in.

Testing Explicit Projection

We have three kinds of project, but we've tested only one. Let's test explicit projection using this query:

```
SELECT `day`, `missing`, `month` FROM cp.`regex/simple.samp`
```

As an exercise, use the techniques described earlier to test this query. Begin by printing the results as CSV, and then create a validation test. Hint: to specify a null value when building the expected rows, simply pass a Java `null`. Check the code in GitHub for the answer.

Testing Empty Projection

Finally, let's verify that projection works for a `COUNT(*)` query:

```
SELECT COUNT(*)  FROM cp.`regex/simple.log1`
```

We know that the query returns exactly one row with a single `BIGINT` column. We can use a shortcut to validate the results:

```
@Test
public void testCount() throws RpcException {
  String sql = "SELECT COUNT(*) FROM cp.`regex/simple.log1`";
  long result = client.queryBuilder().sql(sql).singletonLong();
  assertEquals(3, result);
}
```

Eclipse Users

If the query fails with an error "FUNCTION ERROR: Failure reading Function class," you need to add the function *sources* (yes, sources) to the classpath. Add `drill-java-exec/src/main/java` and `drill-java-exec/target/generated-sources`.

Scaling Up

We've tested with only a simple pattern thus far. Let's modify the test to add the full set of Drill log columns, using the pattern we identified earlier. Because each file extension is associated with a single format plug-in, we cannot use the "samp" extension we've been using. Instead, let's use the actual "log" extension:

```
private static void defineRegexPlugin() throws ExecutionSetupException {

    // Create an instance of the regex config.
    // Note: we can't use the ".log" extension; the Drill .gitignore
    // file ignores such files, so they'll never get committed.
    // Instead, make up a fake suffix.

    RegexFormatConfig sampleConfig = new RegexFormatConfig();
    sampleConfig.extension = "log1";
    sampleConfig.regex = DATE_ONLY_PATTERN;
    sampleConfig.fields = "year, month, day";

    // Full Drill log parser definition.

    RegexFormatConfig logConfig = new RegexFormatConfig();
    logConfig.extension = "log2";
    logConfig.regex = "(\\d\\d\\d\\d)-(\\d\\d)-(\\d\\d) " +
                      "(\\d\\d):(\\d\\d):(\\d\\d),\\d+ " +
                      "\\[([^]]*)] (\\w+)\\s+(\\S+) - (.*)";
    logConfig.fields = "year, month, day, hour, " +
        "minute, second, thread, level, module, message";

    // Define a temporary format plug-in for the "cp" storage plug-in.

    Drillbit drillbit = cluster.drillbit();
    final StoragePluginRegistry pluginRegistry =
        drillbit.getContext().getStorage();
    final FileSystemPlugin plugin =
        (FileSystemPlugin) pluginRegistry.getPlugin("cp");
    final FileSystemConfig pluginConfig =
        (FileSystemConfig) plugin.getConfig();
    pluginConfig.getFormats().put("sample", sampleConfig);
    pluginConfig.getFormats().put("drill-log", logConfig);
    pluginRegistry.createOrUpdate("cp", pluginConfig, false);
}

@Test
public void testFull() throws RpcException {
  String sql = "SELECT * FROM cp.`regex/simple.log2`";
  client.queryBuilder().sql(sql).printCsv();
}
```

The output should be like the following:

```
Running org.apache.drill.exec.store.easy.regex.TestRegexReader...
3 row(s):
year<VARCHAR(OPTIONAL)>,month<VARCHAR(OPTIONAL)>,...
2017,12,17,10,52,41,main,INFO,o.a.d.e.e.f.Function...
2017,12,18,10,52,37,main,INFO,o.a.drill.common.config....
2017,12,19,11,12,27,main,ERROR,o.apache.drill.exec.server....
Total rows returned : 3.  Returned in 1751ms.
```

Success!

You've now fully tested the plug-in, and it is ready for actual use. As noted, we took some shortcuts for convenience so that we could go back and do some performance tuning. We'll leave the performance tuning to you and instead focus on how to put the plug-in into production as well as how to offer the plug-in to the Drill community.

Additional Details

By following the pattern described here, you should be able to create your own simple format plug-in. There are few additional topics that can be helpful in advanced cases.

File Chunks

The Hadoop model is to store large amounts of data in each file and then read file "chunks" in parallel. For simplicity, this assumes that files are not "splittable": that chunks of the file cannot be read in parallel. Depending on the file format, you can add this kind of support. Drill logs are not splittable because a single message can span multiple lines. However, simpler formats (such as CSV) can be splittable if each record corresponds to a single line. To read a split, you scan the file looking for the first record separator (such as a newline in CSV) and then begin parsing with the next line. The text reader (the so-called `CompliantTextReader`) offers an example.

Default Format Configuration

Prior sections showed two ways to create a configuration for your plug-in. You used the Drill Web Console to create it interactively. You also wrote code to set it up for tests. This is fine for development, but impractical for production users. If you're going to share your plug-in with others, you probably want it to be configured by default. (For example, for our plug-in, we might want to offer a configuration for Drill logs "out of the box.")

When Drill first starts on a brand-new installation, it initializes the initial set of format configurations from the following file: */drill-java-exec/src/main/resources/bootstrap-storage-plugins.json*.

Modularity

Ideally, we'd add this configuration in our regex project. Format plug-in configuration is, however, a detail of the storage plug-in configuration. The configuration for the default `dfs` storage plug-in resides in Drill's `java-exec` module, so we must add our configuration there. The ability to add configuration as a file within our format plug-in project would be a nice enhancement, but is not available today.

Drill reads the bootstrap file only once: when Drill connects to ZooKeeper and finds that no configuration information has yet been stored. If you add (or modify) a format plug-in afterward, you must manually create the configuration using Drill's web console. You can also use the REST API.

First, let's add our bootstrap configuration. Again, if we were defining a new storage plug-in, we'd define a bootstrap file in our module. But because we are creating an Easy format plug-in, we modify the existing Drill file to add the following section just after the last existing format entry for the `dfs` storage configuration:

```
"drill-log": {
    type: "regex",
    extension: "log1",
    regex: "(\\d\\d\\d\\d)-(\\d\\d)-(\\d\\d) \
            (\\d\\d):(\\d\\d):(\\d\\d),\\d+ \\[([^]]*)] \
            (\\w+)\\s+(\\S+) - (.*)",
    fields: "year, month, day, hour, minute, second, \
             thread, level, module, message"
}
```

(Note that this code is formatted for this book; your code must be on a single line for the `regex` and `fields` items.)

Be sure to add a comma after the `"csvh"` section to separate it from the new section.

To test this, delete the ZooKeeper state as described previously. Build Drill with these changes in place, then start Drill and visit the Web Console. Go to the Storage tab and click Update next to the `dfs` plug-in. Your format configuration should appear in the `formats` section.

Next Steps

With a working format plug-in, you next must choose how to maintain the code. You have three choices:

1. Contribute the code to the Drill project via a *pull request*.

2. Maintain your own private branch of the Drill code that includes your plug-in code.

---

3. Move your plug-in code to a separate Maven project which you maintain outside of the Drill project.

Drill is an open source project and encourages contributions. If your plug-in might be useful to others, consider contributing your plug-in code to Drill. That way, our plug-in will be part of future Drill releases. If, however, the plug-in works with a format unique to your project or company, then you may want to keep the code separate from Drill.

Production Build

The preceding steps showed you how to create your plug-in within the Drill project itself by creating a new module within the `contrib` module. In this case, it is very easy to move your plug-in into production. Just build all of Drill and replace your current Drill distribution with the new one in the *distribution/target/apache-drill-version/ apache-drill-version* directory. (Yes, *apache-drill-version* appears twice.) Your plug-in will appear in the jars directory where Drill will pick it up.

If you plan to offer your plug-in to the Drill project, your plug-in code should reside in the *contrib* project, as in the preceding example. Your code is simply an additional set of Java classes and resource files added to the Drill JARs and Drill distribution. So, to deploy your plug-in, just do a full build of Drill and replace your existing Drill installation with your custom-built one.

Contributing to Drill: The Pull Request

If you want to contribute your code to Drill, the first step is to ensure your files contain the Apache copyright header and conform to the Drill coding standards. (If you used the Drill Maven file, it already enforced these rules.)

The next step is to submit a *pull request* against the Apache Drill GitHub project. The details are beyond the scope of this book, but they are pretty standard for Apache. Ask on the Drill "dev" mailing list for details.

Maintaining Your Branch

If your plug-in will remain private, you can keep it in Drill by maintaining your own private fork of the Drill repo. You'll want to "rebase" your branch from time to time with the latest Drill revisions.

You should have created your plug-in in a branch from the master branch within the Drill Git repository. This example used the branch `regex-plugin`. Assuming that your only changes are the plug-in code that you've maintained in your own branch, you can keep your branch up to date as follows:

1. Use `git checkout master` to check out the master branch.

2. Use `git pull upstream master` to pull down the latest changes to `master` (assuming that you've used the default name "upstream" for the Apache Drill repo).

3. Use `git checkout regex-plugin` to switch back to your branch.

4. Use `git rebase master` to rebase your code on top of the latest master.

5. Rebuild Drill.

Create a Plug-In Project

Another, perhaps simpler, option for a private plug-in is to move the code to its own project.

Create a standard Maven project, as described earlier.

The *pom.xml* file contains the bare minimum (this project has no external dependencies):

```
<project xsi:schemaLocation="http://maven.apache.org/POM/4.0.0 \
                     http://maven.apache.org/xsd/maven-4.0.0.xsd"
  xmlns="http://maven.apache.org/POM/4.0.0"
  xmlns:xsi="http://www.w3.org/2001/XMLSchema-instance">
  <modelVersion>4.0.0</modelVersion>

  <parent>
    <artifactId>drill-contrib-parent</artifactId>
    <groupId>org.apache.drill.contrib</groupId>
    <version>1.15.0-SNAPSHOT</version>
  </parent>

  <artifactId>drill-format-regex</artifactId>
  <name>contrib/regex-format-plugin</name>

  <dependencies>
    <dependency>
     <groupId>org.apache.drill.exec</groupId>
     <artifactId>drill-java-exec</artifactId>
     <version>${project.version}</version>
    </dependency>
    <dependency>
     <groupId>org.apache.drill</groupId>
     <artifactId>drill-common</artifactId>
     <version>${project.version}</version>
    </dependency>
  <dependency>
     <groupId>org.apache.drill.exec</groupId>
     <artifactId>drill-java-exec</artifactId>
```

```
        <version>${project.version}</version>
        <classifier>tests</classifier>
        <scope>test</scope>
    </dependency>
    <dependency>
        <groupId>org.apache.drill</groupId>
        <artifactId>drill-common</artifactId>
        <version>${project.version}</version>
        <classifier>tests</classifier>
        <scope>test</scope>
        </exclusions>
    </dependency>
  </dependencies>
</project>
```

Replace the version number in this code example with the version of Drill that you want to use.

Then, you need to instruct Drill that this is a plug-in by adding a (empty) *drill-module.conf file*. If you wanted to add any boot-time options, you would add them here, but this plug-in has none. See the other format plug-in projects for more sophisticated examples.

Conclusion

This chapter discussed how to create a format plug-in using the Easy framework. Practice creating a plug-in of your own. As you dig deeper, you will find that Drill's own source code is the best source of examples: review how other format plug-ins work for ideas. (Just be aware that Drill is constantly evolving; some of the older code uses patterns that are now a bit antiquated.)

Drill has a second kind of plug-in: the storage plug-in. Storage plug-ins access data sources beyond a distributed file system (DFS). For example, HBase, Kafka, and JDBC. Storage plug-ins introduce another large set of mechanisms to implement. Again, look at existing storage plug-ins and ask questions on the dev list to discover what has to be done. The use of the test framework shown here will greatly reduce your edit-compile-debug cycle times so that you can try things incrementally.

CHAPTER 13

Unique Uses of Drill

As you have seen, Apache Drill is capable of querying all kinds of data, large and small, in a variety of different systems. This chapter highlights some examples of unique use cases in which Drill has made complex analysis easy. The first example demonstrates how to use Drill's suite of geometric functions as well as the image metadata format plug-in to identify photos taken within a geographic region. Next, you will see a demonstration of a situation in which writing a format plug-in was very helpful, for working with Excel files. Finally, we cover several use cases in which analysts greatly expanded Drill's functionality by creating UDFs.

Finding Photos Taken Within a Geographic Region

In Drill 1.14, two features were added that made this use case possible: the ability to analyze Exchangeable Image File (EXIF) metadata,[1] and a collection of geographic information system (GIS) functions allowing all kinds of functionality, including the ability to search within defined geographic areas or polygons as well as the ability to create these polygons. Drill's GIS functionality largely follows the GIS functionality found in PostGIS.[2]

The first thing you need to do is to extract the fields that contain the latitude and longitude in the EXIF metadata. The example that follows demonstrates how to access the geocoordinates of an image in Drill (note that not all images will contain these fields):

---

1 EXIF metadata (*https://en.wikipedia.org/wiki/Exif*) contains information about an image or any digital media. The metadata includes information about the device that captured the media and more.

2 You can find a complete list of Drill's GIS functions in Appendix A.

```
SELECT t.GPS.GPSLatitude AS lat, t.GPS.GPSLongitude AS lon
FROM dfs.`photo1.jpg` AS t;
```

The next thing you need to do is convert these coordinates into a point object that you can use as a filter. You can accomplish this by using the `ST_Point(long, lat)` function, which converts text or fields into a binary geometry that can be used in subsequent GIS functions:

```
SELECT ST_Point(t.GPS.GPSLongitude, t.GPS.GPSLatitude) AS geom
FROM dfs.`photo1.jpg` AS t;
```

Now that you know how to generate the points from the images, the final step is to use the `ST_Within(point, polygon)` function in the `WHERE` clause to filter out the rows that are not within that polygon. You can also use the `ST_DWithin()` function to filter by distance from a given point. The next example demonstrates the final query, which scans a directory and returns the metadata for any photos within a given polygon—in this case, San Jose, CA:

```
SELECT *
FROM dfs.pics.`*.jpg`
WHERE ST_Within(
    ST_Point(t.GPS.GPSLongitude, t.GPS.GPSLatitude),
    ST_GeomFromText(
      'POLYGON((-121.95 37.28, -121.94 37.35, -121.84 37.35, -121.84 37.28, \
         -121.95 37.28))'
      )
);
```

Drilling Excel Files

Charles has worked for a management consultancy in the past, and in many instances has been asked to assist in helping a client out with "big data," which is a US government term for a shared drive full of random Excel files. Although this may seem like a trivial task, analyzing this data can be quite time-consuming, especially if the files themselves are large or there are a great deal of them.

Unfortunately, Drill cannot natively query Excel files. As of Office 2007, Microsoft adopted an XML format (*https://en.wikipedia.org/wiki/Office_Open_XML*) with the idea of enabling its data to be read by other applications. Luckily, there are open source Java libraries to parse the Office Open XML format, and because Excel files are by their nature tabular data, and the data is self-describing, these files lend themselves well to being read by Drill. Therefore, enabling Drill to query Excel files can dramatically reduce the amount of time and effort it takes to analyze this kind of data.

You learned how to write a custom format plug-in in Chapter 12, and this section demonstrates a practical use case for writing one. You can find the complete code for this storage plug-in on GitHub (*https://github.com/cgivre/drill-excel-plugin*).

The pom.xml File

The first step in writing the Excel plug-in is identifying the dependencies. Essentially, the format plug-in will be a wrapper for the Apache POI libraries, which are a collection of Java libraries that read the Office Open XML files.[3] You must include these libraries in the dependencies in your *pom.xml* file, as shown here:

```
<dependency>
    <groupId>org.apache.poi</groupId>
    <artifactId>poi</artifactId>
    <version>3.17</version>
</dependency>
<dependency>
    <groupId>org.apache.poi</groupId>
    <artifactId>poi-ooxml</artifactId>
    <version>3.17</version>
</dependency>
<dependency>
    <groupId>org.apache.poi</groupId>
    <artifactId>poi-ooxml-schemas</artifactId>
    <version>3.17</version>
</dependency>
<dependency>
    <groupId>org.apache.poi</groupId>
    <artifactId>poi-scratchpad</artifactId>
    <version>3.17</version>
</dependency>
<dependency>
    <groupId>org.apache.poi</groupId>
    <artifactId>ooxml-schemas</artifactId>
    <version>1.1</version>
</dependency>
<dependency>
    <groupId>org.apache.poi</groupId>
    <artifactId>openxml4j</artifactId>
    <version>1.0-beta</version>
</dependency>
```

After you have written the *pom.xml* file, the next step is to write the format plug-in, which in this case consists of the ExcelFormatPlugin class, which implements the EasyFormatPlugin interface; the ExcelFormatPluginConfig class, which implements the FormatPluginConfig interface; and finally the ExcelRecordReader class, which extends the AbstractRecordReader class.

Most of the code for ExcelFormatPlugin and ExcelFormatPluginConfig is boilerplate code, with the only real modifications being configuration variables that are

---

3 For more information, check out the complete documentation for the Apache POI libraries (*https:// poi.apache.org*).

passed to the record reader. Because Excel files often have headers, footers, and other nontabular content, it is useful for the user to be able to define a region in the spreadsheet where the data is and ignore the rest. Therefore, the Excel format plug-in has configuration variables indicating the first and last column and row where the data exists.

The Excel Custom Record Reader

The `ExcelRecordReader` class is where most of the work actually happens. The `setup()` function, shown in the code that follows, sets up the `RecordReader` and defines all the variables that are needed for reading the rest of the data. As with UDFs, the `setup()` function in this interface is executed once, and the `next()` function is executed for each row of your data. Because it is possible in Excel to determine the number of columns in the spreadsheet as well as the header names, the format plug-in will perform both of these operations.

Because this plug-in implements the `EasyFormatInterface`, the example that follows creates a workbook object that represents the spreadsheet in memory. The first thing that you have to do is get the column headers and data types:

```
//Get the workbook
this.workbook = new XSSFWorkbook(this.fsStream.getWrappedStream());

//Evaluate formulae
FormulaEvaluator evaluator = workbook.getCreationHelper()
                                     .createFormulaEvaluator();

//Get the sheet
this.sheet = workbook.getSheetAt(0);
this.workbook.setMissingCellPolicy(Row.MissingCellPolicy
                                      .CREATE_NULL_AS_BLANK);

//Get the field names
int columnCount = sheet.getRow(0).getPhysicalNumberOfCells();
this.excelFieldNames = new String[columnCount];
this.rowIterator = sheet.iterator();

if (rowIterator.hasNext()) {
   while (this.lineCount < config.headerRow) {
      Row row = rowIterator.next();
      this.lineCount++;
   }
}
Row row = rowIterator.next();
this.totalColumnCount = row.getLastCellNum();
```

In the preceding code, the second line creates a `FormulaEvaluator` object. You will use this object when you read in the lines of data to evaluate any cells that contain Excel formulae. The next two lines get the appropriate sheet and set the appropriate missing cell policy.

The next step is to get the dimensions of the data and then set up the data types of the columns and their names. The library we are using allows you to determine whether a cell contains a numeric value or a string; after you've done that, you can extract the value from the cell. This will become the column name. Here is the full code for the setup() function:

```java
public void setup(final OperatorContext context,
                  final OutputMutator output)
                  throws ExecutionSetupException {
  this.writer = new VectorContainerWriter(output);
  try {
    this.workbook = new XSSFWorkbook(this.fsStream
                                       .getWrappedStream());

    //Evaluate formulae
    FormulaEvaluator evaluator = workbook.getCreationHelper()
                                  .createFormulaEvaluator();
    this.sheet = workbook.getSheetAt(0);
    this.workbook.setMissingCellPolicy(Row
                                        .MissingCellPolicy
                                        .CREATE_NULL_AS_BLANK);

    //Get the field names
    int columnCount = sheet.getRow(0).getPhysicalNumberOfCells();
    this.excelFieldNames = new String[columnCount];
    this.rowIterator = sheet.iterator();

    if (rowIterator.hasNext()) {
      while (this.lineCount < config.headerRow) {
        Row row = rowIterator.next();
        this.lineCount++;
      }
      Row row = rowIterator.next();
      this.totalColumnCount = row.getLastCellNum();

      Iterator<Cell> cellIterator = row.cellIterator();
      int colPosition = 0;
      while (cellIterator.hasNext()) {
        Cell cell = cellIterator.next();
        CellValue cellValue = evaluator.evaluate(cell);
        switch (cellValue.getCellTypeEnum()) {
          case STRING:
            this.excelFieldNames[colPosition] = cell
                          .getStringCellValue()
                          .replaceAll("_", "__")
                          .replace(PARSER_WILDCARD, SAFE_WILDCARD)
                          .replaceAll("\\.", SAFE_SEPARATOR);
          break;
          case NUMERIC:
            this.excelFieldNames[colPosition] = String
                                    .valueOf(cell
                                    .getNumericCellValue());
```

```
          break;
        }
        colPosition++;
      }
    }
  } catch (java.io.IOException e) {
    throw UserException.dataReadError(e).build(logger);
  }
}
```

The other method that you must implement is the next() method, which is executed on every row of data and maps the cells to the appropriate columns or vectors. The function that follows contains a lot of boilerplate code, but the next() function maps the data to the appropriate columns:

```
public int next() {
    this.writer.allocate();
    this.writer.reset();

    //Get the configuration variables
    int skipRows = config.headerRow;
    int recordCount = 0;
    int sheetCount = workbook.getNumberOfSheets();
    int lastRow = config.lastRow;

    //Create the base MapWriter
    BaseWriter.MapWriter map = this.writer.rootAsMap();
    int colPosition = 0;
    FormulaEvaluator evaluator = workbook.getCreationHelper()
                                .createFormulaEvaluator();

    try {

        //Iterate through the rows
        while (recordCount > lastRow && rowIterator.hasNext()) {
          lineCount++;
          if (recordCount > 0) {
            this.writer.setPosition(recordCount);
            map.start();
          }
          //Get the row
          Row row = rowIterator.next();
          //Get a cell iterator
          Iterator<Cell> cellIterator = row.cellIterator();

          colPosition = 0;
          String fieldName;
          if (row.getLastCellNum() < totalColumnCount) {
            System.out.println("Wrong number of columns in row.");
          }

          //Iterate through the columns
```

```java
for (int cn = 0; cn < totalColumnCount; cn++) {

  Cell cell = row.getCell(cn);

  CellValue cellValue = evaluator.evaluate(cell);
  fieldName = excelFieldNames[colPosition];

  //Assign values to appropriate columns
  if (cellValue == null) {
    String fieldValue = "";
    byte[] bytes = fieldValue.getBytes("UTF-8");
    this.buffer.setBytes(0, bytes, 0, bytes.length);
    map.varChar(fieldName).writeVarChar(0, bytes.length,
                                        buffer);
  } else {
    switch (cellValue.getCellTypeEnum()) {
      case NUMERIC:
        if (DateUtil.isCellDateFormatted(cell)) {
          map.timeStamp(fieldName).writeTimeStamp(cell
                            .getDateCellValue()
                            .getTime());
        } else {
          double fieldNumValue = cell.getNumericCellValue();
          map.float8(fieldName).writeFloat8(fieldNumValue);
        }
        break;
      case STRING:
        String fieldValue = "";
        fieldValue = cellValue.formatAsString();
        if (fieldValue.length() > 1) {
          fieldValue = fieldValue.substring(1);
          fieldValue = fieldValue.substring(0,
                                    fieldValue.length() - 1);
        }

        byte[] bytes = fieldValue.getBytes("UTF-8");
        this.buffer.setBytes(0, bytes, 0, bytes.length);
        map.varChar(fieldName).writeVarChar(0,
                                    bytes.length, buffer);
        break;
      case FORMULA:
        break;
      case BLANK:
        break;
    }
  }
  colPosition++;
}
map.end();
recordCount++;
}
```

```
      this.writer.setValueCount(recordCount);
      return recordCount;

    } catch (final Exception e) {
      throw UserException.dataReadError(e).build(logger);
    }
  }
}
```

Using the Excel Format Plug-in

After you have built and installed the format plug-in, the next step is to set up the format in the appropriate storage plug-in. Here are the default settings:

```
"excel": {
  "type": "excel",
  "extensions": ["xlsx"],
  "headerRow": 0,
  "lastRow": 1000000,
  "sheetNumber": 0,
  "firstColumn": 0,
  "lastColumn": 0
}
```

Because Excel files often contain formatting and other nondata cells, it is useful to be able to define a region within the spreadsheet where the data exists, and the variables lastRow, firstColumn, and lastColumn enable you to do that. Additionally, the headerRow variable allows you set the row index of the column headers. Remember that the indexing starts at zero. You can also set the sheetNumber to query various sheets within the Excel files.

At this point, you are ready to query Excel files as if they were any other data table in Drill! As noted earlier, the Excel plug-in will interpret data types from the Excel file, so there is no need to use the CAST() and TO_ functions for calculations.

Next, we'll explore a few practical examples where analysts created UDFs to solve particular problems in Drill. These might serve as an inspiration for your own customization efforts.

Network Packet Analysis (PCAP) with Drill

A core component of any network security program is analyzing raw data that is coming over the wire. This raw network data is captured in a format called Packet Capture (PCAP) or PCAP Next Generation (PCAP-NG) and can be challenging to analyze because it is a binary format. One of the most common tools for analyzing PCAP data is called Wireshark (*http://wireshark.org*). Even though Wireshark is a capable tool, it is limited in that it can only analyze data that fits in your system's memory.

Drill can query a PCAP or PCAP-NG file and retrieve fields including the following:

- Protocol type (TCP/UDP)
- Source/destination IP address
- Source/destination port
- Source/destination MAC address
- Date and time of packet creation
- Packet length
- TCP session number and flags
- The packet data in binary form

Querying PCAP or PCAP-NG requires no additional configuration settings, so out of the box, your Drill installation can query them both.

Examples of Queries Using PCAP Data Files

Let's take the example of finding a SYN scan. If you are not familiar with the technique, a SYN scan is a passive technique intended to identify open ports on a victim machine. A SYN scan works by the attacker first attempting to open a connection on a victim machine by sending a TCP SYN packet. Next, if the port is open, the victim will respond with a SYN/ACK packet. If this were a normal connection, the client would respond with an ACK packet and a connection would be opened. However, in this case, because the goal is simply to determine open ports, the attacker does not send the final ACK packet.

Using the example file *synscan.pcap*,[4] if you execute the following query, you will see an example of a SYN scan in progress. First, let's see if we can find examples of sessions with more than one packet. By aggregating on the TCP session ID and counting the number of packets, we can find these suspicious connections. The following query illustrates how to do that:

```
SELECT tcp_session, COUNT(*) AS packet_count
FROM dfs.test.`synscan.pcap`
GROUP BY tcp_session HAVING COUNT(*) > 1
```

Figure 13-1 shows the results of this query.

---

4 The source of this file is available from Chris Sanders's website (*http://chrissanders.org/packet-captures/*).

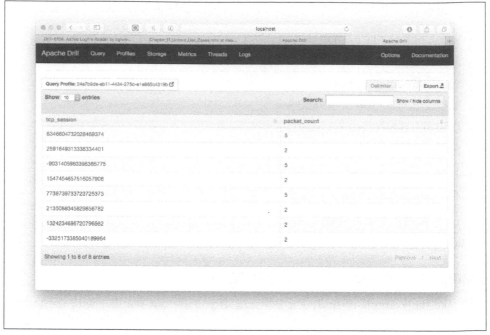

Figure 13-1. SYN scan query results

Next, we could run queries on each of the session IDs, but let's take a look at the first one, containing five packets. This next query retrieves the sessions:

```
SELECT *
FROM dfs.test.`synscan.pcap`
WHERE tcp_session=6346604732028469374
```

In Figure 13-2, you can see the results of this query. The important column to note is the `tcp_parsed_flags` column.

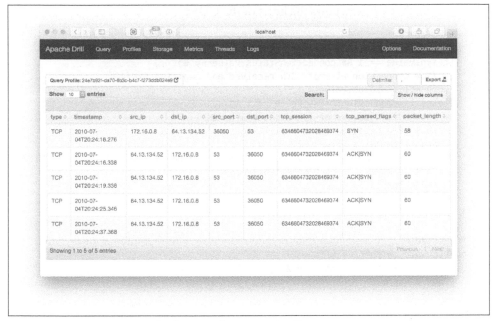

Figure 13-2. SYN scan results (some columns omitted)

In this example, note the exact pattern of a SYN scan. The first packet is a SYN packet followed by a series of ACK/SYN packets with no corresponding ACK packet.

Automating the process using an aggregate function

As you can see in the previous example, it is possible to identify possible SYN scan attacks with a series of SQL queries. However, another way to approach this is to write an aggregate function that returns true or false depending on whether a given session is a syn-flood attempt. We have already covered the mechanics of writing UDFs in detail in previous chapters, and the complete code for this UDF is in the book's GitHub repository.

Here's the pseudocode for such an aggregate function:

1. Group by the TCP session ID.
2. If there is a SYN flag set, increment a counter variable.
3. If the session has seen the SYN flag and there is an ACK flag set (SYN/ACK), increment the counter.
4. If the session is never closed (ACK never received), return true; otherwise, return false.

The example that follows shows the heart of the UDF:[5]

```java
@Override
public void add() {
  if(syn.value == 1 && connectionStatus.value == 0){
    //New connection attempt  SYN received and awaiting SYN/ACK
    connectionStatus.value = 1;
  } else if(connectionStatus.value == 1 && synAck.value == 1){
    //Connection status of 2 indicates SYN/ACK
    //has been received and are awaiting the final ACK
    connectionStatus.value = 2;
  } else if(connectionStatus.value == 2 && syn.value == 0 && ack.value == 1) {
    //ACK received, connection established
    connectionStatus.value = 3;
  }
}

@Override
public void output() {
  if(connectionStatus.value == 2) {
    out.value = 1;
  } else {
    out.value = 0;
  }
}

@Override
public void reset() {
  connectionStatus.value = 0;
}
```

After you have installed the UDF, you could call the function using the following query:

```sql
SELECT tcp_session,
    is_syn_scan(tcp_session, tcp_flags_syn, tcp_flags_ack)
FROM file.pcap
GROUP BY tcp_session
```

Alternatively, you could use the function in the WHERE clause to identify session IDs that are possible SYN scan attempts, as in the following query:

```sql
SELECT tcp_session
FROM file.pcap
GROUP BY tcp_session
HAVING is_syn_scan(tcp_session, tcp_flags_syn, tcp_flags_ack)
```

The results of this query would display the sessions that are possible SYN scans.

---

5 In this example, there are many ways of parsing the TCP flags; however, this UDF is implemented to maximize readability and hence does not use any techniques that use bit shifting.

Analyzing Twitter Data with Drill

Data from Twitter has proven to be a valuable source for a wide range of analytic questions. Although there are many libraries and sources for Twitter data, in many instances they omit the metadata that is quite valuable for analysis.

To deal with this problem, Bob Rudis of Rapid7 wrote a collection of UDFs (*https://github.com/hrbrmstr/drill-twitter-text*) to extract metadata from tweets. These UDFs include the following:

tw_parse_tweet(VARCHAR)
: Parses the tweet text and returns a map column with the following named values:

  weightedLength
  : (INT) Indicates the overall length of the tweet with code points weighted per the ranges defined in the configuration file.

  permillage
  : (INT) Indicates the proportion (per thousand) of the weighted length in comparison to the max weighted length. A value >1,000 indicates input text that is longer than the allowable maximum.

  isValid
  : (BOOLEAN) Indicates whether input text length corresponds to a valid result.

  display_start/display_end
  : (INT) Provide indices identifying the inclusive start and exclusive end of the displayable content of the Tweet.

  valid_start/valid_end
  : (INT) Provide indices identifying the inclusive start and exclusive end of the valid content of the Tweet.

tw_extract_hashtags(VARCHAR)
: Extracts all hashtags in the tweet text into a list that can be FLATTEN()ed.

tw_extract_screennames(VARCHAR)
: Extracts all screen names in the tweet text into a list that can be FLATTEN()ed.

tw_extract_urls(VARCHAR)
: Extracts all URLs in the tweet text into a list that can be FLATTEN()ed.

tw_extract_reply_screenname()
: Extracts the reply screen name (if any) from the tweet text into a VARCHAR.

This collection of functions is a great example of writing a custom UDF to extract artifacts from data.

Using Drill in a Machine Learning Pipeline

Let's begin with the bad news: you cannot do machine learning directly in Drill. However, Drill can be a useful component in a machine learning pipeline. Figure 13-3 illustrates the various phases of the machine learning process. The complete code for this example is posted in the *UDFs* folder of the book's GitHub repository, under *machine_learning*.

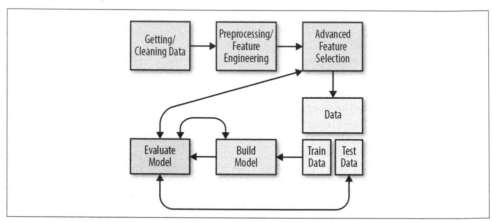

Figure 13-3. The supervised machine learning pipeline

Making Predictions Within Drill

Even though you can't train a model in Drill, after you've built one, you can use that model to make predictions with data that Drill can query. We demonstrate this using H2O, a notebooking product focused on machine learning to build a model and serialize it. Then, we wrap it in a custom UDF.

The H2O platform (*http://h2o.ai*) is very useful for developing machine learning models, but one of its key features is that after you have built and trained a model, you can serialize and export the model as either a Plain Old Java Object (POJO) or a Maven Old Java Object (MOJO).[6]

Building and Serializing a Model

The first step is building and serializing a model in H2O. The code that follows (from the H2O documentation) demonstrates how to create and train a model—in this case using sample data—and save it as a MOJO. If you are familiar with machine learning in Python, the general pattern should look familiar to you. H2O also features an R interface, and you can do the same thing in R:

---

6 POJOs and MOJOs are ways of serializing an object for reuse in other programs, similar to Python pickles.

```
#Example code from
#http://docs.h2o.ai/h2o/latest-stable/h2o-docs/productionizing.html

import h2o
from h2o.estimators.gbm
import H2OGradientBoostingEstimator

h2o.init()
h2o_df = h2o.load_dataset("prostate.csv")
h2o_df["CAPSULE"] = h2o_df["CAPSULE"].asfactor()
model=H2OGradientBoostingEstimator(distribution="bernoulli",
                    ntrees=100,
                    max_depth=4,
                    learn_rate=0.1)

#Train the model
model.train(y="CAPSULE",
            x=["AGE","RACE","PSA","GLEASON"],
            training_frame=h2o_df)

#Save the model as a MOJO
modelfile = model.download_mojo(path="experiment/",
                                get_genmodel_jar=True)
```

After you've executed this code, you will have a JAR file in a folder called *experiment*. You will need to copy this as well as the *h2o-genmodel.jar* file to your Drill site folder, as described in "Building and Installing Your UDF" on page 211.

Writing the UDF Wrapper

Now that you have the JAR files for the model, the next step is to write a UDF that wraps the functionality of the model. Because you will be using data of identical structure to that with which you trained your model, your prediction function in your UDF must have the same structure as the data that you used to train the model.

MOJO Models Accept Only Doubles as Input

When creating a wrapper function for an H2O MOJO, remember that all your features must be Java doubles. Therefore, all your input parameters must be converted to doubles.

Example 13-1 shows the setup() function for the Drill UDF. There are five input parameters that are all Float8Holders and correspond to the structure of the original data. The @Workspace annotation contains the actual model, which we initialize in the setup() function and use in the eval() function.

Example 13-1. Intro and setup() function for H20 wrapper

```
@FunctionTemplate(name = "binomal_prediction",
    scope = FunctionTemplate.FunctionScope.SIMPLE,
    nulls = FunctionTemplate.NullHandling.NULL_IF_NULL)

public static class Binomal_Prediction implements DrillSimpleFunc {

  @Param
  Float8Holder age;

  @Param
  Float8Holder race;

  @Param
  Float8Holder dcaps;

  @Param
  Float8Holder vol;

  @Param
  Float8Holder gleason;

  @Workspace
  hex.genmodel.easy.EasyPredictModelWrapper model;

  @Output
  BitHolder out;

  @Override
  public void setup() {
    try {
      model = new hex.genmodel.easy
                        .EasyPredictModelWrapper(hex.genmodel
                        .MojoModel
.load("/Users/cgivre/experiment/GBM_model_python_1527558187517_1.zip"));
    } catch (Exception e){
      //Handle exception
    }
  }
}
```

The `eval()` function in the UDF is really quite simple, as well. All it needs to do is map the values from the input into an H20 `RowData` object and then call the model's `predictBinomial()` function. This model is a classifier, so you can access the prediction probabilities as well by calling the `predictBinomial()` function on the results of the `eval()` function, as demonstrated here:

```
public void eval() {
  hex.genmodel.easy.RowData row = new hex.genmodel.easy.RowData();
  row.put("AGE", age.value);
  row.put("RACE", race.value);
```

```
    row.put("DCAPS", dcaps.value);
    row.put("VOL", vol.value);
    row.put("GLEASON", gleason.value);

    try {
      hex.genmodel.easy.prediction.BinomialModelPrediction p = model
                                          .predictBinomial(row);
      if(p.label.equals("1")) {
        out.value = 1;
      } else {
        out.value = 0;
      }
    } catch(Exception e) {
      //Handle exception
    }
  }
}
```

You can see that this UDF returns true or false depending on the model's prediction. H20 has other types of models, for regression, clustering, and more. If you use one of those, the prediction functions are slightly different.

Making Predictions Using the UDF

After you have installed the wrapper UDF, you can use it in a query to obtain a list of predictions, as shown here:

```
SELECT binomial_prediction(`age`,
       `race`,
       `dcaps`,
       `vol`,
       `gleason`) AS prediction
FROM dfs.book.`ml_sample.csvh`
LIMIT 5
```

This query would yield results like those shown in Table 13-1.

Table 13-1. Machine learning prediction results

Prediction
TRUE
TRUE
FALSE
TRUE
FALSE

Conclusion

In this final chapter, you have seen several examples of how Drill can facilitate a wide variety of data analyses, including network security, image metadata, and even machine learning. By extending the code base with some simple UDFs and format plug-ins, its possible to extend Drill even further and unlock all kinds of data for rapid ad hoc analysis.

List of Drill Functions

This appendix contains a list of Apache Drill functions that are available in queries as of Drill 1.14. Because Drill is a rapidly evolving open source tool, this list is current at the time of writing but will certainly grow.

Aggregate and Window Functions

Drill has many functions that perform aggregate operations on a column or columns of data. You should use these functions (see Table A-1) in conjunction with the GROUP BY clause, as shown here:

```
SELECT col1, AVG(column) AS col_avg
FROM data
GROUP BY col1
```

Table A-1. Drill aggregate functions

Function	Output	Description
AVG(*column*)	Same as data argument type	Returns the average of the expression
COUNT(*)	BIGINT	Returns the number of rows
COUNT(DISTINCT)	BIGINT	Returns the number of unique values and the number of times they occurred
MAX(*column*)	Same as argument type	Returns the largest value in the expression
MIN(*column*)	Same as argument type	Returns the smallest value in the expression
STDDEV(*column*)	DECIMAL	Returns the standard deviation of the column
STDDEV_POP(*column*)	DECIMAL	Returns the sample standard deviate of input column
STDDEV_SAMP(*column*)	DECIMAL	Returns the population standard deviate of input column

Function	Output	Description
SUM(*column*)	Same as argument type	Returns the sum of the given column
VARIANCE(*column*)	DECIMAL	Sample variance of input values (sample standard deviation squared)
VAR_POP(*column*)	DECIMAL	Population variance of input values (the population standard deviation squared)
VAR_SAMP(*column*)	DECIMAL	Sample variance of input values (sample standard deviation squared)

Window Functions

In addition to the standard aggregate functions, Drill has a collection of windowing functions (see Table A-2). Their functionality is described in Chapter 4. In addition to the functions listed here, you can also use AVG(), COUNT(), MIN(), MAX(), and SUM() in windowing queries.

Table A-2. Drill window functions

Function	Return type	Description
CUME_DIST()	DOUBLE	Calculates the relative rank of the current row within the window: rows preceding/total rows
DENSE_RANK()	BIGINT	Returns the rank of the row within the window; does not create gaps in the event of duplicate values
FIRST_VALUE()	Same as input	Returns the first value in the window
LAG()	Same as input	Returns the value after the current value in the window, NULL if none exists
LAST_VALUE()	Same as input	Returns the last value in the window
LEAD()	Same as input	Returns the value prior to the current value in the window, or NULL if none exists
NTILE()	INT	Divides the rows for each window into a number of ranked groups; requires the ORDER BY clause in the OVER() clause
PERCENT_RANK()	DOUBLE	Calculates the percent rank of the current row within the window: (rank − 1) / (rows − 1)
RANK()	BIGINT	Similar to DENSE_RANK() but includes rows with equal values in the calculation
ROW_NUMBER()	BIGINT	Returns the number of the row within the window

Cryptological and Hashing Functions

The functions listed in Table A-3 all implement various cryptological or hashing algorithms.

Table A-3. Cryptological and hashing functions

Function	Output	Description
AES_DECRYPT(*text*,*key*)	VARCHAR	Decrypts the given text using the AES algorithm
AES_ENCRYPT(*text*,*key*)	VARCHAR	Encrypts the given text using the AES algorithm
MD2(*text*)	VARCHAR	Returns the MD2 digest of a given input string
MD5(*text*)	VARCHAR	Returns the MD5 digest of a given input string
SHA(*text*)/SHA1(*text*)	VARCHAR	Returns the SHA-1 160-bit checksum for a string
SHA2(*text*)/SHA256(*text*)	VARCHAR	Returns the SHA-256 checksum for a string
SHA384(*text*)	VARCHAR	Returns the SHA-384 digest of a string
SHA512(*text*)	VARCHAR	Returns the SHA-512 digest of a string

Data Conversion Functions

The functions listed in Table A-4 are used to convert data from one type to another. Their usage is covered in Chapters 4 and 5. Drill primarily uses Joda formatting for its formatting strings.[1]

Table A-4. Data conversion functions

Function	Output	Description
CAST(*field* AS *data_type*)	data_type	Used to convert an expression into another data type. Possible values include INT, BIGINT, DOUBLE, FLOAT, DATE, TIME, TIMESTAMP, INTERVAL DAY, INTERVAL YEAR, BOOLEAN, and VARCHAR.
CONVERT_FROM(*column*,*type*) CONVERT_TO(*column*,*type*)	type type	Transform a known binary representation/encoding to a Drill internal format. Use CONVERT_TO() and CONVERT_FROM() instead of the CAST() function for converting VARBINARY data types. You will need these functions to query HBase, as discussed in Chapter 6.
DRILLTYPEOF()	VARCHAR	Similar to TYPEOF() but returns the internal Drill names.
MODEOF(*field*)	VARCHAR	Returns the cardinality of a column: NULL, NOT NULL, NULLABLE, or ARRAY.
SQLTYPEOF(*field*)	VARCHAR	Returns the data type of a field using SQL names.

---

1 A complete table of Joda formatting characters is available on the Apache Drill website (*http://bit.ly/2CKr6WZ*).

Function	Output	Description
TO_CHAR(*expression,format*)	VARCHAR	Converts a field to a VARCHAR. You can use this to reformat dates.
TO_DATE(*expression,format*)	DATE	Converts a field into a DATE data type.
TO_NUMBER(*expression,format*)	DECIMAL	Converts a field into a DECIMAL data type.
TO_TIMESTAMP(*expression,format*)	TIMESTAMP	Converts a field into a Drill TIMESTAMP.
TYPEOF(*field*)	VARCHAR	Returns the data type of a field.

Geospatial Functions

As of version 1.14, Drill contains a suite of geographic information system (GIS) functions. Most of the functionality follows that of PostGIS. To use these functions, your spatial data must be defined in the Well-Known Text (WKT) representation format (*https://en.wikipedia.org/wiki/Well-known_text*). The WKT format allows you to represent points, lines, polygons, and other geometric shapes. Following are two example WKT strings:

```
POINT (30 10)
POLYGON ((30 10, 40 40, 20 40, 10 20, 30 10))
```

Drill stores points as binary, so to read or plot these points, you need to convert them using the ST_AsText() and ST_GeoFromText() functions. Table A-5 lists the GIS functions.

Table A-5. Drill GIS functions

Function	Output	Description
ST_AsGeoJSON(*geometry*)	VARCHAR	Returns the geometry as a GeoJSON element.
ST_AsJSON(*geometry*)	VARCHAR	Returns JSON representation of the geometry.
ST_AsText(*geometry*)	VARCHAR	Return a the WKT representation of the geometry/geography without SRID metadata
ST_Buffer(*geometry, radius*)	GEOMETRY	Returns a geometry that represents all points whose distance from this geometry is less than or equal to *radius*.
ST_Contains(*geometry_a, geometry_b*)	BOOLEAN	Returns true if no points of *geometry_b* lie outside of *geometry_a* and at least one point of the interior of *geometry_b* is in the interior of *geometry_a*.
ST_Crosses(*geometry_a, geometry_b*)	BOOLEAN	Returns true if the supplied geometries have some but not all interior points in common.
ST_Difference(*geometry_a, geometry_b*)	GEOMETRY	Returns a geometry that represents the part of *geometry_a* that does not intersect with *geometry_b*.
ST_Disjoint(*geometry_a, geometry_b*)	BOOLEAN	Returns true if the two geometries do not spatially intersect.

Function	Output	Description
ST_Distance(*geometry_a*, *geometry_b*)	DOUBLE	For geometry types, returns the 2D Cartesian distance between two geometries in projected units. For geography types, defaults to returning the minimum geodesic distance between two geographies in meters.
ST_DWithin(*geometry_a*, *geometry_b*, *distance*)	BOOLEAN	Returns true if the geometries are within the specified distance of one another.
ST_Envelope(*geometry*)	GEOMETRY	Returns a geometry representing the double-precision bounding box of the supplied geometry. The polygon is defined by the corner points of the bounding box: ((MINX, MINY), (MINX, MAXY), (MAXX, MAXY), (MAXX, MINY), (MINX, MINY)).
ST_GeoFromText(*text*,[*SRID*])	GEOMETRY	Returns a specified ST_Geometry value from the WKT representation. If the spatial reference ID (SRID) is included as the second argument the function returns a geometry that includes this SRID as part of its metadata.
ST_Equals(*geometry_a*, *geometry_b*)	BOOLEAN	Returns true if the given geometries represent the same geometry. Directionality is ignored.
ST_Intersects(*geometry_a*, *geometry_b*)	BOOLEAN	Returns true if the geometries/geographies "spatially intersect in 2D" (share any portion of space) and false if they don't (they are disjoint).
ST_Overlaps(*geometry_a*, *geometry_b*)	BOOLEAN	Returns true if the geometries share space and are of the same dimension, but are not completely contained by each other.
ST_Point(*long*, *lat*)	GEOMETRY	Returns an ST_Point with the given coordinate values.
ST_Relate(*geometry_a*, *geometry_b* [,intersectionMatrixPattern])	BOOLEAN	Returns true if *geometry_a* is spatially related to *geometry_b*, determined by testing for intersections between the interior, boundary, and exterior of the two geometries as specified by the values in the intersection matrix pattern. If no intersection matrix pattern is passed in, returns the maximum intersection matrix pattern that relates the two geometries.
ST_Touches(*geometry_a*, *geometry_b*)	BOOLEAN	Returns true if the geometries have at least one point in common, but their interiors do not intersect.
ST_Transform(*geometry_a* [*Source_SRID*, *Target_SRID*])	GEOMETRY	Returns a new geometry with its coordinates transformed to a different spatial reference.

Function	Output	Description
ST_Union(*geometry_a, geometry_b*)	GEOMETRY	Returns a geometry that represents the point set union of the geometries.
ST_Union_Aggregate(*Geometry*)	GEOMETRY	Returns a geometry that represents the point set union of the geometries. Note: This function is an aggregate function and should be used with GROUP BY.
ST_Within(*geometry_a, geometry_b*)	BOOLEAN	Returns true if *geometry_a* is completely inside *geometry_b*.
ST_X(*geometry*)	DOUBLE	Returns the *x* coordinate of the point, or NaN if not available.
ST_XMax(*geometry*)	DOUBLE	Returns the *x* maxima of a 2D or 3D bounding box or a geometry.
ST_XMin(*geometry*)	DOUBLE	Returns the *x* minima of a 2D or 3D bounding box or a geometry.
ST_Y(*geometry*)	DOUBLE	Return the *y* coordinate of the point, or NaN if not available.
ST_YMax(*geometry*)	DOUBLE	Returns the *y* maxima of a 2D or 3D bounding box or a geometry.
ST_YMin(*geometry*)	DOUBLE	Returns the *y* minima of a 2D or 3D bounding box or a geometry.

Math and Trigonometric Functions

All the mathematic and trigonometric functions (see Table A-6) accept all numeric types, with the exception of LSHIFT() and RSHIFT(), which do not accept floating-point data types. The complete documentation for these functions is available on the Apache Drill website (*https://drill.apache.org/docs/math-and-trig/*).

Table A-6. Drill math and trigonometric functions

Function	Output	Description
ABS(*x*)	Same as input	Returns the absolute value of the input
ACOS(*x*)	DOUBLE	Returns the inverse cosine of angle *x* in radians
ASIN(*x*)	DOUBLE	Returns the inverse sine of angle *x* in radians
ATAN(*x*)	DOUBLE	Returns the inverse tangent of angle *x* in radians
CBRT(*x*)	DOUBLE	Returns the cube root of the input value
CEIL(*x*)/CEILING(*x*)	Same as input	Returns the smallest integer not less than *x*
COS(*x*)	DOUBLE	Returns the cosine of angle *x* in radians
COSH(*x*)	DOUBLE	Returns the hyperbolic cosine of angle *x* in radians
DEGREES(*x*)	DOUBLE	Converts *x* radians into degrees
E()	DOUBLE	Returns Euler's number (2.718...)
EXP(*x*)	DOUBLE	Returns e to the power of *x*
FLOOR(*x*)	DOUBLE	Returns the largest integer not greater than *x*

Function	Output	Description
LOG(x)	DOUBLE	Returns the natural log (base e) of x
LOG(x,y)	DOUBLE	Returns the log base x to the y power
LOG10(x)	DOUBLE	Returns the log (base 10) of x
LSHIFT(x,y)	Same as input	Shifts the binary x by y times to the left
MOD(x,y)	DOUBLE	Returns the remainder of x divided by y
NEGATIVE(x)	Same as input	Returns x as a negative number
PI	DOUBLE	Returns pi (3.14...)
POW(x,y)	DOUBLE	Returns the value of x to the y power
RADIANS(x)	DOUBLE	Converts x degrees into radians
RAND()	DOUBLE	Returns a pseudorandom number from 0–1
ROUND(x)	Same as input	Rounds to the nearest integer
ROUND(x,y)	DECIMAL	Rounds x to y decimal places
RSHIFT(x,y)	Same as input	Shifts the binary x by y times to the right
SIGN(x)	INT	Returns the sign of x
SIN(x)	DOUBLE	Returns the sine of angle x in radians
SINH(x)	DOUBLE	Returns the hyperbolic sine of angle x in radians
SQRT(x)	Same as input	Returns the square root of x
TAN(x)	DOUBLE	Returns the tangent of angle x in radians
TANH(x)	DOUBLE	Returns the hyperbolic tangent of angle x in radians
TRUNC($x,[y]$)	Same as input	Truncates x to y decimal places

Networking Functions

These functions listed in Table A-7 are useful when you are using Drill to analyze network and security data. The functions starting with IS_ are intended to be used in the WHERE clause of a query.

Analyzing IP Addresses

IPv4 addresses in dotted-decimal notation are actually representations of 32-bit integers. For analytic purposes, it is very helpful to convert IP addresses back into their 32-bit representations because this allows you to sort and filter the addresses much more easily than when using the dotted-decimal notation. Drill provides two functions, INET_ATON() and INET_NTOA(), that convert IPv4 addresses to and from 32-bit integers.

For instance, if you wanted to get an ordered list of IP addresses, sorting with the standard ORDER BY operator would get you results in ASCII order, but if you wanted the IPs in the correct sort order, you could sort them with the following query:

```
SELECT fields
FROM data
ORDER BY INET_ATON(`ip_field`) ASC
```

Additionally, if you wanted to find IP addresses within a particular range you could use these functions to do so, as shown here:

```
SELECT *
FROM data
WHERE
  INET_ATON(`ip_field`)
    BETWEEN INET_ATON('192.168.0.1')
    AND INET_ATON('192.168.0.150'
```

Table A-7. Networking functions

Function	Output	Description
ADDRESS_COUNT(inputCIDR)	INTEGER	Returns the number of IP addresses in the input CIDR block
BROADCAST_ADDRESS(inputCIDR)	VARCHAR	Returns the broadcast address of a given CIDR block
HIGH_ADDRESS(inputCIDR)	VARCHAR	Returns the highest address in a given input CIDR block
INET_ATON(IPv4)	INTEGER	Returns an IPv4 address represented as an INTEGER
INET_NTOA(IPv4)	VARCHAR	Returns an IP address in dotted-decimal notation given an IPv4 address in integer notation
IN_NETWORK(ip, inputCIDR)	BOOLEAN	Returns true or false depending the input IP is in the input CIDR block
IS_VALID_IP(ip)	BOOLEAN	Returns true or false depending on whether the input IP is a valid IP address
IS_VALID_IPv4(IPv4)	BOOLEAN	Returns true or false depending on whether the input IP is a valid IPv4 address
IS_VALID_IPv6(IPv4)	BOOLEAN	Returns true or false depending on whether the input IP is a valid IPv6 address
LOW_ADDRESS(inputCIDR)	VARCHAR	Returns the lowest address in a given CIDR block
NETMASK(inputCIDR)	VARCHAR	Returns the netmask of the input CIDR block

Null Handling Functions

Drill provides two functions to deal with null data: COALESCE(*field*[,list of expressions]) and NULLIF(*expression1, expression2*). See Table A-8 for more Drill null handling functions.

Table A-8. Drill null handling functions and operators

Function	Output	Description
field IS FALSE	BOOLEAN	True if the BOOLEAN field is false (not true or NULL)
field IS NULL	BOOLEAN	True if the field is NULL
field IS TRUE	BOOLEAN	True if the BOOLEAN field is true
field IS NOT FALSE	BOOLEAN	Opposite of IS FALSE
field IS NOT NULL	BOOLEAN	True if the field is not NULL
field IS NOT TRUE	BOOLEAN	Opposite of IS TRUE
IS_PRIVATE_IP(*IPv4*)	BOOLEAN	Returns true or false depending on whether the input IP is a private IPv4 address
COALESCE(field[,list of expressions])	Varies	Returns the first non-null expression in the list
ISFALSE(field)	BOOLEAN	Same as IS FALSE
ISNULL(field)	BOOLEAN	Same as IS NULL
ISTRUE(field)	BOOLEAN	Same as IS TRUE
ISNOTFALSE(field)	BOOLEAN	Same as IS NOT FALSE
ISNOTNULL(field)	BOOLEAN	Same as IS NOT NULL
ISNOTTRUE(field)	BOOLEAN	Same as IS NOT TRUE
NULLIF(expr1, expr2)	Varies	Returns the first expression if the two are not equal, or NULL if they are equal

The COALESCE() function is the most general. In the following query, if a row in field1 is null, the null value will be replaced with 0:

```
SELECT COALESCE(`field1`, 0) FROM...
```

The NULLIF(*expression1, expression2*) function returns the first expression if the two are not equal, or null if they are equal.

String Manipulation Functions

The functions listed in Table A-9 are designed to be useful when analyzing strings.

Table A-9. String manipulation functions[a]

Function	Output	Description
ASCII(*text*)	INTEGER	Returns the ASCII code of the first character of the input string.
BINARY_STRING(*text*)	VARBINARY	Converts a hex-encoded string into VARBINARY.
BIT_LENGTH(*text*)	INTEGER	Returns the bit length of a string.
BTRIM(*text*,*from*)	VARCHAR	Removes the longest string containing only characters from *FROM* from the start of the text.
BYTE_SUBSTR(*text*, [*start*, *end*])	VARBINARY or VARCHAR	Returns in binary format a substring of a string. Length arguments are integers and are optional.
CHAR_LENGTH(*text*) CHARACTER_LENGTH(*text*) LENGTH(*text*)	INTEGER	Returns the length of the string.
CHR(*int*)	VARCHAR	Returns the character corresponding to an ASCII code.
CONCAT(*text*, *text1*, *text2*)	VARCHAR	Concatenates strings; can also be accomplished with the || operator.
ILIKE(*text1*,*regex*,[*escape*])	BOOLEAN	Performs a case-insensitive string comparison.
INITCAP(*text1*)	VARCHAR	Converts a string using initial capitals.
LIKE(*text*,*regex*,[*escape*]), SIMILAR(*text*,*regex*,[*escape*]), SIMILAR_TO(*text*,*regex*,[*escape*])	BOOLEAN	Performs a regex string comparison.
LEFT(*string*, *n*)	VARCHAR	Returns the first *n* characters in the string. When *n* is negative, returns all but the last *n* characters.
LENGTHUTF8(*text*)	INTEGER	Returns the UTF8 length of a string.
LOWER(*text*)	VARCHAR	Converts text to lowercase.
LPAD(*text*,*length*,[*fill_text*])	VARCHAR	Pads a string to a specified length by adding the fill or a space to the beginning of the string.
LTRIM(*text1*,*text2*)	VARCHAR	Removes any characters from the beginning of *text1* that match the characters in *text2*.
OCTET_LENGTH(*text*)	INTEGER	Returns the octet length of *text*.
POSITION(*substring* IN *string*)	INTEGER	Returns the index of a substring.

Function	Output	Description
REGEXP_MATCHES(*source,pattern*)	BOOLEAN	Returns true or false depending on whether the string matches the regex. Note: this function uses standard rather than SQL regexes.
REGEXP_REPLACE(*source, pattern,replacement*)	VARCHAR	Replaces text that matches a regex. *pat tern* must be a Java-compatible regex.
REPEAT(*text,n*), REPEATSTR(*text,n*)	VARCHAR	Repeats *text n* times.
REPLACE(*text,from,to*)	VARCHAR	Replaces all occurrences in *text* of substring *from* with substring *to*.
REVERSE(*text*)	VARCHAR	Reverses a given string.
RIGHT(*text,n*)	VARCHAR	Returns the last *n* characters in the string. When *n* is negative, returns all but the first *n* characters.
RPAD(*text,length,[fill_text]*)	VARCHAR	Pads a string to a specified length by adding the fill or a space to the end of the string.
RTRIM(*text1,text2*)	VARCHAR	Removes any characters from the end of *text1* that match the characters in *text2*.
SPLIT(*text,delimiter*)	ARRAY	Splits the given string using the delimiter.
SPLIT_PART(*text,split_text, index*)	VARCHAR	Splits the given string using the *split_text*.
STRING_BINARY(*text*)	VARCHAR	Converts VARBINARY text into a hex-encoded string.
STRPOS(*haystack,needle*)	INTEGER	Returns the location of a substring in a string.
SUBSTR(*text,start, times*),SUB STRING(*text,start, times*)	VARCHAR	Extracts characters from position 1 − *start* of the string. *times* is optional.
TOASCII(*in,encoding*)	VARCHAR	Converts a string to ASCII from another encoding.
TRIM([*leading|trailing|both*] *string1*, FROM *string2*)	VARCHAR	Removes characters from *string2* that match *string1*.
UPPER(*text*)	VARCHAR	Converts a string to uppercase.
URL_DECODE(*text*)	VARCHAR	Decodes a URL-encoded string.
URL_ENCODE(*text*)	VARCHAR	Returns a URL-encoded string.

[a] Complete documentation is available at the Apache Drill website (*https://drill.apache.org/docs/string-manipulation/*).

Approximate String Matching Functions

As of version 1.14, Drill contains a collection of phonetic and other functions that you can use for approximate string matching.

Phonetic Functions

Phonetic functions implement various algorithms that map a word to a code or string based on how the word sounds. The idea behind these algorithms is to find words that sound similar to a known word.

In Drill, these functions (see Table A-10) are best used as shown in the following query, which demonstrates how to find words that sound like the name "Jaime":

```
SELECT fields
FROM data
WHERE SOUNDEX('jaime') = SOUNDEX(`first_name`)
```

Table A-10. Drill phonetic functions

Function	Output	Description
CAVERPHONE1(*text*)	VARCHAR	Implements the Caverphone 1.0 algorithm created by the Caversham Project at the University of Otago.
CAVERPHONE2(*text*)	VARCHAR	Implements the Caverphone 2.0 algorithm created by the Caversham Project at the University of Otago.
COLOGNE_PHONETIC(*text*)	VARCHAR	Encodes a string into a Cologne Phonetic value. The Kölner Phonetik is a phonetic algorithm that is optimized for the German language, related to the soundex algorithm.
DM_SOUNDEX(*text*)	VARCHAR	Encodes a string into a Daitch-Mokotoff Soundex value, a refinement of the Russell and American Soundex algorithms yielding greater accuracy in matching especially Slavish and Yiddish surnames with similar pronunciation.
DOUBLE_METAPHONE(*text*)	VARCHAR	Implements the double metaphone phonetic algorithm.
MATCH_RATING_ENCODER(*text*)	VARCHAR	Implements the Match Rating Encoder developed by Western Airlines.
METAPHONE(*text*)	VARCHAR	Implements the metaphone algorithm.
NYSIIS(*text*)	VARCHAR	Implements the New York State Identification and Intelligence System (NYSIIS) Phonetic Code, a phonetic algorithm devised in 1970 that features an accuracy increase of 2.7% over the traditional Soundex algorithm.
REFINED_SOUNDEX(*text*)	VARCHAR	Encodes a string into a refined Soundex value.
SOUNDEX(*text*)	VARCHAR	Encodes a string into a Soundex value.

String Distance Functions

As of version 1.14, Drill implements a number of functions that calculate the distance between strings. This distance can be used to match strings that are similar to one another.

Consider a situation in which you might have addresses manually entered into a database. These entries might not be entered consistently, and thus it would be difficult to match rows using standard BOOLEAN operators. For instance, the address 35 Elm Street might be entered as 35 Elm St., or 35 N. Elm St., or 35 North Elm St. The following query demonstrates how you might use a string distance function to match such data:

```
SELECT fields
FROM data
WHERE COSINE_DISTANCE(`address`, '35 Elm Street') < 1.0
```

Table A-11. String distance functions

Function	Output	Description
COSINE_DISTANCE(*text1*,*text2*)	DOUBLE	Calculates the cosine distance between two strings.
FUZZY_STRING(*text1*,*text2*)	DOUBLE	Calculates the fuzzy score, a matching algorithm that is similar to the searching algorithms implemented in editors such as Sublime Text, TextMate, Atom, and others.
JACCARD_DISTANCE(*text1*,*text2*)	DOUBLE	Returns the Jaccard distance between two strings.
JARO_DISTANCE(*text1*,*text2*)	DOUBLE	Returns the Jaro distance between two strings, a similarity algorithm indicating the percentage of matched characters between two character sequences.
LEVENSHTEIN_DISTANCE(*text1*,*text2*)	DOUBLE	Returns the Levenshtein distance between two strings.
LONGEST_COMMON_SUBSTRING_DISTANCE(*text1*,*text2*)	DOUBLE	Returns the length of the longest substring that the two strings have in common. This algorithm is inefficient and should not be used in large datasets.

Drill Formatting Strings

Apache Drill uses Joda formatting strings for date and time formatting, as shown in Table B-1.

Table B-1. Number formatting characters

Symbol	Location	Meaning
0	Number	Digit.
#	Number	Digit, zero shows as absent.
.	Number	Decimal separator or monetary decimal separator.
-	Number	Minus sign.
,	Number	Grouping separator.
E	Number	Separates mantissa and exponent in scientific notation. Does not need to be quoted in prefix or suffix.
;	Subpattern boundary	Separates positive and negative subpatterns.
%	Prefix or suffix	Multiplies by 100 and shows as percentage.
‰ (030)	Prefix or suffix	Multiplies by 1,000 and shows as per-mille value.
¤ (0A4)	Prefix or suffix	Currency sign, replaced by currency symbol. If doubled, replaced by international currency symbol. If present in a pattern, the monetary decimal separator is used instead of the decimal separator.
'	Prefix or suffix	Used to quote special characters in a prefix or suffix; for example, "'#'#'" formats 123 to ""#123"". To create a single quote itself, use two in a row: "# o''clock".

Drill uses the characters shown in Table B-2 for date formats. Note that these are case-sensitive.

Table B-2. Joda date formatting characters

Symbol	Meaning	Presentation	Examples
G	era	text	AD
C	century of era (≥0)	number	20
Y	year of era (≥0)	year	1996
x	weekyear	year	1996
w	week of weekyear	number	27
e	day of week	number	2
E	day of week	text	Tuesday; Tue
y	year	year	1996
D	day of year	number	189
M	month of year	month	July; Jul; 07
d	day of month	number	10
a	halfday of day	text	PM
K	hour of halfday (0–11)	number	0
h	clockhour of halfday (1–12) number	12	
H	hour of day (0–23)	number	0
k	clockhour of day (1–24)	number	24
m	minute of hour	number	30
s	second of minute	number	55
S	fraction of second	number	978
z	time zone	text	Pacific Standard Time; PST
Z	time zone offset/ID	zone	−0800; −08:00; America/Los_Angeles
'	single quotation mark, escape for text delimiter	literal	

Index

Symbols

$DRILL_SITE variable, 177

7-zip, 11

? (question mark), parameter substitution with, 113

@JsonProperty annotations, 228

@Output annotations, 216

@Param annotations, 207

@Workspace annotations, 216

` ` (backticks)

enclosing column names with spaces or same as reserved words, 62

in names not valid SQL or same as SQL keyword, 138

{ } (curly braces), map notation in JSON, 68

{ } (square brackets), referencing individual array items, 66

A

absolute references in Drill UDFs, 208

access credentials for Amazon S3, 101

access keys for Amazon S3, in Hadoop, 185

including in core-site.xml config file, 186

admission control, 188

queues for small and large queries, 188

setting memory for small and large queries, 189

timeout in query queues, 189

aggregate functions, 55-58

aggregate UDFs, 201

comparison with window functions, 59-62

reference of functions available as of Drill 1.14, 277

using to check for syn flood attacks, 269

writing aggregate UDFs, 215

aggregate function API, 216

example, Kendall's rank correlation coefficient, 217-220

all-text mode, 70, 165, 168, 173

ALTER SESSION statement, 111

ALTER SESSION SET, 70

turning on admission control, 188

using scripting to add parameters to a query, 174

Amazon EC2, Drill running in, 19

Amazon S3, 100, 133

getting access credentials for, 101

Hive data stored on, 95

reads and network performance, 194

using for storage in Drill deployment, 185-188

access keys stored with Hadoop, 186

defining Amazon S3 storage configuration, 187

distributing the configuration, 187

standalone Drill, Hadoop configuration file, 186

troubleshooting configuration, 187

Amazon Simple Storage Service (see Amazon S3)

Amazon Web Services (see AWS)

analyzing complex and nested data (see querying complex and nested data)

ANSI standards

date format, 50

SQL, 2, 34

Apache Calcite (see Calcite)

Apache Drill (see Drill)

F

fields field in storage plug-in, 84
file formats
    defining in regex format plug-in, 222
    Drill support for, 2
file storage plug-in, 137
file type inference, 136, 140-142
    (see also data source inference)
    file format variations, 141
    format inference, 141
    format plug-ins and format configuration, 140
filesystems
    Drill spport for distributed filesystems, 3
    insufficient file splits causing query performance problem, 195
    local configuration pointing to local filesystem, 137
filling empty values, 249
filters, 40, 48
    filtering results from window function, 61
finding and filtering valid credit card numbers, writing Drill UDF for, 201
FLATTEN function, 73
FoodMart sample dataset, 135
Foreman (Drill server), 21
form submissions, analyzing for malicious activity, 82
format configurations, 140
format field in storage plug-in, 84
format inference, 141
format plug-ins, 140, 221-257
    additional details for advanced cases, 253-257
        contributing to Drill, pull request, 255
        creating a plug-in project, 256
        default format configuration, 253
        file chunks, 253
        maintaining the code, next steps, 254
        maintaining your branch of Drill repo, 255
        production build, 255
    creating Easy format plug-in, 222-226
        cautions before starting, 226
        creating plug-in package, 225
        Drill module configuration, 225
        Maven pom.xml file, 223-225
        plug-in configuration, 226

    creating regex plug-in configuration class, 227-230
        copyright headers and code format, 228
        fixing configuration problems, 229
        testing the configuration, 228
        troubleshooting, 230
    creating regex plug-in format class, 230-236
        configuring RAT to check copyright header, 233
        creating test file, 232
        creating unit test, 234
        efficient debugging, 233
        how Drill finds your plug-ins, 235
    example regex plug-in, 221
    Excel plug-in, 261-266
    record reader for regex format plug-in, 236-250
        column projection accounting, 242
        columnar structure in Drill, 246
        defining column names, 241
        defining vectors, 247
        error handling, 239
        loading data into vectors, 248
        opening a file as an input stream, 245
        project all, 243
        project none, 243
        project some, 243
        projection, 241
        reading data, 248
        record batches, 246
        regex parsing, 240
        releasing resources, 249
        setup, 240
        testing the reader shell, 238
    testing the record reader, 250-253
        scaling up, 252
        testing empty projection, 251
        testing explicit projection, 251
        testing wildcard (SELECT *) case, 250
format strings
    log format string, 77
    log format strings from Apache server, 78
    reference listing of Drill format strings, 291
FormatCreator class, 235
FormatPlugin class, 235
fragments, 192
    (see also major fragments; minor fragments)
    currently running, drill.fragments.running, 194

SQL session state, 22
statement execution, 26
    data representation, 27
statement preparation, 22
    distribution, 25
    logical and physical plans, 24
    parsing and semantic analysis, 24
operators, 24
    metrics on, in monitoring of Drill queries, 194
OPTIONAL cardinality, 246
Oracle, 90
    configuring Drill to query a database, 91
Oracle Java SE Development Kit 8 (JDK 8), 10, 15
output value, defining for Drill UDFs, 207
OutputMutator class, 247

P

Pandas DataFrame, 112
    transfer of query results into with drillpy, 113
    transfer of query results into with pydrill, 113
parallelizing of internal operators, 26
parameter substitution in queries, 113
Parquet format, 65
    Drill encouraging ETL of data in, 134
    Drill working best with, 133
    querying Parquet files from Drill via Hive, 97
    using Drill with, 168
        schema evolution in Parquet, 169
parse_query function, 81
parse_url function, 81
parse_user_agent function, 68, 79
parsing SQL statements, 24
PARTITION BY clause, 59, 172
partitioning, 43, 134
    dependence on use cases, 43
    of data directories, 169-173
        defining a table workspace, 172
PATH environment variable, 10
    adding Drill to, on macOS or Linux, 13
Pattern class, 240
PCAP (Packet Capture), 266
    (see also network packet analysis (PCAP) with Drill)
PCAP Next Generation (PCAP-NG), 266

    (see also network packet analysis (PCAP) with Drill)
performance
    of Drill, 4
    of Drill queries, determining cause with monitoring metrics, 195
    schema-on-read and, 4
phonetic functions, 288
PHP
    connecting to Drill with
        installing the connector, 119
        interacting with Drill from PHP, 120
        querying Drill from PHP, 120
        using the connector, 119
    querying Drill with, 119-121
physical plan for queries, 24
    distribution across nodes, 25
Pig, 6
Plain Old Java Objects (POJOs), 272
planner.cpu_load_average session option, 192
POINT_AGGREGATE scope, 216
pom.xml file (see Maven)
PostgreSQL, 90
    configuring Drill to query, 91
preparation phase (SQL statements), 22
    (see also statement prepartion by Drill)
Presto, 7, 18
production, 175
    (see also deploying Drill in production)
    plug-in configurations in, 230
    production build, including contributed format plug-in, 255
    production installation of Drill, 176
Project operator, 29
projection, 241
    column projection accounting, 242
    project all, 243
    project none, 243
    project some, 243
    testing empty projection in record reader, 251
    testing explicit projection in record reader, 251
projection push-down, 231
pull request, contributing code to Drill via, 255
Python, 4
    connecting to Drill with, 112-116
        using drillpy to query Drill, 112
        using JayDeBeApi modules, 114

upstream, 25
URLs
    JDBC connection URL for Drill in dis-
        tributed mode, 108
    JDBC onnection URL for Drill in embedded
        mode, 108
URS in web server logs, analyzing with Drill, 80
USE command, 37, 111, 174
    declaring a default schema, 139
    USE DATABASE, 22
    USE WORKSPACE, 22
user agent strings from web server log, query-
    ing, 68, 79
user, defining specifically for Drill in produc-
    tion deployment, 190
user-defined functions (UDFs), 201-220
    aggregate function API, 216
    aggregate function checking for syn-flood
        attempts, 269
    analyzing Twitter data, 271
    complex functions returning maps or
        arrays, 212-215
    example aggregate UDF, Kendall's rank cor-
        relation coefficient, 217-220
    how UDFs work in Drill, 202
        configuring your development environ-
            ment, 203
    structure of simple Drill UDF, 203
        buiilding and installing your UDF, 211
        converting simple function into Drill
            UDF, 209
        function file, 205
        pom.xml file, 203
        simple function API, 209
    use case, finding and filtering valid credit
        card numbers, 201
    using in Drill deployment, 190
    wrapper for machine learning model func-
        tionality, 273-275
        making predictions with, 275
    writing aggregate UDFs, 215
UserException class, 239
using the @JsonTypeName annotations, 227
UTC, setting up Drill to use, 53

V

value vectors, 28, 246
    (see also vectors)
VARCHAR type, 45, 70, 147

nullable VARCHAR columns, 243
vectors, 223, 236
    defining, 247
    loading data into, 248
versioning, Drill plug-in configurations not
    versioned, 230
views, 134
    capturing schema mapping in, 173
    creating, 53
visualizations
    building using Drill and Superset, 130-132
    dynamically redrawing in Zeppelin, 126
    using Drill with other visualization tools,
        132

W

web interface for drill, 33
    no sessions or USE operator, 38
web server logs, querying with Drill, 77-82
    analyzing URLs and query strings, 80
    configuring Drill to read HTTPD web
        server logs, 77
    querying the web server logs, 78
Well-Known Text (WKT) representation for-
    mat for spatial data, 280
wget command, 177
WHERE clause
    fields to include to improve performance of
        Kafa queries, 99
    variables causing Zeppelin to dynamically
        redraw visualization, 126
whitespace
    in JSON, 71
    spaces in column names, 62
wildcards
    in directory names, 43
    wildcard projection, 148
window functions, 58
    comparison with aggregate functions, 59-62
    reference of functions available as of Drill
        1.14, 278
    summary of, 59
Windows
    configuring for Drill and installing, 10
    configuring ODBC on, 110
    downloading and installing Maven, 197
    new lines encoded with carriage return
        character (\r), 63
    no support for Superset, 128

worker Drillbit servers, 21
workspaces, 137
    and directory queries, 139
    becoming default schema, 139
    defining, 36
    defining a table workspace, 172
    specifying in Drill SQL query, 35
    using for variables carried over between
        function iterations, 210

X

XML format (Excel files), 260

Y

YARN, 17
    using as cluster manager in Drill-on-YARN
        deployment, 195
YYYY-MM-DD date format, 51

Z

Zeppelin
    exploring data with Zeppelin and Drill,
        122-127
    adding interactivity in Zeppelin, 126
    configuring Zeppelin to query Drill, 123
    querying Drill from Zeppelin notebook,
        124
ZooKeeper, 9
    clearning Dill's state in, 229
    configuration variables in JDBC URL for
        Drill connection, 108
    configurations stored in, 226
    configuring, 178
    connecting to Drill via single ZooKeeper
        instance or multinode cluster, 109
    coordination of Drill cluster, 19
    Drill-on-YARN clusters, configuration, 195
    installation, 176
    installing and configuring ZooKeeper clus-
        ter, 15
    IP addresses of quorum as comma-
        separated list, 93
    quorum hosts and ports, 97
    server, coordinating Drillbits in a cluster, 21
    storage configurations stored in, 136

About the Authors

Charles Givre, CISSP, is a lead data scientist in the CSO for Deutsche Bank and is the program chair for the Strategic Analytics Program at Brandeis University Graduate School for Professional Studies. He has given talks and trainings about data science and security at Strata, BlackHat, and other international conferences and is a PMC member for the Apache Drill project. He holds a BS in Computer Science, a BMus in Trombone Performance from the University of Arizona, and an MA from Brandeis University. Charles blogs at *thedataist.com* and tweets @cgivre. When not coding, you will find him spending time with his wife and children and restoring British sports cars.

Paul Rogers is an Apache Drill PMC member and longtime systems developer. Paul's experience includes Informix (a relational database), Rational (Rational Rose, a UML tool), Versant (an object database), Actuate (an early BI tool vendor), Skytide (an early big data analytics company), Oracle, MapR, and Cloudera. His interests include systems internals: he developed the Drill-on-YARN feature as well as improvements to Drill's vector memory management. Paul holds a BS from UC Santa Barbara and an MBA from UC Berkeley. When not coding, you will find him bicycling or skiing.

Colophon

The animal on the cover of *Learning Apache Drill* is a mandrill (*Mandrillus sphinx*) of the Old World monkey (*Cercopithecidae*) family. The other species assigned to genus Mandrillus is the drill; both were once classified as baboons, which they resemble.

These primates inhabit tropical rainforests in southern Cameroon, Gabon, Congo, and Equatorial Guinea. Mandrills live in large groups known as hordes, and their mating season is from July to September, giving birth between December and April. Mandrills are the world's largest monkey, and they live on an omnivorous diet of fruit and insects.

Mandrills have olive green or dark grey fur and white bellies. Their faces are hairless, and their long snouts have distinctive blue ridges on each side and a red stripe down the middle. Mandrills have colorful rear ends as well, with blue, red, pink, and purple markings surrounding its genitals. These distinct colorations are more pronounced on dominant adult males.

An oversized mandrill weighing up to 130 pounds (60kg) is reported in the Guinness Book of World Records, but mandrills typically weigh between 22–33 pounds (for females) and 40–80 pounds (for males). The mandrill's natural predator is a leopard, though younger mandrills are vulnerable to crowned eagles, African rock pythons, and venomous snakes. Larger adult males will sometimes stand their ground against even leopards, communicating aggression by staring, bobbing their heads, and slapping the ground. Mandrills also communicate with more peaceful presentations of silent bared teeth and head shaking. The mandrill is classified vulnerable by IUCN.

Many of the animals on O'Reilly covers are endangered; all of them are important to the world. To learn more about how you can help, go to *animals.oreilly.com*.

The cover image is from *Lydekker's Royal Natural History*. The cover fonts are URW Typewriter and Guardian Sans. The text font is Adobe Minion Pro; the heading font is Adobe Myriad Condensed; and the code font is Dalton Maag's Ubuntu Mono.

Learn from experts.
Find the answers you need.

Sign up for a **10-day free trial** to get **unlimited access** to all of the content on Safari, including Learning Paths, interactive tutorials, and curated playlists that draw from thousands of ebooks and training videos on a wide range of topics, including data, design, DevOps, management, business—and much more.

Start your free trial at:

oreilly.com/safari

(No credit card required.)

Lightning Source UK Ltd.
Milton Keynes UK
UKHW030102031118
331700UK00001B/2/P